8-/6

David R. Roediger is Kendrick C. Babcock Professor of History at the University of Illinois at Urbana-Champaign. He is the author of, among other books, *The Wages of Whiteness* and *Towards the Abolition of Whiteness*.

How Race Survived US History

*From Settlement and Slavery
to the Obama Phenomenon*

DAVID R. ROEDIGER

VERSO

London • New York

First published by Verso 2008
© David R. Roediger 2008
This paperback edition published by Verso 2010
All rights reserved

3 5 7 9 10 8 6 4

Verso
UK: 6 Meard Street, London W1F 0EG
USA: 20 Jay Street, Brooklyn, NY 11201
www.versobooks.com

Verso is the imprint of New Left Books

ISBN-13: 978-1-84467-434-3

British Library Cataloguing in Publication Data
A catalogue record for this book is available from the British Library

Library of Congress Cataloging-in-Publication Data
A catalog record for this book is available from the Library of Congress

Typeset by Hewer Text UK Ltd, Edinburgh
Printed in the USA by Maple Press

Contents

Acknowledgments

The idea of my doing a wildly ambitious and ridiculously short book on race came from Peter Ginna, when he was at Oxford University Press. Although I ended up doing the book neither with him nor with OUP, his persistence in making the case that such a book was possible is responsible for its existence. My editor at Verso, Tom Penn, has been a remarkably enthusiastic supporter even while taking apart the writing line by line. His attention and ideas have vastly improved the final book, as has the assistance of Charles Peyton and Natalie Howe.

My long-standing intellectual debts are many. Almost every chapter of this book leans heavily on the work of W. E. B. Du Bois, whose brilliance I would never have grasped fully without the mentorship of Sterling Stuckey. Alexander Saxton, the leading student of race and class in US history, has been both friend and inspiration, as was the late George Rawick. I knew Michael Rogin too briefly before his death, but the fact that he and Rawick sometimes suggested that I might be on the right track made me a far bolder writer and a happier person. A number of intellectual/political peers have also become teachers in matters central to this book: these include George Lipsitz, Cheryl Harris, Noel Ignatiev, Lisa Lowe, Ruth Wilson Gilmore, Pedro Cabán, Peter Linebaugh, and Peter Rachleff.

Two very recently departed fellow workers deserve special mention. Susan Porter Benson allowed me to sit in on her brilliant

US history survey lectures at the University of Missouri long ago so that I could learn how to lecture. Each lecture incorporated what would have otherwise seemed to me an impossibly ambitious, simultaneous consideration of race, gender, sexuality and class. The idea that we might tell histories as complicated as real life somehow stuck, although my ability to do so never approached Sue's. In writing *How Race Survived US History*, the thing I most looked forward to was sending a completed version to George Fredrickson, the remarkable historian of comparative race relations with whom I had studied at Northwestern University in Evanston. George died a month before I finished and is greatly missed.

Fellowship support from the Center on Advanced Study at the University of Illinois sped the completion of the manuscript, as did research assistance from Martin Smith and Carmen Thompson. Trying out ideas with students helped me to push arguments further and to avoid at least some mistakes. I am especially grateful for opportunities to deliver recent lectures based on the themes under consideration in this book, at Vanderbilt University, the University of Kentucky, Tulane University, Xavier University, Louisiana State University, the University of Wisconsin-Milwaukee, and Ohio State University's Kirwan Institute. One particularly transformational experience was my involvement in the Conference of the Australian Critical Race and White Studies Association, arranged by the great indigenous scholar Aileen Moreton-Robinson.

Those who answered queries, contributed insights, and read parts of the manuscript are too numerous to mention without fear of forgetting some of them. Taking that risk, I want especially to thank Brendan Roediger, Jean O'Brien-Kehoe, Clarence Lang, Jennifer Pierce, the late Josephine Fowler, Jean Allman, Poshek Fu, Minkah Makalani, Fred Hoxie, Franklin Rosemont, Paul Garon, Sundiata Cha-Jua, Adrian Burgos, and Elizabeth Esch. The best ideas in the chapter on capitalism and race were thought through in close collaboration with Elizabeth, and some of the material on management and race includes work from an ongoing article that we are coauthoring.

Introduction

FREEDOM DREAMS AND CHANGING SAMES

The week in which I finished an early draft of this book featured the first triumph of "Obamamania," following Senator Barack Obama's victory in the primary election caucuses in the overwhelmingly white state of Iowa. For all of five days, the mania's spread to New Hampshire's primaries, if not the nation, looked assured; in the run-up to the primary, polls had Obama's lead stretching comfortably into double digits. Pundits speculated that in one stroke he could knock Hillary Clinton out of the race for the Democratic Party nomination. From George Will and William Bennett on the right, to Andrew Sullivan in the center, to Jesse Jackson on the liberal left, triumphalism reigned, less in support for Obama's still-vague political program but rather because his victory was "ours," putting paid to the idea that white racism permeated US politics. Jackson and others noted Obama's special appeal among younger white voters, pronouncing them more comfortably attuned to new multiracial realities, and ready to see Obama as the embodiment of hopes that the nation was moving beyond race.

And then Clinton comfortably won the New Hampshire primary, running as many as seventeen points better than the polls that had predicted her defeat. Some experts dusted off Pew Research Center studies, mostly concerning elections in the

1990s, on the tendency for white voters to have proceeded far enough beyond race to tell pollsters they would support the African American candidate, but not always far enough to actually pull the election booth lever for that candidate, to explain the gap between Obama's polling numbers and the vote. Others saw the gap as the product of a tendency of whites who would usually abstain from voting coming out to cast ballots for a white candidate in the face of a minority candidate's possible victory.

Whether either view provides a significant explanation for the results of a very complex open primary among the chronically unpredictable electorate of New Hampshire remains questionable. Obamamania continued to unfold, with fair prospects of success. When the Illinois senator's campaign recovered to win in South Carolina's primary, he took 80 percent of the African American vote and 25 percent of the white vote. Despite this, Obama supporters chanted "RACE DOESN'T MATTER!" at his victory celebration in South Carolina, even as the national press, so euphoric a month previously, noted that in no non-caucus state had he exceeded 36 percent of the white vote, and in Democratic primaries at that. But the jarring transition, within less than a month, from positive testimonials for a colorblind future to dissections of a still-lingering white supremacist past, ought to suggest the need for a long view in thinking about race and change. Such a perspective will remind us that insistent proclamations of a new racial day sit uneasily next to patterns of inequality in the present, and not only in the past, as the following salient facts show.

Black males born in 1991, twenty-seven years after the most important of the modern civil rights acts, are estimated to have a 29 percent chance of imprisonment, more than seven times that of whites born in the same year. Latino men are incarcerated at four times the white male rate.

In 2004, 228 years after the Declaration of Independence found all men to have been "created equal," blacks and Latinos suffered poverty at rates nearly three times that of the white majority population. Nearly one in three of their children lived in poverty, as against one in ten white children.

In 2006, fifty-two years after *Brown v. Board of Education* had proclaimed segregated educational establishments to be unequal, black students constituted 2.2 percent of entering first-year students at the University of California, Los Angeles. Of the very few that were admitted, one-fifth were scholarship athletes. At the time of writing reports show that, in 2008, two-thirds of all African American and Latino urban students are in schools where less than 10 percent of the students are white. One black student in six and one Latino in nine attend what Gary Orfield, in a 2003 study at Harvard's Civil Rights Project, calls "apartheid schools," schools that are less than 1 percent white.

In 2003, seventy-nine years after the Indian Citizenship Act was passed, joblessness among Native Americans tripled that of whites. In 1998, as the United States celebrated the 135th anniversary of the Emancipation Proclamation, the net worth of African Americans and Hispanic families in the US was 17.28 percent that of non-Hispanic whites. In the decade since, the disparity has widened further.

Thirty-five years after the War on Poverty, a study by the Center for Labor Market Studies at Northeastern University found that a quarter of African American adult males had been unemployed for the entire year. As Manning Marable has emphasized, over two in five black men between the ages of 55 and 64 years, who as young workers had been the very objects of War on Poverty reforms, were without work for at least parts of 2002.

As I write these words, 75 percent of all active tuberculosis cases in the United States afflict people of color. As Illinois prepares to celebrate a bicentennial of African American emancipation, around the bicentennial of Abraham Lincoln's birth, a majority of its HIV-AIDS cases occur among African Americans.

Race defines the social category into which peoples are sorted, producing and justifying their very different opportunities with regard to wealth and poverty, confinement and freedom, citizenship and alienation, and, as Ruth Wilson Gilmore puts it, life and premature death. Though genetic differences among groups defined as races are inconsequential, race is itself a critically important social fact; one said to be based on biology, as well as on color, and at times on longstanding cultural practices. Race also defines the consciousness of commonality uniting those oppressed as a result of their assumed biology, perceived color, and alleged cultural heritage, as well as the fellow feeling of those defending relative privileges derived from being part of domi- nant—in US history, white—race. The world got along without race for the overwhelming majority of its history. The US has never been without it. How that came to be so is the story of this book.

The durability of white supremacy over long stretches of US history seems especially remarkable given the forces that have apparently been arrayed against it. Most famously, of course, the nation's revolutionary commitments to freedom and equality putatively created an "American dilemma" regarding how to square such values with the enduring practices of slavery and segregation. The Civil War and its aftermath not only underscored these egalitarian principles in blood and enshrined them in Constitutional amendments but also saw the immediate, albeit uncompensated, abolition of slavery, a central institution around which white supremacy and the very idea of race had developed. A century after emancipation, a surge of freedom movements, together with the Cold War imperative to disarm Soviet criticisms by declaring that the American dilemma had been resolved in favor of racial equality, made the dominant existing forms of white supremacy flatly illegal.

If the idea of the United States as upholder of freedom directly challenged the practice of white supremacy, the nation's status as bastion of capitalist success potentially presented more subtle challenges. The allegedly colorblind logic of the phenomenally successful United States industrial system—"coal does not care who mines it," as the saying went—could bring races together at the point of production, where management presumably saw productivity and profit, not color, as the paramount concerns. At times, too, industry could join workers into powerful multi-racial unions where shared grievances bound them together. A related piece of folk wisdom, holding that dollars don't care who spends them, identified consumerism as another realm in which raceless capitalist logic could undermine firm racial lines.

The tremendous need for settlers, for consumers, and especially enduringly for labor, brought migrants from various European "races," as they were called until well into the twentieth century, portraying some of them as less than fully white. The presence of Irish and, later, Southern and Eastern European workers, along with people of Asian and African descent, made anti-immigration race-thinkers fret as insistently in the 1890s and the early twentieth century as they do now regarding the allegedly impending loss of the nation's racial character. In his jeremiads on "race suicide" President Theodore Roosevelt captured the older panic perfectly, fearing the moment of "the Jew, the Russian, the Hungarian [and] the Italian . . . darkly outshading the Americanized descendants of the English . . . the German and the Swede."

The persistence, amidst challenge and change, of white supremacy—Malcolm X has acutely likened its trajectory to various models of the Cadillac, which despite their differences leave the essence of the brand intact—is, to be sure, a human problem; however, it is also an historical and intellectual problem that demands big and bold explanations. Such explanations must engage the patterns of exploitation and of race-thinking produced not only by slavery and Jim Crow but also by settler colonialism, by overseas empire, and by hostility to immigration. The eminent cultural theorist Stuart Hall acutely points out that racism emerges and is recreated from the imperatives of new sets of realities, not just from bad habits of the past; given this, the way that the Cadillac of white supremacy has undergone centuries of model changes, but no changes of substance, becomes still more troubling. How did white supremacy in the US not yield to changes that we generally regard as constant, dramatic, and, in the main, progressive?

I have tried to incorporate my explanations and provocations in a very small book, and one without an elaborate scholarly apparatus. I do so not because much more might not be said and cited, but because a spare, vigorous, and accessible account of the ways white supremacy has lurked, morphed, and survived is most likely to reach large numbers of busy and perhaps skeptical readers. Such readers care about justice but also hear from liberals and conservatives that "race is over," its sell-by date passed with the passage of the civil rights acts of the 1960s, the growth of a new middle class among people of color, globalization, massive post-1965 immigration, intermarriage, the maturing of new world divisions on axes of religion rather than race, and so on.

While this book addresses in its conclusion the prospects for the future of white supremacy, it is also meant as a whole to remind us of the misplaced faith (or fear) that broad legal, demographic, and/or economic trends will make white supremacy a thing of the past, without the need to take deep and conscious anti-racist action, which has been an almost constant feature of United States history. To say as much is not to abandon the dream that white supremacy and race-thinking might be finite, but it is to focus debate on how they might be dismantled. In using "race" rather than "racism" in its title, the book signals its own intended boldness, not a hesitancy to speak plainly. It consistently fore-grounds white supremacy but argues, following the work of Harry Chang and others, that we must constantly and critically explain the purpose, perversity, and persistence of race as a relatively new category in modern history if we are to address racism effectively. *How Race Survived US History* therefore attempts to go beyond telling stories useful only to a movement for racial "equality," and to generate instead an account of the past in order to show the necessity of completely abolishing oppression based on racial categories. It further aims to show how unlikely it is that a force so longstanding, formative, and persistently recreated as white supremacy has been in United States history will be abolished by accident, as a result of the momentum of forces like capitalism or immigration that themselves have no anti-racist agenda.

What follows specifically challenges the idea that past and present forces assumed to be corrosive of white supremacy functioned only or simply in that direction. Thus the very idea of formal equality among industrious free white citizens emerged in and after the American Revolution from creating, measuring, and imagining their social distance from African American slaves and from Indians whose alleged laziness rationalized their dispossession and exploitation. Similarly, for all capitalism's tendency to see workers in terms of their individual productivity, labor recruitment from slavery onwards has focused on workers' race; management in the United States has often used what I call here "race management," judging laborers on their ethnicity, and habitually dividing and pitting laborers against each other along racial lines.

Globalization, now insistently seen as presenting cosmopolitan challenges to racial hierarchies, could prove to be a force to challenge and erode US certainties about specific contours of white supremacy. But racial slavery and settler colonialism, the engines of modern race-making, were also globalizing moments. Connections between race and slavery made elsewhere in the world, especially in Barbados, produced models for white supremacy in North American colonies. Progressives and eugenicists in the early twentieth-century US pooled their knowledge of policies designed to bolster "white men's governments" with rulers and reformers in other white settler societies, especially Australia, New Zealand, South Africa, and Canada.

White supremacy persisted not only by working against the forces of freedom, of openness, and of economic rationality in US history, but also by working through them. Such complexities complicate the verb "survives" in this book's title, in that many of the forces pushing against the logic of racism at the same time validated, created, and recreated white supremacy.

To tell such a full story challenges the book's commitment to stay within a structure allowing the easiest access to the history being described. From the initial material on the origins of white supremacy—and indeed of race itself—in British colonial North America onward, it has only barely been possible to produce chapters short enough to be taken in over a cup of coffee with perhaps a tall refill. The opening chapter on the origins of race, and its successor on race and revolution, set up the book's largest ideas. These include the ones briefly rehearsed above as well as the ways in which white supremacy continuously and powerfully drew upon, and transformed, ideas and practices regarding gender.

Each subsequent chapter organizes itself around explaining a particular puzzle, even as we are taken from the nation's birth to the recent past. How, the chapters ask consecutively, did white supremacy manage to survive free labor and the take-off to industrialization, emancipation and the heroism of black Americans in the Civil War, mass immigration of "inferior" Europeans, and finally modern liberalism, industrial unionism, and civil rights? Might white supremacy and race survive, the Afterword asks, in a more multiracial, interracial, multicultural, cosmopolitan, and even white-minority nation? Might it survive Obamamania?

1

Suddenly White Supremacy:

HOW RACE TOOK HOLD

Writing during World War I, the unsurpassed US historian W. E. B. Du Bois captured how uneasily modern racism sits within the longer run of world history. "The discovery of personal whiteness among the world's peoples," he wrote, "is a very modern thing." "The ancient world would have laughed at such a distinction," he continued, further noting that in the Middle Ages skin color would have provoked nothing more than "mild curiosity." Despite a good deal of scholarship that has tried to read modern notions of race back into such curiosity, Du Bois was, characteristically, right. As late as the beginning of the seventeenth century, male northern European elites did not see themselves as physically white, and were still further from imagining that the word "white" had uses as a noun.

Du Bois' phrasing was acute. Earlier Europeans did of course note differences between their skin colors and those of non-Europeans, but the idea of "personal whiteness"—something that could be owned as an asset and as an identity—was surely a "very modern thing." Though influenced by the ways that anti-Semitism, anti-Islamic crusading and the conquest of Ireland created "others" against whom a "Christian Europe" and its various empires could begin to fashion themselves, personal whiteness would have to await the slave trade and the settler-colonial conquest of indigenous peoples in the Americas. The notion that one could own a skin color—what the legal scholar Cheryl Harris calls "whiteness as property" and the historian George Lipsitz calls the "possessive investment in whiteness"— came into being alongside the reality that only peoples who were, increasingly, stigmatized by their color could be owned and sold as slaves. It matured alongside the equally brutal notion that land on which the suddenly "nonwhite" peoples lived would be better managed by "white" people.

Du Bois' formulation carries with it the hopeful subtext that we might look forward to personal whiteness having an end, just as it had a beginning. But such a profound insight would only take hold within mainstream understandings of the American past much later, after World War II, when historians finally caught up with Du Bois as they wrote with the weight of moral authority produced by the black American and anti-colonial freedom movements. Since the 1950s, historians of the colonization of British North America have produced a compelling picture of when and why such a white identity took hold there. Liberal and radical scholars alike have emphasized that race is not a natural category; rather, racial slavery was a laboriously constructed system. Even in colonies deeply associated with plantation agriculture, it took time for white supremacy to emerge as a centerpiece of the legal and labor systems.

Policing Inequality: The Turns to Slavery and Race

Reflecting both the forward momentum produced by the civil rights movement, and that movement's need for hopeful lessons from history, postwar historians saw a seventeenth-century colonial world in which, at least for a time, "race relations" were less than hierarchical and fixed. At their best, these accounts joined Du Bois in challenging assumptions about the existence of race relations throughout much of human history. Especially in studying early Virginia, historians showed that the bloody logic of premising a system of production on the sweat of slaves, and anchoring a system of social control to the loyalty of poor whites, took time to develop. So did, in their modern senses, the very categories of black and white.

Written in the shadow of an anti-Nazi war and during the modern civil rights movement, the literature on the turn from indentured servitude of Europeans and Africans to the slavery of the latter group as a basis for plantation agriculture carried the political point that racism is anything but natural. Nor, this study adds, was the idea of "race" separable from the actual social practices of white supremacy contained in plantation slavery and the dispossession of the Indians. The historical literature on the rise of race in colonial Virginia, inspired by the civil rights movement, uproots the reactionary common sense that imagines races exist outside of historical circumstances. It locates the rise of personal whiteness squarely in the material realities of class division and of class rule. What happened in Virginia shows that white supremacy did not arise as a result of agitation, or even sentiment, among the white poor desiring to preserve and extend social distance between themselves and Africans. Rather than being an expression of white unity and common interest, the turn to racial slavery was a response to sharp social divisions among settlers and sought to create an ersatz unity among whites, indeed by creating "white" itself as a social and legal category. Events in Virginia provide a critical clue to the enduring nature of white supremacy by unearthing its roots in popular protest and in the elite's recognition of the rage of the poor.

As the early center of African slavery in British North America and the cradle of revolutionary leaders and presidents, Virginia has been the focus for those wanting to understand how a social system could suddenly be built around the idea of "whiteness." Detailed accounts of the colony, by such leading scholars as Edmund Morgan and Oscar Handlin, from its first permanent settlement in 1607, show that there existed at the outset vexed and vague distinctions between black and white, and between servant and slave. Though Virginia was anything but egalitarian in its treatment of the Indians and its labor policies, it nevertheless connected the concepts of slavery and race only gradually. Its early African laborers sometimes worked for a term of service alongside similarly indentured Europeans. Black and white indentured servants shared alcohol, sex, marriage, death, and escapes across what would only later, after slavery, be called the "color line."

Indeed during the first quarter-century of Virginian settler colonialism, life expectancy was so dire, and female servants were so few, that in many cases there was little practical point in stipulating that Africans and their descendants might be enslaved for life. Moreover, Africans constituted relatively few of the colony's workers. As the colony matured, however, life expectancy grew longer and child mortality diminished, and so calls grew to define Africans and their children as slaves for life, a development coinciding with the increasing determination in Europe that enslavement of other Europeans ought not occur while African slavery could. But in the colonies the situation remained fluid a half-century after the first permanent Virginia settlement. Patterns of sociability, love, and resistance continued to bring together Africans and Europeans. Some of the former had acquired land and along with it the confidence to insist on their rights, including the right to command the labor of others. Race, as a series of post-1660 rebellions would show, had little firm meaning in such a land of flux, force, and death.

If, as Morgan argues, laborers in early colonial Virginia could be so brutally exploited because they were "selected for that purpose" from among those deemed "useless" in Europe, many of the exploited refused to live within such limits. They resisted servitude and came to regard grueling work in the colonies as a prelude to, and a claim on, future landowning prosperity. As a result, in the two decades from the 1661 Servants' Plot, when indentured servants rose up in a rebellion over inadequate food rations, to the tobacco riots of 1682, when "cutters and pluckers" destroyed their crops and those of neighbors to protest overproduction, at least ten popular revolts shook Virginia. Like everyday life among the poor, insurrections brought together Africans and Europeans.

The most spectacular example of revolt, Bacon's Rebellion of 1676, took Virginia to the brink of civil war. Broadly arising from the desire for good land among European and African servants and ex-servants, the rebellion therefore also had anti-Indian dimensions, demanding and implementing aggressive policies to speed settlement onto indigenous lands. Bondservants joined those who had recently served out "their time" under the leadership of the young English lawyer and venture capitalist Nathaniel Bacon, laying siege to the capital in Jamestown, burning it, driving Governor William Berkeley into exile, and sustaining insurrection for months. Authorities offered freedom "from their slavery" to "Negroes and servants" who would come over into opposition to the rebellion. Rebels meanwhile feared that they would all be made into "slaves, man, woman & child." Both the promise of liberation and the language registering fear of retribution suggest how imperfectly class predicaments aligned with any firm sense of racial division.

In coming years elites in England and Virginia responded to threats of rebellion by committing to a system in which much more of the colony's work fell to slave labor and, significantly, by exaggerating differences between the oppression of African and European laborers. With the reorganization of the Royal African Company in 1685 and with imperial authorities smiling on "a trade so beneficial to the Kingdom," slave trading became a lynchpin of imperial policy in North America. The turn to a labor force defined by racial slavery happened with startling speed in the late 1600s. By 1709 Africans in slavery for life overwhelmingly outnumbered Europeans held for a term in Virginia, South Carolina, and Maryland.

But it was in systematizing distinctions between Europeans and Africans that the elites created race in its modern sense. Some moves in this direction pre-dated Bacon's Rebellion. Reacting to threats to the system stemming from the way that flight united slaves and servants, colonial lawmakers added a new race-based policy to their penal system of floggings, mutilations, brandings, extensions of periods of servitude, and occasional exemplary executions: beginning in 1661, English servants joining Africans in flight would have existing additions to their periods of indenture doubled as punishment for escape. Legislation also specified that the children of European women in servitude would themselves be servants until the age of twenty, if the child's father was African. Moreover, a European servant bearing an African servant's or slave's child would suffer severe public whipping and see her own service extended by as much as seven years. Following Maryland's 1661 example, Virginia outlawed interracial sex in 1662.

Such policing of solidarity and reproduction between Africans and "white" indentured servants became the basis for a new regime that sought to set poor people apart from each other much more clearly on the basis of "race" in the wake of Bacon's Rebellion. Pass laws restricted the movement of slaves; poor whites patrolled to enforce the laws. Laws required public, often naked, whippings of recalcitrant black slaves but set limits on penal violence against even indentured whites. Beatings awaited any "negroe or other [Indian] slave" attacking "any Christian," according to a 1680 law, putting state power firmly on the side of Europeans in altercations among servants. The term "Christian" increasingly meant "white." Africans would not be defined as such.

While black Virginians could carry arms only in violation of the law, white servants received a musket as part of freedom dues given on completion of a term of indentured servitude. Such dues also included, under 1705 legislation, ten bushels of corn and thirty shillings for men, and fifteen bushels of corn and forty shillings for women. "Afro-American laborers were not to receive freedom dues," T. W. Allen concludes, "since they were not to have freedom." In 1691, the Virginia Assembly passed further legislation in order to prevent "that abominable mixture and spurious issue" resulting from "negroes, mulattoes, and Indians intermarrying with English or other white women, [or] by their unlawful accompanying with one another." The punishment consisted of banishment for man and wife, until a 1705 revision redefined the penalty as a combination of fines and jail for the offending couple, as well as for the minister presiding at their wedding. White women in such relationships suffered especially harsh penalties, even more so if they were servants, as the race-making state invented itself.

Such a pattern did not simply reflect increased supply in African slaves, which remained patchy, nor even enduring advantages in labor costs favoring the use of slaves. Still less did any illusion that Africans presented less threat of rebellion than indentured white servants condition the turn to slave labor. Indeed as Allen put it, a "Turn, turn again" series of policies prevailed. By 1698 colonial authorities began for economic and security reasons to pursue white indentured labor again, seeking to "people the country" and to patrol the plantations against slave resistance. The decisive turn to African slave labor in the late seventeenth century thus responded to the need to avoid a repetition of the interracial uprisings that had so threatened colonial rule in the time of Bacon, and the development itself quickly set into motion class, racial, and demographic changes leading to a fear of slave revolts.

The Colonial World, Freedom, and the Ownership of Skins

The central role of gender, and the penalties for mixing with Indians contained in the critical 1691 legislation, complicate the social interpretation of the dramatic rise of race in Virginia outlined above. Responsive as it was to a long moment in the civil rights movement, the best academic history of colonial Virginia tends to tell an important but foreshortened story focusing on contingent connections among African slavery, labor, and government policies in creating white supremacy. The ways in which settlers also fashioned themselves as "white" out of the process of confronting and dispossessing those whom the British would eventually call "red Indians" have tended to recede in the framing of such a story largely in black and white. Besides this, the centrality of gender to race-making, and connections between ideas from the larger colonial world and the local practices giving rise to white supremacy in North American colonies, have only recently figured much in the story of racial formation. A turn away from Virginia's story, before a return to it, will give a sense of the larger world of social and intellectual forces that created the white race.

South Carolina's history, in particular, challenges Virginia's pre-eminence in the invention of personal whiteness. Nearly a decade before Bacon's Rebellion, the English politician Lord Ashley joined his secretary, the philosopher and bureaucrat John Locke, in the task of writing the Fundamental Constitutions for a group of eight landowners, the Lords Proprietor, who owned most of the colonial settlements in the Carolinas. The document Locke and Ashley produced was fanciful in the extreme, projecting a trans-plantation of feudal social relations so that "landgraves" and "caziques" would perpetually lord it over "leet-men." The document was never formally ratified, still less implemented, by colonists. Indeed, soon after the Fundamental Constitutions were written, the Carolina authorities acknowledged that indentured servants, not serfs, would provide the colony with its European labor and that, on serving out their terms, the indentured would receive land.

Nonetheless the Fundamental Constitutions are significant in that they, along with the earliest proprietors' directives, projected Carolina as a colony to be built on hereditary African slavery. In a series of directives addressing religious tolerance, Locke and Ashley managed to insulate the proprietors from messy questions over whether religious conversion of Africans ought to lead to their emancipation: "Since charity obliges us to wish well to the souls of all men, and religion ought to alter nothing in any man's civil estate or right," they intoned, "it shall be lawful for slaves [to] be of what church or profession any of them shall think best, and, therefore, be as fully members as any freeman." The qualification that followed mattered greatly: "But yet no slave shall hereby be exempted from that civil dominion his master hath over him, but be in all things in the same state and condition he was in before." Two paragraphs later, the same point, which followed the model of a 1667 Virginia law, came in for re-emphasis, expansion and racialization: "Every freeman of Carolina shall have absolute power and authority over his negro slaves, of what opinion or religion soever."

Writing further to define Carolina land policy in 1670, Lord Ashley underscored this movement towards slavery. Although nothing had hitherto been said about the application of "head-rights," those grants of colonial land made to each settler on his arrival, in relation to the arrival of imported slaves, Ashley clarified matters using the old language of religion and the new one of race: "by saying that we grant 150 acres of land for every able man servant in that we mean for negroes as well as Christians." Slaves, of course, could not possess any such land, but their numbers were used to apportion resources to their masters. The apparent inclusion of the slaves' ability and manhood perversely served to empower their owners and attract them to Carolina.

In order to connect the early proprietors' efforts to turn Carolina into a race-making colony with the longer history of the US as a race-making nation, we must linger over questions of geography and of philosophy. As far as the former is concerned, it was of course the case that much of Carolina policy was made not by its inhabitants, but rather by men of the colonial empire like Locke, who never set foot in the colonies. Moreover, those who did come to adventure or to settle often brought experiences from other colonial settings with them. It was the colonists of Barbados who were being courted by promoters of the Carolina colony as potential settlers. These settlers carried with them the lessons learned in colonizing Barbados—namely, that plantation agriculture based on racialized African slavery could work in a British colony. Indeed Barbados, so small that indentured servants could not be attracted by promises of land, turned to African slaves significantly before Virginia did. By 1661, before Locke set about his constitution-writing for Carolina, and before Bacon's Virginia rebellion, Barbados already had a racialized slave code. Its 1668 law on the subject carried the frank title, "An Act declaring the Negro-Slaves of this Island to be Real Estates"—a point sure to resonate with the property-loving Locke. By 1680 the Anglican minister in Barbados, Morgan Godwyn, had already noted that "Those two words, *Negro* and *Slave*" had become synonymous in the case of Barbados. "*White*," he added, had emerged as "the general name for *Europeans*." To attract Barbadian settlers to Carolina was to attract race-thinkers, masters, and aspirants to slaveholding status.

As important as were the grounded experiences of class conflict on the Chesapeake, those experiences also existed in a wider Atlantic and British imperial context. In that wider context, clear examples of perpetual African slavery and of a slave-based mode of production were available and well known before Bacon's Rebellion. Africans were marketed as subject to lifelong bondage. Important in its own right for understanding the colonial period in general, the insight that race was made in a transnational race-making world will also be critical as we come to grips with race in the national history of the United States.

Locke's prominent role in Carolina helps us to explore the deep philosophical connections between white supremacy and freedom. Locke was far from being the most revolutionary philosopher of natural rights in seventeenth- and eighteenth-century Europe. But we can reconcile the relative tepidness of his political theory with the intense resonances of his work for slaveholding dissenters if we see him more as a colonial functionary and planner, working at the moment of the rise of personal whiteness within a slave-based colony that featured large inequalities among whites. He was, according to one recent, and admiring, account, virtually unsurpassed "in knowledge of colonial life, foreign peoples, slavery and the slave trade." It was in the context of his successful investments in slave trading and colonization that Locke became a Carolina "landgrave," and attended some 372 meetings of the Board of Trade and Plantations after also serving as secretary of the earlier Council of Trade and Plantations. Locke's activities as a colonial functionary informed his ideas, which in turn fit him for prominent roles as planner of a slave-based settlement of colonies.

Navigating a British economic system as it evolved from feudalism to capitalism, and a political context dominated by civil war, Oliver Cromwell's republican commonwealth, and the subsequent restoration of the monarchy, Locke argued that the essence of freedom was not popular government but protection from "absolute arbitrary power." His own preamble to the Carolina constitution set a central goal of the document as "to avoid erecting a numerous democracy." His grounding of natural rights in property, defined broadly enough to include life, labor, and even "happiness," implied no leveling of inequalities of wealth. Weighed down by commitments to feudalism, Locke only hesitantly approached acceptance of what the theorist C. B. McPherson has called "possessive individualism"; the idea that unequal capitalist social relations could still be ones of liberty because all parties possessed their own bodies and could sell labor power in a fair bargain. In Locke's strongest language, man was "master of himself and proprietor of his own person and the actions or labour of it."

But not all men. Locke, far from seeing labor as universal, significantly if uncertainly moved from a hesitant embrace of "possessive individualism" to a straightforward endorsement of the "possessive investment in whiteness." He firmly placed slavery outside of the sphere of possible relations among the English, famously and not quite accurately writing of it as "so vile and miserable an estate" that none of his countrymen would accept or advocate it domestically. But both before and after that declaration, Locke was the architect of policies enabling colonial slavery, and made no serious attempt to reconcile this contradiction. At times he hinted that alleged African (and Indian) deficiencies in commitment to labor and property, and therefore in reason, might justify their enslavement, while at others he wildly claimed that all African slaves (and somehow their children) were legitimate war captives and that the state of war continued.

Such lines of thought either based enslavement in raw power or made possessive individualism a racial matter, in that Africans, being black, did not possess their own laboring selves and therefore lay outside of civilization and of appeals to reason. The inevitable scholarly debate over whether or not Locke was a "racist" necessarily flounders in that he was more precisely a thinker, policy maker and investor who made the idea of race both possible and necessary. The ideology of personal whiteness—the state-supported practice, and increasingly widespread belief, that "whites" ultimately owned their laboring bodies—encouraged the belief that Europeans possessed a skin that was more valuable than the skin of Africans, even if those Europeans were "leet-men" in the colonies, or British beggars whose "crime" Locke advocated punishing with years of forced labor.

Indians' Lands, Settlers' Divisions, and the Racial Logic of Dispossession

But the skins of African and European laborers' bodies cannot be the whole story of the sudden, durable rise of race-thinking in British North America. Including Indian "others" in the story of how personal whiteness came to be forces us to see the powerful and lasting ways in which white supremacy transformed settlers' identities by attaching itself to freedom and to ideas concerning gender—even in colonies without significant commitments to slave-based agriculture or to artisanal production and transport work by slaves. The logic of dispossession bespoke changes in how "whites" thought of themselves, of their households, and of their lands, as well as how they thought of those removed from the land.

From the early colonial period, variants of the question posed in

1609 by the Virginia promoter Robert Gray recurred: "By what right . . . can we enter into the land of these Savages, take away their rightful inheritance from them, and plant ourselves in their places, being unwronged or unprovoked by them?" The question was largely postponed in boosterist plans for Virginia, in New England, and later in South Carolina. Founding documents could ill afford to describe a scenario of carnage, and therefore held that there was ample land for all, and that relations of mutuality and Christian charity could make the English far different colonizers from the Spanish. That founding optimism persisted in an on-again, off-again tendency of elites and planners to exercise some restraint in expanding onto Indian lands. The desire to minimize costly conflicts and bad publicity often mixed with economic considerations in urging caution. A slower pace of expansion dovetailed at critical moments with interests among sectors of the elite in keeping white labor available for exploitation in ways it would not be if the back country areas quickly opened, with a commitment to trading relations with Indians fitting the mercantilist ethos of colonization, and with the practice of reserving claims to huge tracts of back country land for powerful men not yet in a position to exploit those tracts. Conversely, the landless and those aspiring to break through to elite status were tempted to demand, or simply undertake themselves, more aggressive anti-Indian policies so that settler colonialism produced both anti-Indian white identities and divisions among Europeans.

By the 1620s and 1630s in both Virginia and New England, the tensions attendant on colonization left plenty of room for talk of colonists being wronged and provoked by the indigenous peoples, and of Indians thereby forfeiting their rights to land, labor, and life. Such tensions left less room for the Indians to see the British as kinder and gentler than other colonizers. Gray's reference to "these Savages" came to be elaborated into a telling justification for dispossession. The allegedly *savage* behavior and habits of Indians—fixing on the term and idea was a particularly English colonial obsession—took the word's evolution from one vaguely suggestive of the wild and the woodsy to firm associations with brutality, bestiality, and the absence of settled forms of agricultural production or town life supposedly characteristic of "civilization."

During the fierce 1625 reprisals for an earlier attack on the Virginia colonies, the English travel writer Samuel Purchas clarified that what opened Indians to wholesale retaliation and expropriation far transcended military matters. They were savages, and their savagery inhered mainly in their living in that "unmanned wild Countrey, which they range rather than inhabit"—a way of Indian life tolerable if a fur-trading economy were contemplated, but galling for the colonialists when they decided land was needed for tobacco production. Similar land pressures developed as family farms were subjected to increasing generational division in New England because families were large and lives relatively long. The fact that many Indian groups, especially those near the first colonial settlements, practiced agriculture and horticulture as well as hunting and fishing starkly revealed that the arguments for dispossession of "savages" were ideologically based and economically driven. Ronald Bailey counts the voyage of the *Desire* in 1638 as the first participation by a New England vessel in the slave trade. But the Salem-based ship exported Indian slaves from New England rather than importing Africans to North America; it left Massachusetts laden with captured Pequod Indians to be traded as slaves in the West Indies. Myths of Indian savagery, doubling as arguments for their dispossession, spread despite these myths being "contrary to known fact," as the colonial historian Francis Jennings acidly remarks. Indeed, Indians traded their surplus produce with the colonists, whose livelihoods—indeed lives—were at times saved by these exchanges.

As early as 1629 Massachusetts Governor John Winthrop predicated legal claims to land on the fiction that settlers had entered a *vacuum domicilium*, not because he literally thought the territory empty of Indians but because their alleged failure to "subdue" the land forfeited their right to it and "disappeared" them as legal claimants. Writing in 1758, the early Swiss expert on international law Emmerich de Vattel counted incursions on the Indian empires in Peru and Mexico as "notorious usurpation," but reserved judgment on the North American cases, because "the peoples of those vast tracts of land rather roamed over them than inhabited them." Some years later, US Chief Justice John Marshall similarly grounded what he revealingly termed the "right to extinguish Indian title of occupancy" in the early United States through the myth that Indians were "fierce savages whose occupation was war and whose subsistence was drawn chiefly from the forest."

The powerful connections Locke made among reason, labor, and property made him a fit philosopher of the impulse to dispossess "savages." His insistence that "in the beginning all the world was America," however, made the colonies a model for the deep history of a humanity in which all were born free, thus implying that settlers and even the colonial state should not exercise arbitrary power over Indians. Moreover, in marketing the new colonial venture in Carolina, Locke and his associates shrewdly replayed the outworn Virginia dream of peaceful Indian/settler relations on plentiful land rather than advertising the probability of a perpetual state of war with "savages." The need for at least temporary alliances with tribes often arose from conflicts with other European colonial powers, a situation that militated against not only the possibility of imagining a unitary "Indian" presence but also that of a unitary "white" one. Instructions to Carolina colonists in the founding period included, "You are not to suffer anyone to take up land [within] two miles and a halfe of any Indian Towne" and even "Noe Indian upon any occasion or pretense is to be made a slave or without his owne consent to be carried out of our country." The latter was counted as a "temporary law" and both certainly proved to be such. But their presence does suggest a need for allies and at times a "hopeing to draw ye Indians into" the colonial project.

Such ideas and precedents proved over time to be easily superseded. Up to 1715, South Carolina exported more enslaved

Indians than it imported enslaved Africans. By 1707, as Carolina settlers ranching cattle encroached on the land of the Yamasee people, hitherto trading and military partners who organized the important commerce in deerskins and in forced labor, the authorities implemented an early version of reservation policy, acting to "limit the Bounds" of their erstwhile allies. In the bitter Yamasee War that followed eight years later, the central divide was between Indian and white, not African and white, and black slaves were not only armed for self-defense but used as front line troops on the settlers' side.

Locke eventually rationalized eloquently in casting the dispossession of Indians as the engine of progress. His second treatise on government closely considered the case of Indian polities "whom nature . . . furnished as liberally as any other people, with the materials of plenty." Nonetheless, he held, "for want of improving it by labour, [they] have not one hundredth part of the conveniences we enjoy: and a king of a large and fruitful territory there, feeds, lodges, and is clad worse than a day-labourer in England." Locke reckoned that the products of land of the same size and "natural intrinsic value" produced a thousandfold more value "to mankind"—he knew this by reckoning what produce was brought to market and for what price—if under English cultivation rather than Indian control. It is undoubtedly true that English modes of agricultural production differed from all of the varied practices of tribes in North America. Puritan officialdom used migratory patterns of Indian communities to argue that only the small minority who remained behind to farm had "subdued" the land, and should therefore not be dispossessed. But Locke put the key difference between Indians and Europeans squarely in terms of money and markets.

Moreover, what Locke valorized about English and colonial agriculture—what he asserted made such agriculture excel the alleged Indian inability to "subdue" land—alerts us to the ways in which long-established conflicts among "whites" over access to resources helped to justify taking Indian land. He asked:

what would a man value ten thousand . . . acres of excellent *land,* ready cultivated, and well stocked too with cattle, in the middle of the inland parts of *America,* where he had no hopes of commerce with other parts of the world, to draw *money* to him by the sale of the product? It would not be worth the inclosing, and we should see him give up again to the wild common of nature, whatever was more than would supply the conveniencies of life to be had there for him and his family.

Locke's own italics mark *land, America* and *money* as keywords in this critical passage. He links the absence of the last of these among Indians to their letting land "lie waste," blaming not just historical accident but also their willful refusal to have "joined with the rest of mankind in the use of common money."

But two other keywords in the passage—"common" and "inclosing"—show that Locke's logic reflects the bitter conflicts in the land where he lived. The birth of capitalism in England hinged precisely on those words, defined as it was by the enclosure of previously common land. The vast, bounded agricultural enterprise that Locke projects into the New World as an ideal was the desideratum of English commercial agriculture and—since the disappearance of the possibility of sustaining self and family using wood, animals, and plants from the commons drove the rural poor to wage labor and to a desperate bargaining position as workers—of manufacturers as well. As Peter Linebaugh's dramatic history shows, the Charter of the Forest sections of the Magna Charta that granted the right "to common" still seemed worth defending to many in the British countryside before, as, and even after Locke wrote. So, when Locke used interchangeably the phrases "lie in waste" and "lie in common" to describe supposedly dysfunctional land use, he expressed not an "English" viewpoint but his own position in a class conflict between emerging capitalist elites and the rural poor over the continuation of the commons.

Locke's fear that land in the colonies might "return to the wild

common" reflected a wider concern among early colonial authorities. The bounty of the New World, it was feared, would lead
settlers to follow the Indians in choosing to favor life and leisure
over what Locke praised as the hoarding of gold and silver. In
some cases Puritan settlers enjoined hard and above all steady
work, and encouraged postponing gratification of desires. But
settlement was not a decade old when in Massachusetts Thomas
Morton joyously erected a maypole and led a group of settlers in
dancing, frolicking, and drinking with Indians. At about the same
time in Virginia Captain John Smith and other leaders had as much
of a problem with "lazy Englishmen" as with "idle Indians," to
use Edmund Morgan's distinction. But even Smith, remembered
for his "if you don't work you don't eat" rigor, could demand
only a four-hour work day, with "pastimes and merry exercise"
filling in the remaining schedule.

The ways in which access to property was made to turn on
who was saved and sedentary versus who was lazy and foot-
loose lead us to complexities in the emergence of modern
white supremacy. "Heathen," "barbarian," and "savage"—
words applied in various ways and degrees to victims
of modern colonialism in its Irish testing grounds and in North
America—did not directly refer to biology, the hallmark of
nineteenth-century white supremacy, nor even to skin color.
Instead, these totalizing views emerged from colonizers' discussions about indigenous peoples' lack of Christianity, or the
absence of what colonizers could recognize as the practice of
settled agricultural production. What Allen calls "religio-racism"
in Ireland links these early justifications for the dispossession
of native peoples with the anti-black racism that informed
slavery—since Africans as well as Indians were said to be savage,
barbarous, and heathen. As much as anti-black and anti-Indian
initiatives marked different moments in a race-making process,
they were never entirely separate.

Back to Bacon and on to Lubberland: Slavery, Settlement, and Gender in Race-Making

A return to Bacon's Rebellion offers the opportunity to see the ways in which the gendered invention of the white race took shape around both slavery and settler colonialism, and to consider the complex part that race-making played in creating and constraining ideas about American freedom. Bacon's July 30 1676 "Declaration in the Name of the People" excoriated Governor Berkeley for having failed to move decisively against the Native Americans, "barbarous heathen" who might have "with ease beene destroyed." Linking the liberty of the people to Indian removal, Bacon's Rebellion was an interracial movement of the European and African poor, but it was never only that. Especially in its early stages, in the winter and spring of 1675 and 1676, class-based resistance in the US colonies mobilized around demands for a more thoroughly genocidal anti-Indian policy. Rebel leaders were less willing than colonial officials to countenance even temporary alliances with peaceful tribes, and more willing to regard obscure local disputes as a cause to destroy whole peoples, as New Englanders did in the contemporaneous and incredibly bloody King Philip's War of 1675.

Yet this anti-Indian Bacon has been somewhat eclipsed by accounts that take perhaps too much inspiration from seeing his rebellion as simply "interracial." These readings often separate his initial activities, centering on anti-Indian adventures, from his nobler focus later in 1676 on a mobilization of the poor for civil war, if not social revolution. However, Bacon himself died in October 1676, and those who see his movement as fundamentally anti-colonial or as incipiently revolutionary do not linger long over details of his largely unsavory career. But his commitment to the extermination of Native Americans, the "barbarous heathen," cannot easily be waved aside, as it positioned him to lead a movement of white indentured servants who, having worked their time, harbored dreams of freedom centered on gaining possession of vacated land.

White supremacy situated itself at some times in opposition to a "red" other and at others to a "black" one. While Indians were the first to suffer wholesale atrocities at the hands of settlers, terror was typically directed at individual tribes rather than at Indians as a whole. One reason that it took so long for Indians to "become red" in the settlers' imaginations and in colonial policies, was that the imperatives of colonization encouraged identifying differences among groups of indigenous peoples rather than homogenizing them into a single race. Shaping these imperatives were familiar economic and military factors, such as those over which Bacon and Berkeley clashed in calculating the costs of rapid expansion in lives and in loss of allies. As a governor, the latter wished to maintain mercantile ties with the same local tribespeople Bacon threatened to exterminate.

Nor were lines necessarily clearly and permanently drawn. Settlers pushing for more rapid expansion wanted new opportunities and fortunes, rather than new worlds and new ideas about race. Well into his campaign against native peoples, Bacon could still loyally cast himself as an aspiring member of the traditional elites, as opposed to as an aspiring revolutionary, when he wrote to Berkeley. He argued that, if properly led, anti-Indian expeditions could ease social tensions among colonizers. Among his forces, Bacon reported, "the Exclaiming concerning forts and [taxes] has been suppressed and the discourse . . . of the people is against the Indians." Near the top of Bacon's list of charges against Berkeley we find "assumeing monopoly of the beaver trade," a depredation Bacon linked to soft policies on Berkeley's part towards Indians. But Bacon himself also aspired for a time to making his fortune in the fur trade—and on Berkeley's account provoked hostility of "innocent and courteous Indians" by demanding tribute in the form of "beavors."

That Berkeley, Bacon, and even a freewheeling, pro-Indian fur trader like Thomas Morton all at times viewed the colonies as mercantile stations gathering beaver, deer, Indian slaves, and other products from the hinterlands, rather than only as sites of commercial agriculture, complicated and postponed genocidal impulses. Mercantile goals combined with security concerns to encourage continued colonial distinctions between Indian tribes and individuals, who were often seen as allies and trading partners, not as an undifferentiated race. Trade could act as a brake on the development and enclosure of the back country, producing temporary "middle grounds" rather than sharp racial distinctions. Clashes among Europeans over the pace, cost, and wisdom of expansion fractured any sense of common personal whiteness, even as settler colonialism profoundly formed a sense of white entitlement to settled property in the longer run.

From the point of view of settler colonial elites, policy-making towards Indians, exploitation of African slavery, and manipulating poor white loyalty interacted in intricate ways during this time. To imagine a modern, white supremacist racial order emerging in any simple way out of "whites" suddenly defining themselves as such by virtue of contemplating Africans as a group to be enslaved and exploited thus would be to oversimplify matters considerably. Although contacts with Indians, who when conquered and enslaved were generally exported, were more fleeting than African/white relations, subtle processes also operated to complicate such distinctions. Africans and Indians mixed in the minds of settlers and in real life, often in communities of resistance such as those that formed in some of Virginia's swamps. Religio-racism ensured that white attitudes toward friendly Indians could turn murderous on a dime, as in Bacon's Rebellion, and early demands on behalf of "the [white] people," calling for state violence to enforce hierarchies prioritizing the rights of Europeans, were much more likely to be directed against Indian tribes than against African slaves.

The category of "African" meanwhile also remained internally differentiated, and not only because there continued to exist a minority of free blacks after the late seventeenth- and early eighteenth-century transition to massive use of slave labor. Slavery depended on the exploitation of particular skills of different ethnic groups in Africa. Nowhere was this more the case than in South

Carolina, where slave traders and masters attended closely to matching commodities with the knowledge and skill of specific African ethnicities and regions. The truly sophisticated masters at times sought skilled labor from the peoples of Senegambia and other African rice-producing regions to grow that crop in Carolina. As the French writer Abbé Raynal noted of Carolinian rice production later in the eighteenth century: "This [rice] production grows by the care of the Negroes."

Rice was far from the only "black" enterprise in which managers took African ethnicity into account. Cattle production, fishing, basketry, and maritime work all also came to be associated with specific African peoples. Taking into account that New World purchasers of slave labor associated particular African ethnicities with greater health, and with specific patterns of productivity and resistance, the term "African"—like that of "Indian"—was constantly being both deployed in different contexts and deconstructed. Likewise, those imported into the common horror of slavery initially no more saw themselves as having a common identity than did "whites" or "red Indians." They preserved practices of their specific African ethnicities; only over time did they creatively "exchange their country marks" to build a common African American identity.

Such realities provide further vital clues as to the future staying power of the white supremacist social system, and of the race-thinking accompanying it, being created in the late seventeenth century. White supremacy defined not just a set of racial attitudes and prejudices, but a new social order. Created out of the colonizers' constant and businesslike judgments as to the talents and strengths of enslaved and conquered peoples, white supremacy could easily survive possible panics over the dependence of the colonizer/slaveholder on the very people newly defined as "of color." For masters, slavers, overseers, and traders, the activities of race-making and of managing constantly overlapped. Managing a colony through fluctuating preferences for white indentured labor or for African slaves, managing the pace of expansion onto Indian lands, choosing what kind of Indian labor to rely upon in fur trading, and assembling the "proper assortment" of slaves to accomplish given productive tasks, made "race management" an enduring feature of American life after 1700—a workaday reality created and recreated over time.

In the early eighteenth century, race, gender, and labor— Indian, African, and white—came together tellingly with the Virginian planter and writer William Byrd II's survey of the disputed "boundary line" between Virginia and North Carolina. Byrd provided a dystopian but rapt travelogue of back-country poor whiteness, in Lubberland as he called it. For Byrd, the commons had returned, or rather, had never been abolished here: he wrote, "there is no place in the world where the inhabitants live with less labor . . . by the great felicity of the climate, the easiness of raising provisions, and the slothfulness of the people."

We rightly read such lines less as reportage rather than as expressions of the desire of the powerful for everyone to work harder, but there can be little doubt that the appeal of a return to the commons held attractions even for those who criticized it most harshly. Such appeals shaded into a utopian belief that the New World offered the realization of the longstanding popular fable of the existence of a Land of Cockaigne, a tale inspiring the marvelous modern utopian song "Big Rock Candy Mountain." In that charmed land, wonderful food, drink, sex, holidays, and indeed fountains of youth materialized, even though work was forbidden.

Although Thomas More premised his famous 1563 *Utopia* on the dispossession of the native inhabitants who left land "idle and waste," living in the colonies at times encouraged other senses of how Indians and utopia were connected. For Morton, as for many other European colonials, Native American life generated a powerful and concrete sense of attractive alternative ways to be. Although at the beginning of the colonial period choosing to live among Indians was a capital crime in various places, by that period's end Hector St. John Crevecoeur wrote in 1781 of thousands of colonists who had become "new made Indians," living as "half cultivators and half hunters" or who, worse still, had "degenerated altogether into the hunting state."

Such realities gave both urgency and form to ruling elites' invention of the "savage" Indian. As it rationalized dispossession of "lazy" Indians, the stress on "savagery" underwrote the possibility of satisfying demands for land among settlers, decisively contributing to the idea that "whiteness is property." The indictment of the Indian savage also implied an opposite: the idealized, industrious, and manly settler. Even when the latter ideal went unrealized among "lazy" and poor Europeans, it was not given up easily. Byrd, for example, obsessed endlessly on the patterns of whites' contact and cohabitation with Indians and with escaped African slaves in Lubberland, but stopped short of calling it a mixed-race area. Insisting on the "poor whiteness" of lubbers, Byrd let the adjective "poor" describe at once their economic degradation and their inadequate performance of superior racial status.

Byrd's reflections were, however, as much about gender as about race. He inherited a substantial seventeenth-century European tradition of anti-"savage" imperial writing that claimed to have the best interests of native women at heart—a form tragically familiar to us as we hear contemporary justifications of the Anglo-American occupations of Iraq and Afghanistan. Ignoring complex gender divisions of labor in Indian agriculture and horticulture, and seeing hunting and fishing as the opposite of labor, settlers could convince themselves that Indian men lived by exploiting, and even "enslaving" the women in their households, while male colonists effectively "husbanded"—a synonymous verb for "subdued"—the land. Rhode Island's Roger Williams described the incredible "burthens" such "poor women" in Indian tribes literally carried, not in order to praise their strength but to lament their degradation, and thereby to indict from another angle "savage" Indian men. In Virginia, John Smith found that "the women and children" performed any "worke," such as it was, done by Indians. The practice, or at least ideal, of keeping European wives out of field labor became at times a hallmark of colonial civilization, in which patriarchs protected their women not only from Indians but also allegedly from hard work, helping to fix the place of white women as privileged but in need of protection.

Historical criteria of European color, beauty, and class allowed the definition of "white woman" to emerge with relative ease, though it allowed for sharp distinctions between those who qualified for full inclusion and those who did not. As Gary Taylor's cultural and intellectual history of early European whiteness shows, through the time of early colonization, European men—even the famously pale English—were not represented as being of a white color in art or literature: negative connotations of illness, absence of vigor, and effeminacy ensured as much. John Locke, fittingly enough, was one of the first Englishmen to be represented by an artist as white, almost to the point of translucence. In marked contrast, "pallor" was an established feminine ideal, at least for the elite women who could maintain a whiteness born of avoiding outdoor labor. The color of the "brown wench," in Europe before colonization, and in Lubberland after, marked her as available for exploitation. Thus the categorizing of all European women in the colonies as "white" signaled a bold and powerfully gendered moment in the strategy of creating cross-class loyalty to the state based on whiteness, although the ideal was bound to break down regularly in daily, class-divided life.

In fact early colonization often featured wildly skewed male-over-female sex ratios among settlers, giving rise to sexual violence against both wives and indentured white female servants. Nonetheless in constructing a counterpoint to the Native American "other," and in defaming pro-Indian settler-dissenters like Thomas Morton, colonial rulers fancied themselves as models of civilized gender relations. As such they found yet another reason to brand Indians as savages, whose dispossession promised to benefit not only humanity generally but Indian women specifically, albeit in ways that remained obscure. Byrd worked both sides of this street, sympathizing with overworked Indian women and with the "white" women of Lubberland, likewise seen as doing the work of their uncivilized men. The "lubber" men, he charged, un-racing and un-sexing them in the same stroke, "just like the Indians, impose all work upon their women" in order to "loiter away their lives."

Some varieties of Protestantism spread an ethic that insisted on deferring gratification in order to enforce ever-stricter standards of sexual repression, or at least louder announcement of such standards and greater guilt over any failure to stick to them. Here again the articulation of an ideal white masculinity could work to reconcile opposites, including self-righteousness and sexual abandon. Byrd combined his wholly abstract but "civilized" defense of women with a chronicle of his own career of sexual adventuring, sexual coercion, and sexual violence involving Indian, European, and enslaved African women. He also collected folklore regarding the insatiable sexual appetites of women. Over his life of writing, and sometimes within a single passage, he alternated between repenting and exalting in his misbehaviors. He ended a description of his sexual attack on a cleaning woman with "I kissed and felt her, for which God forgive me." The period of his life in which he toured Lubberland was one in which he tried, Kathleen Brown writes, to "construct a public persona of sexual self-restraint," portraying himself as a sometime rescuer of Indian, black, and lubber women, themselves wanton, when his underlings "employ'd force" sexually. Projecting sexual abandon onto women, increasingly and leeringly onto "non-white" and "poor white" women, but glorying in his white masculine power, he managed to be at once a libertine and a Protestant. Nowhere was this more apparent than in Lubberland, which functioned, as Matt Wray observes, as a "sexual playground" in fantasy and fact for Byrd.

The peculiar way in which "white" settlers, slave masters, and slave traders could be pulled towards involvement in such a playground while insisting that they had no part in creating or enjoying it, is best captured by George Rawick's acute provocations on the ways that projecting their sexual desires onto racial others bore testament to the deep contradictions among Europeans learning new regimes of capitalist repression. "The Englishman met the West African as a reformed sinner meets a comrade of his previous debaucheries," Rawick wrote, adding that such a sinner "often creates a pornography of his former life." In new colonial worlds, the settler and the slave trader imagined the racial other as "living as he once did or as he still unconsciously desires to live." Frequently backsliding and always fearful of doing so, he "cannot leave alone" fantasies of the sexual behavior of those whom he enslaves. Rawick clinches his point by arguing that in fantasizing that African women copulated with apes, Englishmen expressed their own fears as to where their own losses of control might end.

Interestingly, Locke's *On Human Understanding* organized itself for long sections around precisely the fantasy—he characteristically treated it as fact—of African women giving birth to the children of apes, specifically of "Guinea [West African] drills." In Locke's hands, the fantasy is so charged with meanings of sex and race that it animates an otherwise hopelessly dry consideration of the definition of "species." Writing on apes, sex, and race, Locke generates the first extended and explicit philosophical discussions of the relation between whiteness and humanity by placing Africans within the animal world.

The ways in which the invention of racial distinctions spoke to gender and sexual crises among Europeans, and within their individual psyches, thus bring us back from anti-Indian to anti-African ideologies as mainsprings of race-thinking. The logic of "whiteness as property," what Du Bois called "personal whiteness," emerged out of the turn to slave modes of production and out of the dispossession of the Indians. Even as European elite women were idealized as "white" long before their male counterparts, African women were for a time even more insistently and fetishistically connected to the animal world than were African men. Colonial accounts of African women and apes, as well as obsessive descriptions and drawings of female Africans' breasts, came amidst crises in gender and masculinity among whites.

These crises generated in 1691 a reformulation of firm legal distinctions between white and African women. That law set out to undermine daily gendered interactions between African and European laborers, to punish what was coming to be seen as sex across a color line—unless, of course, that sex was coerced by a white, often slaveholding, man. As the behavior of Byrd's men towards "lubber" women underlines, such a law did not make such poor white women free or secure, but did put them in a different position from the enslaved. Formerly, they would have been unambiguously "wenches," with the adjective "nasty" and perhaps, given work outdoors, "brown" thrown in for good measure. Now, a collection of remorseless material realities set them apart from enslaved African women. Where race, gender, and sex were concerned the transformations had begun well before Bacon's Rebellion and accelerated after. In 1662 the General Assembly in Virginia, admitting ambiguities in prior practices—Elizabeth Key, the child of an English father and an enslaved African mother, had won a freedom suit in 1659— declared "that all children borne in this country shalbe held bond or free only according to the condition of the mother." Although the 1662 act did not quite invent personal whiteness—it used "Christian," to identify European settlers, which applied to only relatively few African women in the colony—important and durable distinctions were being drawn. In extending punishments for consensual interracial sex the 1691 law did use the word "white" as a defining term for the first time in Virginia law. Since European women had long practiced the newly outlawed behavior, the first law naming a "white" race was also a piece of repressive legislation against some whites.

But in the same period laws also specified that Europeans possessed privileges that Africans did not. Whether a lubber or the most respected "good wife" in the colony, "white" women could only give birth to free children. Enslaved African women, on the other hand, could only legally give birth to property. At law, then, the master's sexual violence against slave women potentially increased his property. As Sharon Block argues, such dynamics made rape itself "part of the architecture of early American racial and gender hierarchies." By the early eighteenth century a new world of race and terror, one featuring powerful connections among race, class, property, gender, violence, and sex, had emerged. That white supremacist world would prove most difficult to dismantle.

2

Slavery's Shadow, Empire's Edge:

HOW WHITE SUPREMACY SURVIVED
DECLARATIONS OF INDEPENDENCE

As the American revolutionary process gained momentum through direct actions against the 1765 Stamp Act, Britain's first attempt to impose direct taxation on the colonies, the Charleston (South Carolina) merchant Henry Laurens tempered worry with bemusement. Laurens, among the largest slave traders based in the colonies, described "a peculiar incident, revealing in what dread the citizens lived among the black savages with whom they surrounded themselves." The foreboding "was furnished . . . by some negroes who, apparently in thoughtless imitation, began to cry, 'Liberty.'" Even as he wished away the event's gravity, Laurens added, "The city was thrown under arms for 10 to 14 days." Just over a decade later Laurens, whose own house had been mobbed by Stamp Act protesters who saw it as a symbol of reaction, finally overcame his longstanding inclination to side with British authorities against the revolutionary struggle. By then a substantial rice planter, he made his leap in outraged response to British offers of freedom for slaves willing to desert their rebellious masters and aid the British. The revolutionaries welcomed Laurens, who by 1777 presided over the Continental Congress, the de facto colonial government.

A very different fate awaited Crispus Attucks, an Afro-Indian escaped slave who was shot and killed by the British in the 1770

Boston Massacre. The lawyer and later US president John Adams defended the British soldiers in the legal proceedings that followed. He branded the murdered anti-British fighters as "obscure and inconsiderable," a "motley rabble of saucy boys, negroes and molattoes [sic], Irish teagues and outlandish Jack Tarrs." Attucks came in for special abuse, as ringleader and as someone "whose very looks [were] enough to terrify any person." By 1773, Adams would himself be protesting against the Tea Act and other abuses. He issued one of his hottest letters to the Massachusetts governor under a pseudonym: Crispus Attucks.

Similarly the celebrated Boston Tea Party protests stood among many whose participants used "Indian disguise," often referred to as consisting of wearing Native American clothing and "blackening" the skin, to create unity and encourage audacity in the revolutionaries. The iconography of the American Revolution portrayed colonists as noble, but victimized, Native Americans. Virginia's revolutionary militias frequently carried "tommyhawks." Meanwhile, atrocities against the real Indians were rife. In one battle in native "Indian Country," patriot hero George Rogers Clark had captives bound and tomahawked in the sight of those yet to be attacked. Revolutionary Pennsylvania offered incredible sums for Indian scalps and counted among its heroes the Paxton Boys, perpetrators of the notorious December 1763 massacre of Indians in Pennsylvania; later, they themselves joined General George Washington's ranks, "dressed and painted" in "redface." Even as the Declaration of Independence was about to be signed, Adams fretted not just about British power but about the forces inside the freedom movement that Attucks embodied. Writing to his wife to "laugh" at her early calls for considerations of women's rights, Adams allowed that what he called "our struggle" had regrettably "loosened the bands of Government everywhere . . . Children and Apprentices were disobedient . . . Indians slighted their guardians and Negroes grew insolent to their Masters." When he later acknowledged that the "blood of the martyrs" of the Boston Massacre "proved to be the seed of the congregation" of revolutionaries, Adams felt no need to admit that the Revolution belonged to Attucks specifically as much and more than it did to him.

The incredible about-faces, breakthroughs, transformations, retreats, and blind spots suggested by such small, contradictory stories capture something of the settlers' capacity for spectacular change as the US created itself. Historians have remarked upon the sense of possibility contained in the idea of the American Revolution as a "contagion of liberty," a process alternately exhilarating and worrisome for elite men like Laurens and Adams. And yet in helping us to answer how white supremacy survived the Declaration of Independence, even as promising a framework as the contagion of liberty can lead to a scripted, unsatisfying set of answers.

As the example of Adams shows, colonial elites fancied, though uneasily, that liberty radiated out from them. But the real story moved in much more dramatic, dialectical, and longstanding patterns. The New York City Revolt of 1741, centering on a series of insurrectionary fires, promised freedom to slaves and paradise to a variety of poor people living on the margins of freedom, poverty, and the law. Its principal players included "Negro Peg" (Irish despite her nickname) and her black lover, John Gwin. The most extensive contemporary account termed the plot a "Conspiracy formed by Some White People, in Conjunction with Negro and other Slaves." It directed its rhetorical fire against "white" (that is, elite white) people. It was variously considered an Irish, a Spanish, a "Popish," or a "Negro" plot. Thirty Africans and four whites were executed in the wake of the plot, usually in the most brutal and public ways possible. A white leader and a black leader, "hung on the gibbet" and then displayed alongside each other, exchanged races, so the story went, as they decayed. The hair, features, and color of the white corpse were all said to have changed miraculously as the white rebel John Hughson took on "the symmetry of a negro beauty." Here was contagious liberty with a vengeance. Like Attucks' death such

dramas informed, emboldened, and terrified more cautious revolutionaries. But such freedom dreams could not bequeath a
racially egalitarian vision to the American Revolution as a whole.

Overwhelmingly, the Revolution comes down to us as a set of
treasured founding documents, ideas, and ideals produced by
literate and usually propertied leaders. In part because the classic
formulation of the "contagion of liberty" idea developed in a
corpus of intellectual history, scholars often assume that literate
and powerful revolutionaries laid out advanced ideas about freedom that other groups then adopted and applied to their own
plights. This assumption, that "in the beginning there were the
words of elites," has its logic. Because the Declaration of Independence, and to a lesser extent the Constitution, are such
seminal texts of liberation, appealed to by future generations of
freedom fighters at home and abroad, their words are rightly taken
as being carefully chosen and enduringly important facts. However, these texts also reflected the sharp limits of the Founding
Fathers where opposition to white supremacy was concerned.
Liberty could only be so contagious.

The very power of such documents, along with the fact that
their evasions and elisions on race and slavery are more significant
than the few words they manage to say on the subject, makes
understanding their contexts as imperative as it is difficult. The
decision to declare independence while retaining slavery has long
underpinned the liberal approach to race where both history and
policy are concerned in the US, something that further burdens
and narrows our understanding of the Revolution where race is
concerned. Conceived as a paradox, or more famously as the
"American dilemma," such an approach laments the distance
between the founders' universalistic ideals of equality and their
easy compromises with slavery. However, in most cases the
critique quickly gives way in practice to some mixture of fatalism
and patriotism. A flattened context is reasserted, and we learn that
little of the world was antislavery at the time, so that the founders'
vision of freedom, being second to none at the time, could only go

so far. The two horns of the American dilemma thus remain distinct, with the infinitely nobler half—commitment to equality—separate from, and largely unsullied by, the practice of racism. Appeals to this nobler half become the key to resolving the dilemma, not with urgency but in an imagined long term spanning centuries.

Reading the Declaration of Independence in light of an American dilemma, and attempting to square the circle regarding freedom and slaveholding, forces us to see the document in black and white, in racial terms. In lingering over the declaration's silence regarding whether enslaved Africans had a place among "all men" who were "created equal," we can miss the document's characterization of Native Americans, "the merciless Indian savages, whose known rule of warfare is an undistinguished destruction of all ages, sexes and conditions." Unhappily the most sustained "contagion of liberty" actually practiced by the new nation centered on imagining its own manifest destiny to spread across the continent. To omit consideration of such realities leaves us understanding the staying power of neither empire nor slavery. The vast expansion of US settler colonialism, especially embodied in the 1803 Louisiana Purchase, was justified as securing and extending an empire of liberty. The acquisition of this vast swathe of land ensured that the white supremacy attending settler colonialism would be an ongoing central theme of the nation's story. Moreover, geographical expansion meant that slavery, far from being gradually dismantled as many revolutionaries hoped, would long survive—indeed the number of slaves quadrupled nationally between 1803 and the Civil War.

What follows explores how the revolutionary US proclaimed liberty at the same time as expanding slavery and dispossession. I hope to retain the sense of wild possibility that a formulation like "contagion of liberty" conveys at its best, but to show that liberty, as settlers understood it, did not simply stand in opposition to slavery and white supremacy. Instead the very idea of freedom, and the prospects of gaining it, took shape within existing and evolving systems of exploitation. Spaces in which to struggle for the broadest meanings of liberty did open up in a long, electric revolutionary process. However, the logic and practice dictated by the first successful war of national liberation in the shadow of slavery and on the edge of empire also made the new nation resistant to any strains of contagion attacking white supremacy. The contradictions of the "contagion of liberty" became most clear at moments when elites imagined the new nation's citizens, or decided on its shape and its expansion.

A wonderful subtlety in W. E. B. Du Bois's early study of the slave trade and US nation-building clarifies how we can, and why we must, move beyond the American dilemma. With studied ambiguity, Du Bois held that through 1787 it would have "needed an exceptionally clear and discerning mind . . . to deny that slavery and the slave-trade in the US of America were doomed to early annihilation." His words force us to see the real and extended possibilities for slaves' liberation in a long revolutionary process. Du Bois' reference to 1787 saw the Constitution itself as a marker of the dashing of revolutionary hopes regarding antislavery. However, he went much further than mere analysis of the words of documents produced by revolutionary leaders. That the slave was both threat and commodity informed the very terms and extent of opposition to the slave trade. Indeed when Du Bois enumerated six reasons that the slave trade had seemed doomed to a speedy disappearance until 1787, only one had anything to do with the "rights of man." That reason was sandwiched between slavery's economic failure outside the far South and the renewed appreciation of "the old fear of slave insurrection" that arose in the context of war. Other reasons cited by Du Bois included purely market considerations, namely that planters and traders wishing to raise slave prices domestically stood among the "strongest partisans" of a movement promising to limit supplies of slaves by curtailing the international trade.

While there was, in Du Bois' view, a tension between slavery and revolutionary ideals, there was no actual movement based on "a great moral protest against an iniquitous traffic." Based neither on "timeless truths" nor an organized movement, but on the exigencies of war and coalition, hopes for black freedom suffered betrayal. By 1800, Du Bois notes, there were about 900,000 slaves in the US, a figure that had grown by 28 percent in the previous ten years. This figure totaled more than those in bondage in all the British colonies put together. It equaled the total number of slaves held in all French, Dutch, Portuguese, and Spanish possessions. The post-revolutionary growth of bondage resulted from enslavement of the newborn in numbers unprecedented and unmatched in the Atlantic world. It also reflected the continuing importation of slaves from Africa and the West Indies.

Contagious Liberty as Afterthought, Military Response, and Crime

If the British conservative Samuel Johnson were correct, there would be little need to ask how white supremacy survived the American Revolution. According to Johnson, revolutionaries were hardly in agonies over an American dilemma. Instead the hypocritical "demigods of independence," organizing for their own freedom, doubled as the brutal enforcers of African slavery. In 1775, as rebellion against British rule matured, Johnson argued that the widespread practice of slavery made Americans' claims of deep commitment to human freedom, and claims of "being enslaved" themselves, ring hollow. "If slavery thus be fatally contagious," he asked, disdaining assertions that royal actions in the colonies threatened all British liberties, "how is it that we hear the loudest *yelps* for liberty among the drivers of negroes?"

Some months later, Thomas Jefferson had a forceful answer for Johnson. Influenced by Benjamin Franklin, who had earlier parried Johnson's charges, Jefferson's draft of the Declaration of Independence threw the accusations of hypocrisy right back into British faces. Jefferson made slavery and the slave trade the last and longest of a crescendo of indictments against imperial authority. It was for Jefferson the British Crown that had "waged cruel war against human nature itself, violating its most sacred rights of life and liberty in the persons of a distant people who never offended him, captivating and carrying them into slavery" or to "miserable death." Moreover, the colonized had attempted to legislate against "this execrable commerce," only to see the king block their efforts. Thus the colonists and their slaves alike were victims of tyranny from the same source.

As far as commitment to universal liberty is concerned, Johnson and Jefferson each wrote from such a compromised position that the words of both can be dismissed as posturing. Johnson defended the nation most central to slave trading during the century in which he wrote. His mannered outrage was that of a British enemy of colonial freedom—one capable of frankly urging the "subjection of Americans" whom he regarded as a "race of convicts"—rather than an abolitionist. For his part, through a long career as revolutionary and statesman, Jefferson kept in chains hundreds of people whom he personally owned, including several of his own children. Jefferson simply dropped all mention of slaves' sacred rights from the Declaration of Independence as soon as fellow leaders balked at his raising such issues, even in critiquing the king.

Nonetheless the opposing positions of Johnson and Jefferson teach us much about why the spread of what Du Bois called the "new philosophy of 'Freedom'" proves both indispensable and insufficient in charting the challenges that the Revolution posed to slavery. Johnson was clearly right that revolutionaries worried most about their own "slavery." Considered broadly, revolutionaries strikingly conformed to Johnson's caricatures of them on that score. Even when we allow that they inherited a British dissenting political tradition in which arguments to defend rights in terms of a stark dichotomy between individual liberty and figurative "slavery," it is clear that everyday life in the colonies—even in New England one household in six held a slave—made slavery far more than a metaphor. Aggrieved colonials spoke of their own "real slavery," implausibly but painstakingly linking their travails to race-based miseries inflicted by them. The white Virginian Arthur Lee displayed, if unconsciously, what F. Nwabueze Okoye has bitterly and aptly called "a detailed familiarity with the elements of the Afro-American experience" in responding to the threats posed by a 1766 piece of British legislation. Extravagantly imagining himself as the victim of those "wantonly cruel in the execution of despotic power," Lee wrote, "I see already men torn from their weeping and distressed families, without hope, without redress, never to return . . . I see every endearing tie of father, husband, son and brother, torn asunder, unrespited, unpitied, unreprieved . . . forever." Philadelphia's Richard Wells explicitly raised the specter that colonists would be treated as "Guinea slaves." He then apologized at once for having to use that "horrid simile."

Franklin, a longtime slaveholder and sometime abolitionist in a city where 10 percent of his fellow Philadelphia artisans owned slaves at the time of the Revolution, emphasized to Johnson how fully inappropriate it was to treat him as a "slave." Like Adams, Franklin occasionally adopted an African American persona to write pseudonymously, in part to underline his claim that Britain wanted to "make American whites black." Such rhetoric became, as David Waldstreicher puts it, a "kind of signature" of Franklin's revolutionary prose. As Johnson's remarks on the colonists as a "convict" race imply, Franklin's paranoia reflected a fanciful but not wholly unfounded position. Apologists for British Empire did at times impugn the racial qualities of colonists, citing either their alleged criminal or indentured origins or emphasizing their physical environment in America as the cause of biological deterioration across generations. Jefferson, who described his own misadventures with slave trading and inherited debts as turning him into "a species of property annexed to certain mercantile houses in London," took care to respond to charges of such degeneration, even defending in his notebooks the vigor of North America's fauna.

When the historian Edmund Morgan wrote that Americans "bought their independence with slave labor," his words resonated because they revealed the source of wealth, power, and time to organize among the slaveholding Founding Fathers. Slavery also grounded master/revolutionaries' habits of command, and their fears of being commanded, in their everyday experiences of bossing and brutalizing black labor. The British conservative Edmund Burke understood as much when he urged compromise with colonial radicals because slaveholding made them formidable enemies who were "most . . . jealous of their freedom" because they were themselves experienced in the "haughtiness of domination."

To allow Johnson's counter-revolutionary cynicism to overly inform our historical analysis misses as much as it captures. There was some inspired "contagion of liberty" where slavery was concerned. The very idea that contending British and US forces, each deeply entangled with slavery, would argue for their own relative innocence regarding the slaves' plight was itself something new and exciting. If racial slavery was a newcomer on the world's stage, elite, secular opposition to it was younger still. Those criticizing bondage in the names of universal liberty and of moral decency were not so much failing to live up to an established ideal as they were, amid compromises, defining the future of antislavery. However, because they did so within a revolutionary movement in which fears of "slavery" being visited on whites came first and stood foremost, that future would often be difficult and compromised.

Hearing and making extravagant comparisons between themselves and slaves did encourage a growing number of revolutionaries to think that both oppressions deserved to be addressed. Benjamin Rush privately wrote by the late 1760s that he thought it "useless" to campaign against British conspiracies to enslave the colonies while "we continue to keep our fellow creatures in slavery just because their color is different from ours." In 1776 Samuel Hopkins would go further, allowing that colonial oppression was "lighter than a feather" compared to slavery. After African American revolutionaries themselves, those most likely to embrace this line of argument were white radicals wishing to extend the contagion of liberty to matters well beyond representation and taxation. As she tried to open debate on the rights of women, First Lady Abigail Adams warned against disconnecting the issue of chattel slavery from the rights of man. From the time of his own arrival in North America, Tom Paine, among the most consistently freedom-loving of the artisan radicals beginning to contribute mightily to an abolitionist tradition, stood in support of the slave's freedom. He wondered how Americans could "complain so loudly while they held so many hundreds of thousands in slavery; and annually enslave many thousands more."

One of first acts of the associated revolutionary states was the magnificently straightforward, if quickly dishonored, pronouncement: "We will neither import, nor purchase any slave imported after the first day of December next; after which Time, we will wholly discontinue the Slave Trade." By 1779, Rhode Island had outlawed interstate slave trading without the slave's consent. Revolutionary Vermont joined the high-flown language of the declaration on universal natural rights to the abolition of slavery with the weighty word "therefore." As George Washington's presidency began, most of the Northern states had at least a gradual plan of emancipation in effect, with others to follow by 1804, making the region's record on emancipation superior to that of British Canada. The revolutionaries in parts of the North could briefly claim a share of world leadership in antislavery initiatives. Nonetheless ideas about emancipation of slaves developed among revolutionary elites as a postscript to reflections on their own "slavery" and as a calculation of their own economic and national interests. Such realities had deep and enduring impacts, from facilitating the easy dismissal of the "sacred rights" of Africans from the Declaration of Independence, to shaping the way in which the nation's imagination and laws connected race and citizenship for centuries to come.

But there was also concrete reason for the Revolution to set itself against the freedom of slaves from its inception, as we can again see in the differing views of Johnson and Jefferson. Beyond his famous query on opposition to slavery among slave drivers, Johnson also delivered what he hoped would be the Revolution's political and military epitaph by urging that the British military be used to free colonial slaves, thus striking at the colonists' greatest vulnerability by creating "more grateful and honest" subjects from among those freed. By 1776, the counter-revolutionary aggression advocated by Johnson was apparent in British policies that aimed to impress upon rebels the perils of founding a revolution in the shadow of slavery: in key colonial districts the British offered freedom to those who would desert their rebellious masters. In contrast to the nineteenth century, when the notion of the "docile slave" would be used to buttress pro-slavery arguments, there was no doubt that the promise of liberation would provoke a lively response among the enslaved population. Sylvia Frey's monumental work shows that a decade of fierce slave resistance before 1775 had made the British aware that any hints of possible freedom would be eagerly pursued by a sizeable number of slaves. At the time of the Revolution, as the late Winthrop Jordan wonderfully observed, "The Negro . . . was of course presumed to crave liberty."

Britain's bloody and continuing record as a slave power, and its desire not to alienate loyalist slaveholders in North America, consistently made it stop short of wholesale encouragement of slave rebellion, which it once branded "too black, horrid and wicked" to be fully embraced. Strapped British forces at times sold captured African Americans as slaves in order to buy supplies, dropping any claim to be an army of liberation. Nonetheless, first by the hundreds, and eventually by the tens of thousands, slaves found ways to declare their independence during the Revolution. The Virginia defections reached right into General Washington's own slave labor force. In South Carolina the conflict became a three-sided war with as many as 20,000 slaves not just caught in the middle but also asserting their own interests, sometimes dying in bids for freedom. Georgia lost an estimated two-thirds of her prewar slave population and Jefferson's calculation for Virginia—he was much interested in compensation claims and inflated his personal losses—was a loss of 30,000 slaves in a single year. A sharp sense of the extent of slave resistance and of the value of such resistance to the Revolution's enemy helps us greatly to under-stand what Jordan called the "seemingly paradoxical denunciation of both slavery and Negroes" by Jefferson and other revolution-aries.

The draft Declaration of Independence left little doubt as to who was to be blamed and who was to be criminalized for such resistance. The Crown, of course, drew censure for "exciting [slaves] to rise in arms among us," but blame for the actual "crimes," explicitly "murdering," was apportioned to slaves who sought freedom. Always brutally prosecuted, politically charged slave resistance now became not only a crime against order and property, but also against the Revolution itself. Sym-bolic counter-revolutionary political acts, such as having African American drummers in the British army whip captive "Liberty Boys," fueled the fire.

Because British appeals to desert slavery often went out to indentured servants as well as slaves, they raised the specter of a "motley" interracial rebellion within the Revolution of the sort that had so exercised Adams' negative response to the victims of the Boston Massacre. The metaphor of contagion aptly captures the implication that, carried too far, liberty becomes disease. Slaves deserting to the British could, as in the case of the Virginian planter Landon Carter, cause revolutionaries to focus far more intently on recapturing runaways than on the fortunes of the rebellion.

What Du Bois termed "the old fear of slave insurrection" had animated colonists' attempts to limit the slave trade from the early eighteenth century onwards. In the midst of revolutionary war, threats of flight to the British, of fighting alongside them, and even of more everyday forms of resistance, spurred anti-slave trade agitation and in a minority of cases revolutionary emancipation. But slaveholders also spoke acidly of the "contagion of 'ingratitude' " among slaves, regarding this as more worthy of note than any contagion of liberty. The post-revolutionary surge of manumissions and grants of freedom by individual masters resonated with the highest ideals of freedom. But weariness and fear in the face of "betrayal" and resistance by slaves also mattered in setting such liberatory practices into motion.

Emancipation became, among other things, a strategic matter. In 1775, Virginia rebels at the Williamsburg Convention spectacularly resolved that Americans wanted "not only [to] prevent any more Negroes from losing their freedom, but [to] restore it to such as have already unhappily lost it." They chose words perfectly suited to defuse British efforts to enlist slaves against the Revolution. The grudging deployment of African Americans as revolutionary soldiers filled the same purpose. Not long after a period when enlisting a black soldier could carry a jail sentence, Henry Laurens' son broached wild plans to sign up thousands of slaves as soldiers, offering freedom as the incentive for their service and to respond to British efforts to foment slave resistance.

But a wide racial gulf remained between the way in which white revolutionaries conceived of their own relation to liberty and how they thought about freedom for African American slaves. For white Americans, the logic of revolution was that true independence would never be granted but would have to be seized, while among slaves freedom could never be seized but only granted. White freedom would come heroically in highly compressed "revolutionary time," governed by a sense of extreme anticipation that worlds could change overnight. Emancipation of slaves, on the other hand, was to be at best gradual, unfolding over many decades. Conversely, stopping short of the indictment of slaveholding and slave trading, as the Declaration of Independence does, could have appeared to be the key to national unity and therefore the essence of revolutionary wisdom. Some things changed little. When revolutionaries recaptured one of

Washington's escaped white indentured servants in a raid on a British vessel he was, like other whites seized, accorded "great humanity" in treatment. The "Ethiopians" taken in the same raid were "tried for their lives." When the revolutionary artisan Paul Revere rendered Crispus Attucks' likeness in a memorial, he made the face white.

Whiteness and Property: Antidotes to Contagious Liberty

Wishful thinking has often left liberal writers hoping that Jefferson's phrase "life, liberty, and pursuit of happiness" represented a conscious break from the older aphorism "life, liberty, and property," derived from John Locke's writings. This view distances the Declaration from its debts to an explicitly pro-slavery theorist, and implies that the master's title to slaves as property need not have complicated the contagion of liberty too hopelessly. But Jefferson's own pronouncements, as well as the interchangeable uses of "happiness" and "property" in the wording of state constitutions—not to mention the nation's return to "life, liberty, and property" in the Bill of Rights—leave little doubt that the revolutionary leaders continued to lean on Locke, and regarded independence and property as inextricably linked.

Methods of attracting soldiers to the revolutionary army make this point concrete. In March 1784 the legislature in liberated South Carolina reported on the number of slaves still owed to one group of revolutionary war veterans, who were enticed to sign up to the cause with offers of bounty. Similar "negro bounties" went to other South Carolina troops, and to those of other states. In Virginia, more soldiers would have been owed slaves had James Madison's broader 1780 proposal for slave "bonuses" in the revolutionary army been enacted. Even so, the 1784 numbers for slave bounties owed, calculated down to fractions of human, were large and telling. South Carolina recognized in that year claims from General Thomas Sumter's men alone for $570\frac{3}{4}$ adult slaves as well as $44\frac{3}{8}$ slave children. Since by the 1780s demand for slaves outstripped supply, South Carolina issued interest-bearing treasury certificates to meet its obligations. Also granted to veterans were bounties of land that promised to contribute to their economic independence. The relationship of race to property in slaves and in Indian land set stark limits on the contagion of liberty.

Although at the time neither pro-slavery nor white supremacist thought had received much scientific or theological elaboration, the brute fact that some powerful people owned other people loomed large. Occasional arguments were emerging that slavery was a positive good for African souls, or that settler colonialism somehow spurred "civilization" among Indians, while the tentative but troubling beginnings of American racial "science" were emerging in the writings of Jefferson and Benjamin Rush, among others. But it was the reality of slaves as property, not ideas about race, which worked most powerfully to arrest the contagion of liberty. In the early 1780s, the peace process and the British withdrawal featured harsh, protracted debate on what colonists called the "plunders" of slaves who had fled to freedom. It was the ubiquitous Henry Laurens, now one of the negotiators in talks with the British, who made insistence on re-enslavement a founding act of diplomacy for the victorious US. He insisted that the 1783 Treaty of Paris, which formally concluded the revolutionary war, should include language specifying that British withdrawal not involve "carrying away American property, Negroes, &c."

The tragic fate of antislavery revivalist religion offers the best example of the compelling pull of slave property. Having been tarnished by associations with the English Church and counter-revolutionary politics, Anglicanism in the US was further weakened by disestablishment by revolutionary state governments, in the process making Methodism and Baptism well poised to thrive in the new nation; these took strong hold especially in the South. Baptists used the ringing language of "jubilee," drawn from discussions in the Old Testament book of Leviticus about the justice of periodic slave emancipations and redistribution of property, to describe their own urgent commitment to uprooting the "violent deprivation of the rights of nature" that was slavery. Before the Revolution, Methodism's leading light, John Wesley, announced God's judgment on slaveholders and slave traders. In 1784 the denomination's Baltimore Conference sternly promised expulsion of all members not divesting themselves of slaves within two years. After the Revolution, however, both Baptists and Methodists quickly acknowledged that valued members and prospective converts held slave property, with some important doctrinal decisions based on the existence of laity and clergy who innocently came to own slaves through inheritance or marriage.

The power of the planters quickly asserted itself. When Wesley's emissary Thomas Coke toured Virginia in 1784 and 1785 he faced persistent threats from an assassin, from armed mobs, and from a grand jury when he "touched on the subject of slavery." He consequently changed tack, and took to starting sermons by lecturing black listeners "in a very pathetic manner on the Duty of Servants to Masters" in order to be able to continue to speak. Political reform, hopefully in concert with slaveholders, became the preferred Methodist strategy, and a delegation lobbied George Washington in 1785 to join a petition campaign for general emancipation. Washington's negative response predicted the fragility of such appeals to masters. He confusingly cited the contagion of liberty as his reason to abstain from furthering to that contagion: "It would be dangerous to make a frontal attack on a prejudice which is beginning to decrease." By the nineteenth century it was clear that Coke's line on the need for the slaves "to be obedient" would drown out his denomination's antislavery text in the Protestant South. Promising to save souls, though not bodies, such preaching to slaves would become a prominent feature in pro-slavery thought.

Post–revolutionary public policy regarding slaves fleeing to more northerly states that had at least gradual emancipation plans in place made the priorities of property-holders brutally clear. In the Somerset case of 1772, British law had held that a slave brought into Britain might challenge successfully the master's right to imprison him. While the decision focused on technicalities and did not abolish slavery, even in Britain, it did establish at law that positive protection for slave property from local institutions was necessary and that British courts could henceforth decide to value what jurists called the "free air" of Britain over the incoming master's right to hold slave property.

The general failure of the states and of the US as a whole to pick up the logic of the Somerset decision showed the overwhelming influence of revolutionary deference to property. Even amidst fierce defenses of local and state rights in constitutional debates, a national system for returning freedom-minded fugitive slaves to their masters took shape without serious discussion because slaves were so clearly defined as property. The Northwest Ordinance of 1787, for example, opened new states north of the Ohio and east of the Mississippi to settlement. Reflecting the contagion of liberty, it forbade slavery in those areas—but it also promised the return of slaves who had escaped to them. The federal Constitution likewise doubled as a fugitive slave act, echoing the Northwest Ordinance's language. In keeping with the document's avoidance of the word "slavery," Article IV Section 2 of the Constitution provided that those "held to service or labor," but "escaping" into a free state, "shall be delivered up" to owners. In the slight debate on the clause, Carolina delegates were brutally clear in their insistence that "fugitive slaves and servants . . . be delivered up like criminals."

Similarly the course of emancipation in the North reflected respect for ownership of slave property, even at the height of the contagion of liberty. These states, with New Jersey as a partial exception, were not about to compensate masters for emancipated slave property. The adopted alternatives, especially in the emancipationist states with the most slaves, therefore often involved agonizingly gradualist schemes, freeing not adult slaves but their children, who sometimes had to continue in slavery until well into their twenties. With masters thus having long stretches to gain returns on their "investments," nearly 40,000 people remained enslaved in the North as late as 1800, and the institution persisted for many decades thereafter in the supposedly "free" states. Connecticut's 1784 emancipation law was so cautious that the pro-slavery Supreme Court in the infamous 1857 Dred Scott decision would cite it, in trying to discredit the very idea that African Americans had rights. Revolutionary Connecticut had insisted that "the right of property of the master was to be protected" even at the high tide of revolutionary contagions of liberty.

Moreover, freedpeople were seldom quite that. They lived within long, racially charged patterns of litigation, dependency, indenture, discrimination, surveillance, and kinship to loved ones still enslaved that left them as "slaves to the community" if not still to individual masters, much like New England Indians caught in webs of "overseers," indentures, and denials of their very existence. Revolutionary Massachusetts embraced not only emancipation but also harsh laws against interracial marriage. Nevertheless, gradual emancipation proved more than enough to allow many white New Englanders to, as a recent account puts it, "disown slavery," erasing past and present oppression.

In the two other major areas in which the Constitution compromised with slavery debates were fuller, allowing for more explicit accounting of questions of property. The Constitution's framers decided to allow the slave trade to continue in whichever states did not explicitly ban it, with no possible national prohibition until twenty years had passed. Debating this policy, a South Carolina delegate urged Northerners to "consult their interests [remembering that] the increase in slaves . . . will increase the commodities of which they will become the carrier." A Connecticut delegate followed by observing that "What enriches a part enriches the whole." There was no clear North/South split on the slave trade's continuation among those deliberating the Constitution. Upper Southern colonies like Virginia and Maryland, fearing revolt, nurturing the seeds of abolitionism, and having a surplus of slaves to dispose of on the domestic market, opposed the international slave trade. A trade-off between concessions on navigation policy, wanted by some Northerners, and the ability to traffic in humans, especially desired by the Deep South, ensured the defeat of those seeking a speedy end to the Atlantic slave trade. The compromise keeping the international slave trade off the table until 1808 reflected entrenched connections between the slave trade and commerce generally, in both North and South. When colonists spoke broadly of slaves as "the strength and sinews" of their world, the reference was not just to the productivity of plantations but also to the ties of slavery with the whole economy.

The slave trade shaped the history of capital and shipping in the United States, especially in the North. Although confined by colonial empires to less favorable routes and smaller ships, North American vessels managed to conduct substantial slave trading. Trade routes involving Africa and the Caribbean accounted, as Ronald Bailey calculates, for over three-quarters of New England's exports in 1770. The African trade generated revenues that eased somewhat the new nation's chronic, serious balance of payments shortfalls. The Deep South, therefore, hardly stood isolated in debates over the slave trade: Jefferson wrote that his anti-slave trade language in the Declaration was removed "in complaisance to South Carolina & Georgia," but also at the behest of "Northern brethren" whom he thought "felt a little tender [as] they had been pretty considerable carriers" of slaves. By the early nineteenth century, the explosion of cotton production and the expansion of Northern textile factories created expanding webs of economic alliance among New England factory owners and illegal slave traders, New York merchants and Southern slaveholders.

The most mysterious and politically momentous constitutional concession to slavery came near the document's beginning: Article I Section 2 declared that representatives in the House and the electoral college would reflect the "whole number of free Persons including those bound to service for a Term of Years, and

excluding Indians not taxed, three-fifths of all other persons."
Following on a 1783 use of the same 60 percent ratio for counting
slaves to apportion per capita national taxes, the three-fifths
mechanism used in the Constitution flowed from the fact that
the holding of slaves as property was a respected established fact in
the political landscape of the new republic. But the short passage
applying this "federal ratio" to representation as well as to taxes
related to whiteness as property in far more profound ways. While
it made even indentured whites (their race unnamed) into "free
persons," it read Indians (who were named) out of citizenship, and
it counted enslaved "other persons" (named neither racially nor in
their servile position, by what one delegate called an "ashamed"
constitutional convention) not as holders of political power, but as
sources of such power for their own enslavers.

The last point merits special emphasis because the 60 percent or
"three-fifths" clause consistently lends itself to misunderstanding.
In his gloss on the matter in *The Federalist Papers* of 1787–88,
which advocated the ratification of the US Constitution, James
Madison began the confusion by praising the "great propriety" of
the Constitution in treating slaves as having "the mixed character
of persons and property." In fact the compromise was far worse
than Madison implied. The Constitution did not confer any
percentage of legal personhood, still less political power, on slaves.
It used slaves' bodies to give power to those who held slaves,
securing, as Madison himself once put it, "the guardianship of
property." The extent of the pro-slaveholders' advantage was clear
by 1800, when Jefferson won a close presidential race where
apportionment of votes favored the slaveholding states by counting three-fifths of their slaves as if they were voters. By the time of
the Civil War, the slave South began every election with a head
start of over two million votes based on counting three-fifths of
those it held in bondage. Such a concession giving extra political
power to the areas holding property rights in slaves, came at a time
when the US otherwise pioneered in divorcing voting from
property ownership by extending the franchise to the white poor.

The Three-Fifths Compromise underwrote slaveholders' domination of the presidency and key congressional committees. This aggrandizement of planters' power, based on their dependents and property, provides the best evidence for the political philosopher Charles Mills' branding of American revolutionary ideology as "herrenvolk [that is, 'master race'] Lockeanism." That is, the coexistence of slavery, property, aristocracy, and natural rights that animated Locke's Carolina constitution eerily reappeared when the federal Constitution defined its compromises with slaveholding.

Settler Revolutionaries and Indian Enemies

Where Indian policy was concerned, the Founding Fathers clearly spent little time on the horns of an American dilemma. Founders like Jefferson might have seen Native Americans as superior to Africans, as more like whites, and as potential neighbors if they changed their ways of life—even as models to be emulated in some aspects of rebellion, nobility, and governance. But the fact of their defeat at the hands of settler domination, and increasingly settlers' presumption of their impending disappearance, made even the softest version of anti-Indian racism paternalistic at best and subject to quick, brutal reversals. Far from creating more political space for Indians, the American Revolution favored hard versions of anti-Indian policies and fed the messianic faith that white Americans were destined to rule greater and greater swathes of territory on behalf of freedom, and Indians needed to get out of the way if they could not quickly fit themselves onto the fringes of such "progress."

Britain had long hesitated over expansion into the back country at a pace that might provoke costly conflicts with tribes and open possibilities for intrigue by other imperial powers. The Crown ingeniously combined paternalism and imperial right in proclaiming of territory west of the Mississippi River to which it held exclusive claim after the 1763 treaty with France: "We reserve it under our sovereignty, protection and dominion, for the use of Indians." But such restraint sparked grievances across class lines. As Woody Holton's important work on Virginia shows, those aggrieved by such policies included the largest (but often indebted) planters, who had designs on and claims to large tracts. Also chafing were land-hungry squatters who defiantly settled new areas, but complained that the British withheld military protection and legal title. The glue keeping together rich and poor claimants to the land melded anti-British sentiment and, especially as the Revolution proceeded, an anti-Indian white nationalism that could pursue blood and land even at the expense of stable military alliances.

While Jefferson advocated, as Colin Calloway writes, "using friendly tribes to wage war against hostile ones," his language in the Declaration had already branded Indians as "savage" warriors in league with the British. Despite the extremely varied behavior of Indians, the totalizing views of them expressed in the Declaration dominated during the revolutionary war, resulting in astonishing violence visited on Indians by revolutionaries. While most Indian tribes hoped to avoid taking sides, they often fought either for the Revolution or its enemies, in many cases switching after betrayals. But neutrality had its own perils, as the Delaware tribe's converts to Moravian religion (and thus non-violence) learned in 1782 when American militia occupied Gnadenhutten and beat to death ninety-six American Indian converts; men, women, and children. Nor did attempting to side with the revolutionaries guarantee security, given the American willingness to attack allies. In the back country Indians as a group were regarded—and in the wake of the war, were scrupulously remembered by veterans—as the enemy, sometimes in a much more immediate and murderous way than were the British. One commander described the goal of his Indian policy as to "excel them in barbarity." When revolutionaries destroyed crops close to harvest to create cycles of destruction and starvation they realized just such an aspiration.

The fact of hard combat in confused and shifting frontier situations, all sides containing individuals given to committing provocations, goes some distance to explaining this indiscriminate response to highly differentiated Indian actions during the war. As in the earlier so-called French and Indian War of 1754–63, the fact that armies fought both alongside and against Indians proved insufficient to prevent all Indians being identified as a threat, in much the same way that being on the US side in Indochina or Iraq has not protected soldiers from being called "gook" or a "hajji" in our time. But more than mere stereotyping under fire was involved in the case of the Revolution. Prosecuting the war in back country areas as anti-Indian conflict smoothed squatter–planter tensions by providing a common enemy and positioned a variety of whites to claim Indian land after the fighting stopped. Neither side thought enough of its Indian allies to provide substantial mention of them in the Treaty of Paris. By the time the new nation pronounced on trans-Appalachian settlement in the mid-1780s it claimed the right to occupy all of that territory immediately, by virtue of conquering Indians who had supposedly been in league with the British enemy.

The historian Robin Blackburn has described connections between revolution and empire that are at once real and "fantastic." The real connection, for Blackburn, "is that societies that had been internally transformed by revolution thereby acquired social capacities that made economic, cultural, and territorial expansion possible." But, he adds, "the fantastic connection was just as important, in that a deluded revolutionary conceit supposed that empire might elevate and redeem otherwise benighted, recalcitrant native peoples" and produce a "republic One and indivisible." In the post-Revolution United States, it was the inability to implement the sweeping imperial control asserted in the 1780s that provided space for the conceit of elevation and redemption of Indians to emerge. Although weakened, Indian resistance—allegedly and at times actually in concert with European powers and with runaway slaves—frustrated settler efforts to simply occupy the land east of the Mississippi. The cost of such occupation seemed too great for a nation strapped for money and with a slight military presence.

Moreover, insistence on speedy occupancy favored the claims of squatters and poorer prospective settlers, as the former could sweep in to take title based on possession despite claims by eastern elites to legal ownership. The alternative approach, pursued by the propertied elites, was the purchase of Indian territories, albeit under tremendous and sometimes orchestrated pressure from troops and settlers. This was used especially by Henry Knox and later by Jefferson, who tended to define Indians as his "children." The compulsory purchase of territories, he said, encouraged their "civilization" into settled agriculture and husbandry, activities that would require far less space. Those making the transition successfully would disappear through intermarriage into a white American race. A new nation would be built, as Michael Rogin put it, "on Indian graves," but in the short term it was as likely to rely as much on economic processes as on frontal assaults to end tribal presences. Instead Indian graves—which Jefferson had robbed to collect "data" for his *Notes on Virginia*—symbolized in the new national imagination the fact that Native Americans had no ongoing future in the US. Treating their disappearance as both prediction and accomplished fact dismissed the real ability of tribes to slow westward advances. "The dead," Jefferson wrote, "have no rights."

White Citizens, White Nation

The most fascinating and least studied words to appear in drafts of the Declaration of Independence, words which then disappeared in the final document, indicted the British Crown for having exploited divisions among whites. Jefferson charged that the king had "incited treasonable insurrections of our fellow citizens with the allurements of . . . confiscation of property." Elsewhere the draft document saw imperial power as committing offenses violating the "blood" lines of white English colonists. In a doubly bloody phrasing, the draft Declaration charged the king with presiding over an occupation enforced by "not only soldiers of our common blood, but Scotch and foreign mercenaries to invade and deluge us in blood." The approved draft stopped some of the bleeding, referring simply to "foreign mercenaries" whose "perfidy" hearkened back to "barbarous ages."

When bound for the frontier, such non-English white migrants generally appeared not as barbarians but as good potential American settlers, and King George's offense was "to prevent the population of these states [by] obstructing the laws for the naturalization of foreigners" by restricting immigration and delaying "new appropriation of land." Such phrasings suggested how the thorny issue of intra-white divisions could be finessed; the approved Declaration was even more deft, removing reference to insurrections by citizens and settling for the muddy phrase "He [the king] has excited domestic insurrections among us," likely to be read as a reference to slave insurrections. The final draft merged that tempered clause with a subsequent section principally concerning royal complicity in alleged Indian "savagery."

These several attempts to address and smooth over social divisions among whites remind us that beyond the perils of undertaking a revolt while holding massive numbers of slaves, revolutionaries of property also had to worry about sharp differences among those whites whose independence they did proclaim. Indeed some historians have attributed Jefferson's preference for couching issues in terms of happiness rather than property to his realization that the finite nature of the latter would inevitably lead to tension within the revolutionary coalition over the distribution of wealth. In Virginia, for example, in the months before the signing of the Declaration of Independence, class tensions came to the fore at the very moment when, as Michael McDonnell writes, "[white] racial solidarity was most essential." Landon Carter heard poor whites object to having to conduct slave patrols that they said were designed for "keeping a rich man's slaves in order." White convicts and slaves escaped to the British together, and fears of tenant farmer "uprisings" preoccupied rebel strategists. As the revolutionary war continued, those charged with raising an army bumped up against the widespread contention of poor and "middling" farmers that it was one thing for a master, with slaves doing the work, to stay away from crops for long stretches, and quite another for them to do so.

The "republic, One and indivisible" that emerged from the Revolution came to be explicitly identified with whiteness, as did its citizens. When Congress passed the nation's first naturalization law in 1790, it named the race of the imagined American citizen as white. The language reflected an expansiveness among lawmakers who would have grown up harboring certain suspicions of non-British immigrants. Franklin, for instance, had worried before freedom about how little of even the European world was really white "like us," and was disquieted by the "swarthy Swedes." However, the confidence of Revolution, the need to build and defend the new nation, and a transformation of attitudes and realities that made recruiting English settlers seem less ideal and practical made a variety of "whites" seem desirable. The naturalization act, as courts later emphasized, spoke even more powerfully about who was unfit for citizenship, implicitly placing not only slaves and Indians, but also people of color generally, in that category. The young were also excluded from naturalization, underlining that to be dependent was a bar to citizenship. For those male youths who would someday be "free, white, and 21," that bar would be temporary; for slaves it would be permanent and inherited from generation to generation.

The idea that white racial status might confer the right to independent male citizenship could not work magic in causing social divisions among whites to vanish. But the post-revolutionary US did dramatically move to the position that male whiteness conferred sufficient independence to qualify even the propertyless as fit republican citizens and voters. This stance received post-revolutionary challenges, with property qualifications for voting disenfranchising some poor white men on the traditional republican grounds that they were too dependent to vote for their own interests. Free blacks meanwhile did vote in a dwindling number of places into the nineteenth century. But by the 1790s the nation had already produced powerful connections, both real and imagined, between whiteness and republican independence. Citizenship came to divide all white men from the "anti-citizens": blacks and Indians. What Dana Nelson calls "national manhood" pivoted, she argues, on a common whiteness that made white male suffrage both politically critical and a key "ritual" of racial separation.

The 1790s were the optimum time to drive home the point that white independence differed utterly from the natural dependence of slaves, semi-free blacks and Indians. The last decades of the eighteenth century saw a steep decline in dependence among whites. The numbers of white urban indentured servants dipped amid the uncertainties prior to the Revolution. Fighting itself brought freedom in exchange for military service. Among those indentured servants outlasting their period of service, many possessed artisanal skills and advanced not only to wage labor but also to the idealized independence of self-employment. Compared to the rest of the late eighteenth- and early nineteenth-century world and to subsequent periods in the US, white men of the revolutionary generation were far more likely to win personal economic independence, and the patriarchal authority in households that went with it.

White women could also claim citizenship, albeit without political representation, power, or equal property rights. The possibility of such restricted citizenship both conditioned and constrained protests. Wartime sacrifices and labor of nationalist wives and mothers underwrote arguments to "remember the ladies," as Abigail Adams urged. Appeals to a common whiteness, and to nationalism, informed patriarchal dismissals of pleas to consider the rights of women. Arguments for political rights based on the exalted role of "republican motherhood" were fragile enough in any case. They tended to ignore the fact that substantial numbers of women worked in the market economy and not simply as mothers. Moreover any attempt to argue that republican mothers should have direct political roles was subject to being disarmed by the notion that their foundational maternal roles made women already "represented" in government. John Adams replied, in high patriarchal jollity and brutality, to his wife's arguments for the contagion of liberty across gender lines by implying that women ran what critically mattered already. Tom Paine's bad poetry ("O Woman! Lovely Woman!/ Nature made thee to temper Man./ We had been Brutes without you") presaged a long, unhappy history of national liberation exalting women into subordination. In revolutionary iconography, the proud, white, clothed female figure of liberty fantastically represented a new nation, replacing the violated Indian as America's central symbol; however, it did not necessarily confer any more power on white women than did the earlier symbol for America's indigenous peoples.

The harder edge of white patriarchy persistently linked white women with people of color, defining them as groups whose behavior was governed too much by passion and too little by reason, residing outside of market society and unfit for political participation. However, white American women were crucially differentiated from people of color in that they brought forth and mothered the world's finest embodiments of manly independence. They also served, as Benjamin Rush argued in a plea for female education, as "the stewards and guardians of their husbands' property." Praised tellingly as the "fair sex," middle- and upper-class women could more easily claim influence than power, protection than property, whiteness than rights. Such claims best thrived when embedded in civilizing discourses that measured societies and races not by women's rights but by their treatment. These patriarchal views were nurtured by fear of the other: the alleged British calls for slave insurrections, or the Indian captivity narratives that formed so much of the early republic's national literature. When, for example, the brilliant and tragic revolutionary intellectual Mercy Otis Warren focused attention on the need to "soften and civilize" the "rude nations of the interior," she was not moving the focus away from gender. Instead she pioneered efforts to define in gendered terms the imperial expansionism that the white republic came to call Manifest Destiny, which, to borrow Amy Kaplan's phrase, also came to incorporate "Manifest Domesticity."

Empire of Whiteness

Kaplan's insight that the concept of domesticity, too, was a product of racialized transnational and imperial encounters is fundamental to understanding the emergence, in the years just after 1800, of the US as a white nation on the world stage. As the nineteenth century opened, the US entered its first foreign war. The enemy, North Africa's Barbary States, stood accused of harboring Islamic pirates who seized American ships. The multi-racial pirate crews were said to practice "white slavery," a term that would insinuate itself deeply into domestic languages of labor and freedom in the nineteenth century. As one of the captives, William Ray, made clear in his remarkable autobiography, *Horrors of Slavery*, the liberties of sailors underwent relentless assaults on authoritarian-run ships everywhere, whether they ventured near North Africa or not, but the new nation's targeted response to an Islamic threat to "whites" underlined connections between race and independence. The war coincided with harsh Jeffersonian opposition to black emancipation in the Haitian Revolution. He fervently hoped—but rightly doubted the likelihood—for an end to "black government" in Haiti. Preferring race over revolution, he branded Haiti's leaders as "Cannibals of the terrible Republic," underscoring that abroad as well as at home the US would be a white nation in foreign as well as domestic policies.

The moment when consolidation and expansion of the more racially debased forms of the American Revolution definitively substituted for any continued contagions of liberty came with the Louisiana Purchase in 1803. The US's acquisition of this vast swathe of formerly French territory in the central US returned the nation to the edge of empire, as in 1776. But now the empire was not Britain's but its own, facing west. Napoleon Bonaparte himself offered to sell French Louisiana—not only the state but the whole half-nation west of the Mississippi—to the Jefferson administration, an index of the US's emergence as at least a minor player in the world of European imperialism. But the real authors of the deal were ironically the very revolutionaries Jefferson had disdained: the Haitians' freedom struggle had exposed France to losses and perils necessitating the sale. When the historian Henry Adams wrote in 1889 that "the prejudice of race alone blinded the American people to the debt they owed to the desperate courage of 500,000 Haytian negroes who would not be enslaved," he well understood the monumental place of the Louisiana Purchase, and Haiti's role in it, in US history, putting it on a par with the Declaration of Independence and the Constitution.

To specify why Louisiana constituted such a critical endpoint and new departure requires special care. The imperative for further US expansion grew out of an existing logic, and out of plans to settle in a commercially viable way territory already held. In Tennessee's original constitution, its bill of rights had included "free navigation" on the Mississippi River because such a "right" seemed essential to commerce. Jefferson's presidential addresses suggested the desirability of expansion across the Mississippi well before any chance to buy Louisiana presented itself. The allegedly "vacant lands" there became for agrarians the imagined key to providing land, and therefore independence, to a growing nation. Jefferson had long urged that the "civilizating" of tribes in the trans-Appalachian west would be best effectuated by having white settlers to "press upon them" to speed their decisions to transfer land into white private hands. Well before Haitians helped put Louisiana on the market, he had declared Montesquieu's venerable contention, that republics had to be kept small, to be fundamentally wrong: "The reverse," he had discovered, "is the truth." Expansion was a key to trade, freedom, and implementing policy against indigenous peoples.

But this remained a dream until the sudden possibility of buying Louisiana radically changed the framing of national commitments to slavery and colonialism, deepening them and foreclosing the already small chance of alternative possibilities: "Had Jefferson and other Americans been forced to choose between a war with France and no further expansion at that time," as William Appleman Williams observed, "they might have worked out some clear conception of the kind of society they wanted to build." Before the Louisiana Purchase, New England-based Federalist opposition to Jeffersonianism sought stable economic relations with revolutionary Haiti, and raised questions about the growth and spread of slavery. But the consensus that supported Louisiana's acquisition (only five senators voted in opposition) showed how weak such opposition was in the face of mercantile opportunity and nationalist glory. Not only did the ensuing treaty offer citizenship to existing Louisiana slaveholders, but provisions for governing the new territory allowed for the importation of slaves. Federalists made no headway, and failed to prevent the Three-Fifths Compromise being extended south and west, thereby assuring their own demise and the occupancy of the White House by slaveholders empowered by the necessities of ruling an empire.

Prior to the Louisiana Purchase, ex-revolutionaries could and did believe that slavery and the "Indian problem" would be solved in time. The gradualism of emancipation plans by Northern states coexisted with vague, usually private and voluntaristic schemes for eventual Southern emancipation. Proposals to colonize the free black and slave populations back to Africa—Jefferson and others argued that a biracial nation without slavery was impossible—remained propositions unfolding in an unspecified frame of time. Jefferson promised that he would find the propitious moment to intervene decisively against slavery. He urged patience as long patterns of civilization and intermarriage continued among Indians and Europeans on the frontier.

After Louisiana's purchase, the fate of slavery and colonialism would unfold in geographical space at least as much as it did in time. The Mississippi River putatively secured, and the cotton gin perfected, Old Southwest cotton production joined Louisiana's booming sugar industry in its success. Jefferson had urged that intelligent direction of the "process of emancipation and deportation" could replace (and displace) slaves as "free white laborers," moved in to replace blacks in "such slow degrees" that the "evil" of slavery would "wear off insensibly"—in a passage Lincoln still fondly quoted as civil war erupted. But the Louisiana Purchase ensured that "deportees" from Virginia would be sold south and west into a worse slavery. Many more slaves would suffer transportation from their homes in the internal US slave trade and planter migrations of the nineteenth century than had originally been torn from Africa and brought to North America.

The post–Louisiana Purchase uncoupling of revolutionary rhetoric from even vague and deferred commitments to transcend the social and property relations that enforced white supremacy was clearer still in the realm of Indian policy. There, framing the problem in terms of space yielded bloody temporal changes as well. By the time of his second inaugural address in 1805, Jefferson's long view of assimilation was showing signs of strain. All his good intentions, he complained, clashed with cultural patterns so deep as to verge on the biological. His reformist impulses were "combated by the habits of their [the Indians'] bodies." Two years later, responding to Indian resistance, he connected new territories with new strategic options: "If ever we are constrained to lift the hatchet against any tribe, we will never lay it down again till that tribe is exterminated, or driven beyond the Mississippi." Six more years down the line, he spoke of Indians generally, charging that their new alliances with the British "oblige us now to pursue them to extermination, or drive them to new seats beyond our reach."

During the First Seminole War of 1817–18, Andrew Jackson's promise to eradicate in South Florida any "harbor" for escaped slaves there, showed where such logic led. Even so, after the Louisiana Purchase policy could not simply devolve into the deportation of Indians and the expansion of slavery. Any operation attempting to cover such a physical expanse, and bind together such diverse interests with so few forces, was bound to proceed with great unevenness and contradiction. In the short term, the process of expelling Indians had to retain some vestiges of assimilationist optimism and to cultivate Indian allies, in order to avoid being overwhelmed by the tasks before it. Lewis and Clark's celebrated expedition to the Pacific Coast and back in 1804–06 presented as much a trader's description of the new territory as a settler's, suggesting that much of what they surveyed might remain for a while a mercantile hinterland, a place for Indian trading partners, delaying the question of where settlers would bring slavery. But not delaying it forever. The removal of Indians from the land east of the Mississippi, and then hemming them in smaller and smaller territories beyond it, would ensure that the republic would long continue to be built on Indian graves, slave sales, and white supremacy.

Managing to Continue:

HOW RACE SURVIVED CAPITALISM AND FREE LABOR

Flavor of the month economist Robert Murphy, currently popularizing the conservative faith in the infinite capability of market forces, has recently made perhaps the most simplistic case for capitalism's inherent ability to undermine inequality. "Slavery," he wrote, "really makes no sense economically. If you're a slave, then your incentive is to produce the bare minimum to avoid a whipping. But if you're a free laborer, you have an incentive to produce more than the guy next to you, because you'll get paid more." Murphy added that "in a truly free market—even if it started out with some people classified as the 'property' of other people—there would be tremendous incentives for the slaves to buy their freedom from their masters." A writer who thinks that being property is a happy abstraction— Murphy argues elsewhere that the problem for endangered species such as bald eagles lies precisely in their misfortune in not being "owned"—can happily imagine racial bondage succumbing easily to the logic of market forces.

But however pushed to extremes by Murphy, Thomas Sowell, and others far out on the right, the argument that capitalism has progressively undermined both race-thinking and the outmoded social systems that create such thinking, enjoys a pedigree and a logic familiar to every student of an introductory economics course: that the "free enterprise" system prizes labor and capital. Abstract units of labor are endlessly subdivided and traded to generate increasing prosperity in a system in which work, like all else, finds its price based on supply and demand, not on color and culture. When economic historians declare that even the modes of exploitation most associated with racial oppression—slavery and sharecropping—responded to market pressures in ways that made it possible for African American labor to profit and progress, they may be regarded as conservatives, but also honored as innovators.

Moreover, those of us who are opponents of racism, and even of capitalism, often descend from intellectual traditions shared to some degree by Murphy and others like him. Those wishing to abolish slavery, or at least to prevent its spread, rightly argued that the employment of "free labor," working for wages, was morally superior to the use of slaves, and also produced a more efficient outcome. Liberal and radical writers of the late twentieth century inherited from earlier progressive historians a framework viewing the Civil War itself as a contest between the agrarian feudalism of the South and the industrial capitalist ambitions of the North. Early Marxist historians generally agreed, and the most celebrated late twentieth-century Marxist writing on the subject unfortunately resonated with such accounts far more than it did with Marx's own writings on the United States. By contrast, Marx's own words at their best impressively resisted drawing the easy opposition between a backward pre-capitalist South and a progressive capitalist North. For Marx, the contrast was less marked, even as he championed the Union side in the Civil War. "We . . . call the plantation owners in America capitalists," he wrote, because they exist and compete "within a world market based on free labor." Moreover, the transnational emphases of the Marxist tradition have made possible a healthy recognition of the fact that slavery and the expansion of capitalist production did more than simply coexist; rather, this expansion was rooted in slavery. The term "factories" was used to describe the West African staging areas gathering laboring bodies for the slave trade, and then for the production of cotton, making possible in turn the textile "factories" of England and of New England.

Nonetheless Marxist writers have themselves often lost track of the centrality of race in the development of US capitalism, because they too gravitate towards the idea that labor is abstract and that mature capitalism is, or should be, colorblind. Sometimes they have adopted such perspectives for good reason, or at least with good intentions, in attempting to spread the hopeful view that the manifold and deadly historical and cultural divisions that workers bring to their jobs are bound to disappear in the shared experience of exploitation. When Marx and Engels wrote of capital creating a world in "its own image," they observed and imagined a new society, in which national divisions and "various interests and conditions of life within the ranks" of working people would give way as the opposition of labor to capital became the overriding social difference. Marx's logic held that capital homogenizes society because it sees a world made up of units of labor, rather than of races, nationalities or genders. That logic became at times a powerful tool for those who hoped to practice labor solidarity across racial divides.

For such radicals the connection between industrial capitalism and the possible end of white supremacy arose in the context of struggle. In the pine forests of Louisiana just before the outbreak of World War I, African Americans and whites violated the law by meeting and associating with one another. Marxist-influenced organizers who wanted to change the law succeeded in arguing that capitalism itself undermined race-thinking. "Trees," a Brotherhood of Timber Workers supporter assured readers, "don't care who fells them. They make as good a lumber when felled by the hand of a negro [or] a Hindoo . . . as when coming from the hand of a white American citizen. The interests of all who work in the woods . . . are the same." Nor did Marxists monopolize this common sense. Older activists in the Louisiana woods might have read an aphorism appearing in the state's great Radical Republican newspaper, the *New Orleans Tribune*, just after the Civil War.

Under capitalism, the paper held, tying a reformist anti-racism to the supposed logic of capitalism, "Labor equalizes all men; the handicraft of the worker has no color and belongs to no race."

This said, the deep roots of Marxism in classical capitalist political economy make its adoption of the idea that capitalism undermines slavery and racism more than just incidental or tactical. The most searching and good-natured critique of Marxist historians' tendency to divorce the concept of labor from the bodies and cultures of those performing it, Lisa Lowe's remarkable introduction to her *Immigrant Acts* shows the stakes involved in a theoretical challenge to such Marxist abstractions practiced in the name of political economy and even of interracialism. Lowe makes two powerful and related points in order to show why Marxism is both indispensable and inadequate in addressing the history of the US and of the embodied labor that built it.

Immigrant Acts argues that, in tracing the history of the US, Marxism has too often settled for the demarcation of an early, finite period of "primitive accumulation," in which race-making processes like the slave trade and the seizing of native lands mattered greatly. However, Lowe insists that in the world's most developed capitalist nation the connection of race and exploitation was not restricted to this early period but was continued and ramified, driving the accumulation of capital and shaping the nature of government. "In the history of the United States," she writes, "capital has maximized its profits not through rendering labor 'abstract' but precisely through the social productions of 'difference' . . . marked by race, nation, geographical origins, and gender."

Second, Lowe notes a critical but limited advance made by the Marxist tradition. Marx understood that constitutions of capitalist democracies had to contend with the extent to which "each individual man's right to property violates the rights of others." Constitutionally, for Marxists, the idea of political citizenship smoothed the contradiction between the state as a guarantor of measures of equal rights among men, and of the possession of property within highly unequal social orders. But although, abstracted from material conditions, one citizen was formally equal to another, it was only as "the imaginary member of an imaginary sovereignty divested of his real, individual life." Such a citizen pressed claims for justice by assuming an "unreal universality" that left unspoken the real differences that property made in terms of who could in fact accumulate wealth and exercise political power.

However, as Lowe observes, Marx's "critique of citizenship" incorporates some of the same "abstract and universalist propositions" that it skewers. Nowhere in the first half of the nineteenth century was a sense of "natural" rights more widely applied than in the US, but those rights did not attach themselves to anything quite so simple as a false universalism. Instead, rights flowed from a series of concrete distinctions that made adult white men the only full citizens, and conferred on them not only imaginary sovereignty but also significant, and far from universal, concrete advantages in the ability to own property. Specifically, they could securely possess ownership of their own bodies, and at times the bodies of those racially excluded from citizenship, as well as their own land, and at times they could seize the lands of those racially excluded. Given such relative self-possession, it was possible to believe that white men could rise by virtue of controlling their "free labor," and that therefore the new nation would be one whose adult citizens would overwhelmingly be independent of wage labor.

That the spectacular industrial capitalist take-off of the post-revolutionary US produced no firm drive to make labor abstract, raceless, and subject to a level playing field of market forces, nor any successful attempts to insure that free, self-employed labor would be a reality even for white men, are omissions both deserving of discussion. In their place, spectacular economic growth existed alongside proletarianization, the continued enslavement of 4 million black workers, and the forced ethnic cleansing of Indians to beyond the Mississippi. Such realities taught that the benefits of white citizenship were both tenuous and fatefully connected to property. Moreover, they left room for ample confusion about how, and whether, free white labor and white citizenship would pay off. As adult wage labor became more and more common, dreams of economic independence became more and more firmly tied to expansion of the settler population in the West, linking it to anti-Indian campaigns. The ideal of manly independence could devolve into settling for the claim that voting rights and not being a slave amounted to freedom for white, wage-earning men. White citizenship, the particular US form of the "universal" mystifications attending citizenship observed by Marx, thereby helped square the circle of how a revolutionary nation so ideologically committed to economic independence could generate so much dependency on wage labor. But it did so in a way that left undisturbed, indeed even strengthened, commitments to race-thinking. A turn to the history of management and race further deepens Lowe's insights on race and capital by showing that the very idea of management in the history of the US has centered on claiming knowledge of other races. Far from flattening difference by buying undifferentiated units of labor power, US management studiously bought into inequality, preserving and continually recreating race.

Capital and Reproductions of Race in Antebellum US History

The enduring appeal of the argument linking capitalism to the inexorable erosion of race-thinking lies in the fact that not just one but several very different lines of reasoning serially undergird the case for making such a magical connection. When the argument is discredited on one front, therefore, it simply shifts to another. However, one of these lines of argument regarding the pre–Civil War years is particularly easily dismissed. The notion that racial minorities will themselves develop as powerful forces within capitalism, and wield power as such, has been proposed insistently in recent years under the catchphrase "black capitalism." One variant of the argument predicts that the control over capital will lead to minorities governing their own communities and becoming powerful in the nation as a whole. Another sees disposable income as central, stressing that people of color in the US now constitute a market as large as all but a few nations of the world and therefore command influence in a "republic of dollars."

However, the lack of any plausibility for either variant of this argument during the foundational period in which the US nation rose to become a world economic leader is telling. During these years, African Americans overwhelmingly failed to gain property; rather, they were property. For every free black in 1860, there were more than eight slaves. As the Civil War approached, the former group owned scant property while the latter, as slaves, constituted almost $4 billion in other people's property, a value outstripping all US capital investment in railroads and manufacturing through 1860 and roughly equaling the gross national product for that year. Only investment in land outpaced capital investment in slaves.

Slaves were not only owned but also traded, with most Southern states actually exporting slaves to newly opened regions of production. Of the, perhaps, 1 million domestic US slave sales before the Civil War, 40 percent or more were interstate, involving as much as $600 million changing hands; this meant that slaves ranked high on any list of US-produced commodities. Virginia alone may have raised and sold down the river a third of a million slaves in the early national and antebellum periods. Racialized bodies also formed the basis for the great marketed entertainment crazes of the period, whether in the disguise of "blackface," in which white entertainers put on minstrel shows, or in promoter P. T. Barnum's "What Is It?" exhibition, one of many popular shows inviting consumers to form their own ethnological judgments on where lines between races (and between humans and animals) fell.

Yet even among free blacks the republic of dollars produced only further disfranchisement. Though saving at a greater rate, their average wealth stood in 1860 at about a seventh of that of whites—a figure, eerily enough, roughly equal to the ratio in

2000. Sharply discriminated against in programs providing access to federal lands, and in free entry to areas of available land, free blacks owned on average an eighth as much real estate as whites did at the start of the Civil War. Including slaves, whites owned on average well over sixty times as much real estate as African Americans. Income data for the period, which are hard to come by, suggest that free black Americans "voted" with about two-fifths the mean disposable income of whites in the pre–Civil War republic of dollars. Although plantations constituted a significant market for Northern industry and Midwestern foodstuffs, and although the vast management literature on slaves often suggested the ideal array of products for them to consume, all such decisions were mediated by the master. For most of the century after slavery's abolition, national corporations did not systematically pursue African American consumer dollars. Advertisers instead used racial stereotypes like Aunt Jemima and Uncle Ben to appeal to white customers.

None of this is to say that, during the antebellum period, African Americans with property did not play important roles in communities and in protecting their families, sometimes by buying them out of slavery. Nor is it to gainsay the fact that exercising consumer choices produced satisfaction, sometimes even for slaves. But it is to insist that if we imagine dollars as a source of power, the sharp levels of inequality in resources during slavery and beyond have made racial capitalism in the US far more a source of relative black powerlessness than of black power. Just as only a tiny minority of the fraction of black Americans who were free could vote, the free black minority "voted" in the market at extremely disadvantaged levels.

A second line of argument for capitalism's erosion of race-thinking associates capitalism with a firm preference for wage labor, placing it in opposition to earlier relations of mutuality that were gradually superseded by the ability of workers and owners to contract "freely." Looking at the world today we might better argue, following and extending Lowe's analysis, that capital prefers

varying degrees of freedom and bondage, and a full set of
opportunities to exploit the differences in social position among
workers. No pat distinction or decisive break between the interests
of Southern slavery and Northern capital could or did quickly
emerge in the antebellum US.

Multiple economic, cultural, and political ties bound Northern
capital to Southern slavery. Not only did the earlier legal slave
trade provide both finance and models for pooling capital to
Yankee investors, but the illegal post-1808 slave trade continued
to power investment in New England textiles. Sharing risks in
slave voyages was important to the growth of the insurance
industry. The furnishing of masters with goods with which to
provision slaves made a decisive contribution to a critical phase in
the factory production of shoes and to the booming palm-leaf hat
industry. Slave-made profits, as recent controversies have shown,
underwrote elite Northern universities, which were in turn leaders
in the invention of the scientific defenses of white supremacy that
increasingly underpinned pro-slavery arguments.

With cotton accounting for 57 percent of the total value of US
exports just before the Civil War, merchant capitalists and shippers
in New York and elsewhere saw the defense of slavery as critical
not just to their own interests, but also to those of the nation.
Cotton also came north, with the Boston Associates textile group
commanding a substantial share of the market, using it to build the
most visible example of factory production in the antebellum US.
Without such interregional ties it would hardly have been possible
for the small number of large-scale slave owners to dominate
politics and law for so long, even given the constitutional arrangements aggrandizing their power.

Conflicts over how to engineer the next phase of economic and
geographical expansion, and the pressure of slave resistance,
opened up differences between Northern and Southern capital
on the spread of slavery. But there existed durable affinities
between capitalists in the two regions, affinities vital both to
the refusal of significant numbers of Northern political and

economic elites to support the abolition of slavery as a Civil War aim, and to the ramifying connections between race and management. Falling out over where to build railroads, over tariff policy (with the slaveholding South pressing for the free trade principles we now associate with unbridled capitalism) and over how to open the West, slaveholders and Northern capitalists nevertheless shared an abiding commitment to Indian dispossession and to private property.

Indeed the slaveholders' insistence on their "right" to expand into new territories was based on an unwavering focus on the bottom line, with the export of slaves to new territories rescuing areas where the soil was being destroyed by cotton monoculture. Geographical expansion and the huge internal slave trade unified slaveholders. Plantation owners made management and investment decisions fully within a context of transnational capitalism. In 1860, for example, 75 percent of US cotton was exported, while no more than 5 percent of antebellum grain production was sold in foreign markets. Understanding such patterns ensures that we do not opt for the easy explanation that capitalism and trade automatically acted as a solvent for racial inequality, or for the mirror twin of such an explanation—that the real dramas of US history were about "economics" in ways that were somehow separable from race.

The only area of capital investment outpacing slaves was land, so expansion, capitalist development and race-thinking went hand-in-hand. The opening up of new lands to speculation, settlement, and production made more explicit than ever the fact that Native Americans would be the subjects, not the partners, of expanding US capitalism. The most aggressive land grabs and ethnic cleansings were in the South, where the slaveholding soldier and politician Andrew Jackson provided martial and presidential leadership in carrying them out. His role underlined the importance of the South's gerrymandered, slave-based dominance over the national state, the judiciary, and often the officer corps of the military. But what John Hope Franklin has called the South's "militant expansionism," characterized by its particular tendency to "filibuster" far south of the US border, was in fact only an extension of its internal expansionism. Acquiescence of politicians in the North and Northwest, first to Jackson's avowedly extra-legal approach to Indian removal, and then to Georgia's nullification of federal authority in engineering removal of the Cherokees, and to the notorious Indian Removal Act of 1830, bespoke a broad intersectional consensus in support of dispossession.

There were differences in scale between Jackson's extended and far-flung assaults on Southern Indians, and the Black Hawk War of 1832 in Illinois and present-day Wisconsin between a group of Native Americans and the US army. But North and South, Democratic and Whig, the consensus for Indian removal was broad. Indeed in the Black Hawk War a young Abraham Lincoln soldiered with Jackson as his commander-in-chief. Quickening attention as to whether farmers or slave owners would occupy the "free land" being opened to settlement sparked policy debates and occupied the attention of white working-class land reform movements (these were sometimes rhetorically sympathetic to Indians, but in ways lacking political results) as the Civil War approached. Such divisions and debates mattered, but sectional division did not lead to any significant break from settler colonialism, North or South. Denying that Indians held property in a modern sense, the government pressed attacks on the settled, and even slaveholding, groups of Cherokees and Creeks. Such assaults spoke volumes about how anti-Indian campaigns combined what Peter Linebaugh calls "assaults on commoning" with race war directed even against those Indians who embraced private ownership; dispossession easily alternated between appeals to statute and the practice of terror. Native claims were made to seem, as Eric Cheyfitz puts it, "unrepresentable" in courts and legislatures, so much so that Alexis de Tocqueville's famous 1835 homage to *Democracy in America* could pronounce Indian removal as remarkable for its humanity and legality. The impressed de Tocqueville urged that French imperialists in Africa look not to US slavery but to US anti-Indian policies as a model.

The acquisition of Texas, followed in 1846 by the Mexican War, produced an "American 1848," in which the peace settlement ensured that Mexico's loss of land would specifically be the slaveholders' gain. The war brought deep disaffection among soldiers, although some land and labor reformers still joined important sections of capital in favoring it for a time. Its results helped to shift laborers' and farmers' support from the merely aggressive expansionist policies personified by Jackson, to "free soil," anti–Slave Power mobilizations that Lincoln would come to symbolize. However, maturing mainstream political opposition to limitless empire-building on slavery's behalf took racially charged forms, with the 1846 Wilmot Proviso firmly insisting on "white" settlement as the cornerstone of public policy. The 1850s slogan of the rising Republican Party, "Vote yourself a farm," never found a way to acknowledge Indian presence, or to challenge effectively the color bars that closed areas of settlement to African Americans.

Where Mexicans themselves were concerned, the antebellum racial system showed an impressively sophisticated ability to balance the rights of property against what James Baldwin called the "lie of whiteness." Much war propaganda (and some rhetoric arguing against the war or against wholesale annexations still deeper into Mexico) branded Mexicans as either a "mongrel" race or as Indians, incapable of full civilization or self-rule. As Richard Slotkin observes, policymakers and journalists often described the conflict as yet another Indian war, with Ambrose Sevier, Arkansas senator and chairman of the Committee on Foreign Relations, urging the imposition of a reservation system on conquered Mexico. If, as was said, "The Mexicans are *Indians*, aboriginal Indians. Such Indians as Cortez conquered . . . only rendered a little more mischievous by a bastard civilization," such prescriptions made imperial sense, albeit jarring against the troops' observations that Mexico was far more majestically urbanized than the US.

But the logic of imposing anti-Indian policies on Mexicans in the name of white government collided with the reality of powerful, capitalist Mexican landowners, with recognizable legal title to ownership sometimes reinforced by claims to be descendents of Cortez rather than of those whom he had conquered. When peace was established, racist war propaganda could give way to grudging acceptance of the land titles of the Mexican elite in territories seized. In California, for example, political and property rights of the Mexican landowners were respected at law, with land passing into settlers' hands only over time, through fraud, purchase, and intermarriage. State law codified race-thinking leavened by class, defining the Mexican elites as "white" while proscribing the rights of Indians and propertyless Mexican "greasers." During the war gendered language prettified empire and specifically obscured the use of rape as a method of conquest, covering it with rhetoric about love and consent. New York *Sun* editor James Gordon Bennett maintained that Mexico would be "gorgeously" happy when conquered, and specified that "like the Sabine virgin she will soon learn to love her ravisher." After the war, the reality of marriages between white American men and women of landed Mexican families sped the transfer of land out of Mexican hands in California, while the fascination with such relationships in popular culture delivered a judgment against the race and masculinity of even wealthy Mexican men. In New Mexico, as Laura Gómez's *Manifest Destinies* shows, Mexican elites buttressed a "fragile claim" to whiteness by differentiating themselves from nonwhites—at the same time defending Indian slavery as practiced in the territory, supporting African American slavery in the abstract, and helping to enact draconian restrictions on free blacks.

Free Labor and White Citizenship:
Solving the American Dilemma

Speaking at the 1853 Massachusetts state constitutional convention, the lawyer Henry Williams left the ostensible topic of the debate, the secret ballot, to argue for deep connections between the supposed equalities of free citizenship and of free labor:

In a free government like ours employment is simply a contract between parties having equal rights . . . The work to be performed is, by the contract, an equivalent for the money paid . . . The employed is under no greater obligation to the employer than the employer is to the employed . . . they are both freemen—citizens having equal rights, and brethren having one common destiny.

The passage underscores how their "precocious achievement" of full voting citizenship, as David Brody puts it, exposed white US workers to processes described earlier in this chapter, processes in which abstractions regarding equality among citizens seemed to override the fact that some people owned only their own bodies and labor, and others owned far more and could drive hard bargains for that labor.

The closeness of Williams's remarks to the Dred Scott decision four years later suggests that what he did not say about his country, at that time the most free in the world for white men, and the one holding about twice as many slaves as the rest of the Americas combined, matters more than what he did say. By this time even in the North only one free black person in seventeen could vote and the Dred Scott decision of 1857 drove home the fact that none were legally full citizens. In the Scott case, the Court could point to a broad pattern of ill treatment by the nation and almost all states towards African Americans (and, in a curiously extensive commentary for a case not about them, towards Indians). Whether regarding freedom of movement, voting, obtaining a passport, or serving on juries, the Court's majority could make a convincing, if brutal, argument that, as Bernard Mandel wrote, even free blacks were "branded with the stigma of the auction block" by their historical and geographical connections to slavery and to property.

The most famous line in the Scott decision flatly held that African Americans possessed "no rights which the white man was bound to respect." While some voices in the small abolitionist movement in the North did challenge white supremacy as well as slavery, and while Lincoln could argue for protecting black rights even as he despaired of creating a biracial nation, the trend continued in the opposite direction. Just as importantly, the Scott decision specified precisely whose authority over black people it was championing. In a case bedeviled by conservative justices asserting federal power over states' rights to make white supremacy more impervious to uneven local and state practices, the Court resorted in its key formulation to saying that authority on race and rights resided somehow in the "white man" as the embodiment of American power.

To explain the crux of the Dred Scott decision, and to understand how white citizenship specifically shaped the experience of class, we must turn the American dilemma about national ideals of equality fully on its head where race is concerned. In the reality of the antebellum US, there was indeed a profound dilemma regarding the squaring of revolutionary ideas with existing social divisions. But that dilemma focused on class divisions among whites, not on racial justice for African Americans or American Indians. Moreover, far from being its source, white supremacy was typically viewed as providing promising solutions to that dilemma. The dilemma, as lived, arose from the American Revolution's emphasis on independence as a nationalist goal. In the US case, this always meant not only absence of British control at the macro level, but the possibility of the male head of the household being independent of an employer, of an agricultural landlord, and of a master. The Revolution promised a government generally able to deliver on the promise of upward mobility away from wage labor for at least most adult white males.

By the standards of the time, states in the US moved very quickly to embrace universal male suffrage; in doing so they broke from suspicions long held by advocates of republican government that the poor and dependent could not think or vote freely. They did so partly as a result of logic and pressure born of popular participation in the Revolution, but also out of a confidence that expansion of territory and manufacturing could reliably produce a nation of independent farmers and craftsmen. In the short term, dramatic social divisions among native-born whites did decline, especially in terms of indentured servitude. But the problem of wage labor proved to be enduring and expanding. During the war of 1812, Francis Scott Key would write a verse of "The Star-Spangled Banner" in which "the hireling and the slave" counted as the antithesis of all that was free, American, and republican. But US hirelings proliferated with the expansion of capitalist industry and agriculture. By the early nineteenth century, the defining economic freedom of workers in the post-revolutionary US was the "right to quit" a labor arrangement without being subject to criminal penalties.

While Lincoln could still argue in 1859 that labor is "prior to" capital—meaning specifically that in a good society, males labored for wages while young but achieved economic independence as mature heads of households—he emphasized that the power of slaveholders was subverting that "free labor," "free soil" dream. His own state of Illinois, and many of his followers, championed new lands being closed not only to slaveholders but also to African Americans, and to the powerful Indian presence. On the other hand, in parts of the South the owning of as few as one or two slaves could mark the achievement of manly independence by small-farming whites. Southerners proposing to reopen the slave trade in the 1850s thus couched their appeals as egalitarian, promising to create new opportunities and to protect whites from unseemly burdens of labor. Slaveholders and advocates of settler colonial expansion using free labor both responded to the dilemma of a society predicated on economic independence but unable to deliver it. Because independence was seen as a requirement for full patriarchal authority in one's household, as well as full republican citizenship, the stakes in political debates over slavery and expansion were enormous. But those debates did not turn on any American dilemma regarding racial justice.

The US offered, not universal notions of citizenship, but particular aggrandizements of adult white men made fictively equal by their race and gender as well as their labor. Phrases like "free, white, and 21," and "white man's government" proliferated. They spoke profoundly to intersections of age, gender, and race while reassuring listeners that the new nation might still provide pathways for the great majority of proliferating young white "hirelings" to achieve eventual economic independence. Over time, the "property" of being white came to stand in imperfectly, for actually owning a small workshop or farm, with white citizenship signaling independence. Nothing like a conspiracy was required. As late as 1860, after decades of astronomical growth in both the wage- and slave-labor sectors of the working population, more laboring people in the United States still worked for a master who owned them—and could beat, kill, starve, or sell them—than for an employer paying wages. Any notion of what it meant to come under the heading "freeman" necessarily included consideration of racial differences between the white American worker and the black slave. The complex fascination of early US white labor activists with terms like "white slavery" or "wage slavery" reflected the reality that workers were bound to judge their conditions in comparison to slaves. If use of such terms could briefly lend urgency and anxiety to organizational efforts by white workers, metaphors invoking slavery also proved problematic and limiting. Black abolitionists, often runaway slaves, challenged any easy equation of oppression under chattel slavery with that under wage labor. Moreover, white male artisan radicals themselves sometimes hesitated to identify their republican selves with slaves, speaking instead of the future threat of white slavery, or of its reality for women factory workers.

In the long run, the inevitable comparisons of white workers and slaves were as likely to lead to a complacent conclusion that the former were independent, as to the organizing of militant labor. The comparison to slaves was likely to seem pejorative even when put forward by radical artisans. When, for example, the great American revolutionary and abolitionist Tom Paine described the dangers of a white working class becoming "mere Negroes . . .

lazy and careless," the fact that such apparently racist words came from a patriot wanting to build a nation without slaves or a permanent waged population hardly kept them from being offensive to both African Americans and whites. When the British investor Charles W. Janson visited the US in 1807, he reported on one way in which the real American dilemma, of one person serving another for wages in a republic, was being literally addressed. He asked a household worker to see her "master" and was quickly told that she had none, adding "I'd have you know, *man*, that I am no *sarvant*; none but *negers* are *sarvants*." In 1839, the great observer of US life, Frances Trollope, fretted over difficulties in "getting servants" but corrected herself to write "getting help." The former term so implied comparisons to "negurs" that it was "more than petty treason to the republic to call a free citizen a *servant*."

The specific opposition of "negur" and "free citizen" suggests how critically important was the role of the post-revolutionary state in determining how poorer whites would present themselves and their grievances in public discourse. It was the free white citizen who could make claims for rights. The revolutionary and manly idea of being an independent "freeman" was therefore repeatedly reinvented rather than abandoned. Even if the white male head of household owned no productive property, the security of his family remained far different from what was suffered on the trails of tears separating African American families as the internal slave trade boomed, or on the relocation of whole Indian populations to the trans-Mississippi West. Again and again the expansion of white suffrage accompanied the disenfranchisement of "free" blacks, even as popular blackface minstrel shows featured insistent ridicule of black political speech. The "freeman," proper-tied if only in his whiteness, and the African American and American Indian "anti-citizen," were fashioned together, defer-ring any genuine confrontation with an American racial dilemma. Whether such deferral could survive a civil war and the end of slavery would be another question.

Race and the Roots of US Management

Although almost wholly unexplored, the connections between race and labor management in US history are profound. The pioneer labor economist and historian John R. Commons would write in 1907, well after Frederick Taylor had begun to market scientific management as a revolutionary system of studying the time and movements of workers, that US management had shown just one "symptom of originality," namely "playing one race against the other." Commons' striking link between cutting-edge management technique and the bloody history of race contrasts sharply with the images that dominate our thinking in relation to the highly technical US managerial innovations inspired by Taylor, the bloodless efficiency of engineers with stopwatches studying workers. While it would not do to simply substitute the former view for the latter, as though US management were all about race, it should be acknowledged that the idea of race did permeate the processes through which US labor was chosen and bossed. "Race management" came well before scientific management; later, the two coexisted significantly as complementary rather than alternative strategies to extract productivity. To appreciate as much helps us lay bare the inadequacy of assumptions that link race only with the early stages of capitalist production in the US.

In connecting management and race, Commons bespoke long-standing, even foundational, American traditions that we have encountered in previous chapters. As members of both a white settler and a slaveholding society, American colonists developed a sense of their own whiteness by casting their race as uniquely fit to manage land and labor, and by judging how other races might feature in the service of that project. Dispossession of Indians found justification in the supposed inability of indigenous people to "husband," or manage, the resources at their command, while early American management decisions centered on what sort (and quickly on what "race") of coerced labor was most economical, skilled, durable, efficient, and tractable.

After a period in which Indian slavery seemed a possibility, the last century of the colonial period featured the cyclical favoring of white indentured servants or African slaves. Among slaves themselves, management by ethnicity also obtained. Likewise in the fur trade, management was practically defined as judging the abilities and fostering the willingness of specific Indian tribes and individuals to organize and defend the gathering and transport of vast quantities of furs. Ironically, distinctions among groups of indigenous and African peoples were not generally described as "racial," the term being reserved for whole populations of "red" or "black" people, but when national groups within Europe came to be indexed according to their exploitability, talk of Irish and German "races" flowered.

In the nineteenth century, "race management" became formalized into the thoroughly modern practices and discourses that Commons had in mind. The plantation and the factory by then coexisted as the most spectacular sites for management of labor in the Americas; if anything, the latter provided a model for the former. As Robin Blackburn has written, "By gathering the workers under one roof, and subordinating them to one discipline, the new industrial employers were . . . adapting the plantation model (which is why people came to speak of steel 'plants.')" The words "overseer," naming the manager watching and speeding up the labor of slaves, and "supervisor," denoting the manager performing just the same roles in industry, have the same literal meaning.

Antebellum US politics, as well as economics, turned on the relative merits of free versus slave labor. Such discussions easily devolved into considerations of the (dis)advantages of African American labor, in the fields and especially in manufacturing, as against those of "white" labor or of the emerging, distinct "Irish race." In the 1850s, 20 percent of all manufacturing capital was invested in the South, while Southern nationalist slaveholders often led the highly theorized and quantified charge for more such investments. When in 1830 white skilled workers protested to the

federal government over their replacement by slaves in the Nor-
folk Dry Dock, management's response showed how thoroughly
difference could be quantified, and how easily distinctions between slave and free labor slipped into distinctions between black
and white. Management reported that stones "hammered by
White Men" cost precisely $4.05 more than those "hammered
by blacks."

Calculations leading to the replacement of free black workers in
service and seaports in the North by desperately poor Irish
immigrants primarily hinged on the extent to which desperation
made the Irish willing to underbid African Americans in wage
terms. But the switch from one group to the other also featured
wide-ranging discussion as to which "race" was, in management's
view, more suited to labor. When the wealthy New York City
lawyer and despiser of Irish Americans, George Templeton
Strong, maintained that the Irish had "prehensile paws" rather
than hands, his judgment came in the context of extracting labor
from immigrant workers in his own home. The antebellum
replacement of white American-born "helps" in domestic labor
by "servants" of the Irish "race" likewise involved scrutiny and
comparison, as did the turn from native-born to Irish women in
Northern textile mills.

The premium on race management skills permeated the class
structure. Overseers and drivers were prized and hired for their
racial knowledge. Slave markets literally traded on that same
knowledge, however unsystematically acquired, while non-slaveholders were conscripted onto "patrols" literally observing and
managing slaves, and even poor white craft workers in the South
strove to hire a slave as a temporary "third hand." Moreover, the
ripening logic behind speedy removal of even agriculturally based,
"friendly" Indian tribes in the early nineteenth century was clearly
intended to make management of nature the sole province of
white men, grounding their claim to entitlement to the soil.

Southern white antebellum labor organizations lacked the
power, permanence, and ideas to break workers from the idea

that all whites held common interests based in part on the tasks of management of slaves and land. To the meager extent that white workers in the South organized to oppose the threat of their replacement by slave labor, their target was just as likely to be slaves, or even African Americans per se, as it was to be slavery itself. When Virginia's Tredegar Iron Works rapidly expanded in the 1840s it placed slaves in more skilled positions, as well as in the laboring jobs they had traditionally occupied. These developments provoked the most important strike by white workers in the history of the slave South. White workers left their jobs, calling for removal of "the negroes" from skilled work, illustrating how thoroughly intertwined black race and slave status had become. The workers' initiative failed, as did most such efforts, in the face of the masters' political power in a police-state South that cast even the most impeccably white supremacist attempts to limit slaveholders' power as subversive. Even in those relatively rare cases where some white skilled workers enforced bars against slave labor in their trades, their ability to bargain suffered because a threat to turn to bonded labor could always be made. Moreover, many white Southern artisans were not so much non-slaveholders as junior race managers. Renting slaves and aspiring to own them, such artisans responded to white nationalist slogans like "Every laborer a slaveholder."

The most notorious "scientific" pro-slavery thinking to emerge from the Deep South reflected the imperatives of management, claiming superior knowledge of African Americans through empirical approaches: mastering and "improving" them. Along with management whose status and power was maintained through keeping an industrial workforce divided along lines of race, slaveholders also believed that their system produced racial development among Africans. The physician, slaveholder, and University of Louisiana professor Dr. Samuel Cartwright exemplified the coexistence of a managerial and an improving impulse. Writing in the Southern agricultural reform and management journal *De Bow's Review* in 1851 he identified two major African "pathologies." He termed one condition *drapetomania*, the "disease causing negroes to run away," and another *dysaesthesia Aethiopica*, a seemingly "half-asleep" performance on the job. Cartwright's extravagant pseudo-science makes it hard for us to take his claims seriously, but antebellum experts suffered few such qualms. Cartwright at times portrayed the conditions he had invented as individual maladies, and elsewhere regarded slave "diseases" as part of a complex of inherited "racial" inferiorities. He was not merely contradicting himself. Such double vision encapsulates a pattern running through race management, which hinged both on a firm sense of biologically determined white supremacy—defined against what Cartwright called the "peculiarities of the negro"—and on the supposed malleability of African Americans that made management possible.

Cartwright spelled out two distinct ways in which his knowledge stemmed from a manager's wisdom, and proposed a master's and a manager's cures for the African American "diseases" he had himself invented. First, he chided Northern scientists for being blind to diseases so clear to slave owners and overseers who were in daily contact with slaves, claiming that almost all free blacks in the North displayed *dysaesthesic* symptoms, but that their "masterless" status made both diagnosis and treatment impossible outside the South. Cartwright then insisted that the masters' racial knowledge excelled that of overseers. The latter, he complained, wrongly dismissed slave misbehavior as "rascality," rather than observing it scientifically as disease and inferiority. As Du Bois long ago observed, such quasi-scientific advocacy of race management had far-reaching impact on the development of white supremacist thought beyond the South. To the "watching world," a racism designed to manage what Du Bois called "slave industry" seemed "the carefully thought out result of experience and reason."

The solutions Cartwright proposed straddled a line between the two overlapping schools of slave management identified in Walter Johnson's *Soul by Soul*. One school advocated terror in the form of physical beatings, and Cartwright similarly urged "preventively . . .

whipping the devil" out of potential *drapetomaniacs* as a treatment. But Cartwright also advocated management through a terror based not on direct violence but on superior knowledge, on paternalist judgments regarding individual slaves, and ultimately the threat of their sale, taking them away from loved ones. Last but not least, he grounded hope for a "cure" to slave ills in productivity itself: the hardest working slaves improved their mental health because exertion brought oxygen to their brains.

The practice of race management blurred the division between free blacks and slaves in a tangible, not just symbolic, way. The regular exposure in the workplace to danger and filth, and the overwork and subservience that could be particularly demanded of African American workers, free and slave, had spawned a linguistic Americanism. "Nigger work" entered, and endured, in the language, while the related phrase "slave like a nigger" bespoke the thorough amalgamation of race and class. When poor, often immigrant, whites were so desperate for work that they displaced or joined black workers in doing it, they were referred to as "white niggers," or perhaps Irish ones. Such immiseration did not necessarily produce fellow feeling—small armies of historians have managed to unearth but one example of black/white unity during a strike in the entire history of the antebellum North. Instead, it could produce a desire for color bars at work in order to disassociate jobs from black workers, and could generate a militant insistence on being treated as white, rather than as a slave, or even as Irish.

For all the attention paid by antebellum political economists and slave masters to race and productivity, Herman Melville's 1857 novel *The Confidence Man* remains the most revealing text on the far-flung sources and implications of pre–Civil War race management. The story is set on a ship crossing the Ohio River as it proceeds down the Mississippi. When it enters—as the nation seemed about to do itself in 1857 with the pro-slavery Dred Scott decision—a region where all territory is slave territory, characters debate not only abolition and bondage but labor generally. A contractor of bonded labor parading as a sentimental reformer offers to provide a "good boy" to a "misanthrope" skeptical that any young worker would be able to satisfy his need for steady and honest help. In answer to the self-interested reformer's pieties regarding the goodness of all boys, the misanthrope lists a racialized litany of the young workers he has tried: "I speak from fifteen years' experience; five and thirty boys; American, Irish, English, German, African, Mulatto; not to speak of that China boy sent me by one who well knew my perplexities, from California; and that Lascar boy from Bombay. Thug! . . . All rascals, sir, every soul of them; Caucasian or Mongol."

This multiplicity of racial types suggests the ways in which a world labor market enlivened antebellum debates on race management during a decade when calls to reopen the African slave trade became insistent, and when the "coolie trade" from Asia to the Caribbean and elsewhere already framed, as Moon-Ho Jung demonstrates in his *Coolies and Cane*, discussions of slavery and labor in the United States. By Reconstruction in the aftermath of the Civil War pro-"coolie" planters and supporters, betraying what Jung calls an "unyielding fascination with race," briefly saw the importation of Chinese labor as a way to break "Sambo" from the sense that he was "master of the southern situation," as the *New Orleans Times* wrote in 1869. A newspaper in New Iberia, Louisiana, found that most planters preferred Chinese laborers because they were "more easily managed." Even so the praise was for racial competition, along the lines Commons envisioned, as much as for the virtues of either race. Entry of 100,000 Chinese workers would "make the negro a much more reliable laborer." In the West, the building of the Transcontinental Railroad between the Civil War and 1869 featured competition between Chinese and Irish work gangs in highly dangerous situations.

While most such discourse was domestically produced, tied to North/South sectional conflict rooted in slavery and then Reconstruction, Melville rightly insisted on a context of trade, maritime labor, western expansion, and the hubris required for empire as a frame for all discussion of race and management. His passages on labor in *The Confidence Man* come just after discussion of the "metaphysics of Indian-hating," for example, and much of his sea-going fiction describes race and labor. Melville's short story, "The 'Gees," offers a short, enigmatic, and rollicking sketch of how whites, and particularly white managers of maritime work, claimed racial knowledge of the Afro-Portuguese—thus the name "'Gees"—from the Cape Verdean island of Fogo. Melville locates the production of the US racial knowledge that he ridicules within an Atlantic system of commerce, folklore, and, above all, management. As Carolyn Karcher shows, the broader target of Melville's merciless satire is US ethnological writing on race, particularly that of Cartwright. Melville demolishes all such claims of "expert" knowledge and quasi-scientific rigor, perfectly capturing its off-handedness, circularity, and selfishness, without losing sight of its import. In "The 'Gees," ethnology regularly collapses into a ridiculous managerial instruction manual. The most important judgments regarding 'Gees hinge on which ones to hire. Such choices are best left to men "well-versed in 'Gees," men who it transpires are themselves completely ignorant, but who help maintain the hubris necessary to venture out into the imperial-colonial world.

The Modernity of Race Management, There and Here

In 1896, steel magnate Andrew Carnegie would write of the "dubious" ways that indigenous land had been seized, but conclude that nonetheless "upon the whole the management of the land acquired by our race has been for the higher interests of humanity." Indeed, "civilization" made "the acquisition of the land necessary." It was, Carnegie digressed in an article on a boundary dispute in Venezuela, "well that the Maori [in New Zealand] should fade away, and give way to the intelligent, industrious citizen, a member of our race." As Carnegie's *fin-de-siècle* quotation suggests, emancipation hardly ended race management. Having lost its labor force, the large landowning class in the South redoubled an interest in "coolie" labor, and eventually warmed to the possibilities of measuring and pitting Chinese and Southern Italian work forces against African American labor. In the West, meanwhile, the drama of completing a transcontinental railroad relied on playing off Chinese and Irish immigrants against each other.

As the US empire spread significantly beyond North America, the "race" of subject peoples, endlessly subdivided, became a matter of popular education, drawing more and more Americans into the logic of race management. Doubts about the wisdom of contact with "inferior people" were countered with arguments that the excellence of US managerial and scientific expertise mattered as much as the current abilities of the colonized in making imperialism wise and workable. In the wake of the brutal war of occupation against the Philippines, the 1904 World's Fair featured photographs and life displays of the conquered. Each identified group was carefully associated with a specific "breadth of head." The fair-goers could learn or even judge which subgroups of the colonized were racially destined for an early grave, which for productive association with a Singer sewing machine, and which for service as administrators of the colonial occupation.

Indeed the discourse combining race management and scientific engineering techniques matured among US managers outside the country before its widespread adoption at home, though the spread of ideas went in both directions. Arguably the greatest US export in the quarter century after 1890 was the mining engineer. Scientifically trained, such engineers replaced European experts in Asian, Mexican, South American, Australian, and African mines, with South African mines the site of the most spectacular influx of US management. To a great extent this was because the Americans could so confidently claim knowledge gained at the intersection of race and management. Often experienced in Western US mines, where central to all management was the issue of which races and nationalities could live in the "white man's camp," such engineers particularly claimed an ability to know and to boss "native" and racially divided labor.

A central figure in the cult of the Yankee mining engineer, Herbert Hoover, later the secretary of commerce and then president of the United States, gave the name "Golden Age" to the triumph of US engineers in the world's mines. Though billed as the "Doctor of Sick Mines" for his work in spectacular adventure capitalist exploits, bringing managerial efficiency to Africa, China, and isolated areas of Australia, Hoover might more easily have been given the simpler title of "race manager." In Australia, he thought that the "saucy independence" and "loafing proclivities" of local white miners required a counterweight. Hoover assiduously ranked groups of indigenous Australians— but nevertheless called all of them "niggers," and judged all as having "too little intelligence to work very much." He therefore pitted the "races" against each other by importing crews of Italian immigrants. Speaking to a government inquiry into the use of such labor, Hoover's associate explained the logic of the choice: Italians, he reckoned, were more "servile" and "peaceable," but the real benefit lay in the racial competition itself. Management would be "in a mess if they had all aliens or all British." It was "mixed labor" that paid off.

An eager consumer and producer of reports judging the relative efficiency of African, Chinese, and white miners in South Africa, Hoover was accustomed to calculating productivity by weighing "colored shifts" and "colored wages" against those of white labor. His own most extensive calculations on race and management involved Chinese workers. Hoover, who once said that he had opposed "Asiatic immigration" to the US from the moment that he could "think and talk," made much of his early career as an engineer in North China. He continually commented on race and productivity there, at times spinning that data to attract investment in China, and at others to explain why more dramatic gains in efficiency had not been made. In an early prominent appearance before an international congress of engineers in London in 1902, he wrote of the "mulishness" of Chinese miners and of their "capacity for thieving." However, he cheerily concluded, money could be saved on timbers supporting mines because the resulting tragedies only had to be compensated at $30 per death, something he perversely ascribed to "the disregard for human life" among the Chinese.

Hoover's endless ratios for race to productivity varied wildly. In 1900 he supposed that Chinese in mining produced a fifth of what white workers did. Two years later, the Chinese worker had "no equal" in the world for crude labor, though an accompanying chart counted him only a quarter as productive as the "American" in such work, for a twelfth the pay. When he published *Principles of Mining* in 1909, Hoover featured a chart on mines in South Africa displaying data on African and Chinese workers there, although it also included data on Chinese workers in China. He concluded that in simple tasks like shoveling "one white man equals from two to three of the colored races. In more highly skilled work "the average ratio is . . . one to seven, or . . . even eleven."

Hoover's memoirs explained such productivity differences as racial, though all of his writings offer the possibility, common in progressive thought, that enduring cultural habits mattered as much as biology in making race. "Our inventions and machinery came out of our racial instincts and qualities," he held. "Our people learn easily how to make them work efficiently." The Chinese, "a less mechanical-minded people than the European-descended races . . . require many times more men to operate our intricate machines." In this Hoover departed substantially from the editorial view of the influential *Engineering and Mining Journal*, which maintained that "mine operators find it economical to make the best of whatever native labor may be available," and training it up to "American or European" standards, rather than deal with sickly and entitled imported white miners. However, he never argued that nonwhite labor must be barred from unskilled work, only that wages, opportunities, expectations, and conditions of competition should be adjusted by knowledgeable race managers.

When employing nonwhite labor Hoover also indulged in paternal fantasies of racial uplift. Much in keeping with the tradition of slave masters, he balanced racial competition with what was called by the early twentieth century "race development," believing that the Chinese and others could be "much-developed by Western ideas" and US experts. The alternating currents of race management and race development helped give rise to a thoroughly modern US imperialism. Indeed the flagship journal of modern US empire, *Foreign Affairs*, evolved from the tellingly titled *Journal of Race Development*. Just as Fordism at home allowed foremen to set immigrant "races" against each other, even as company-paid social workers could claim to develop "the race" as a whole through education in Americanism and intrusive home visits, US capital and managers overseas promised race development across the board to host country elites, while they made judgments as to the "blood" of potential workers. Elizabeth Esch's accounts of Ford's own simultaneously paternalist and brutalizing management of Brazilian rubber workers are an important case in point.

The ways in which race management coexisted with scientific management in the US deserve our attention as the clearest examples of how fully compatible was the modernity of capitalism with the atavism of race. Melville's misanthrope, sorting haphazardly through racial types to find the perfect worker, seems utterly at odds with the science of management that Frederick Winslow Taylor is credited with inventing in the late nineteenth century. John R. Commons could maintain otherwise, in part because Taylor's ideas always existed alongside, and sometimes adapted aspects of, crude practices of race management. Indeed the famous example which Taylor himself used to educate the public on his system's ability to create "high-priced men" by careful selection and scientific regulation of their movements on the job, suggests overlap between managerial science and race management. For his case study, Taylor chose "Schmidt" as the prototypical worker to retrain into a new regimen, moving a stock of pig iron suddenly made valuable by the Spanish–American War. He did so with group "racial" attributes much in mind. Schmidt's name, and Taylor's description, emphasized that the chosen worker's agreement to submit to the new system, and his ability to produce, flowed in part from his membership of the German "race." Schmidt embodied the strength, doggedness and thrift thought by Taylor to be peculiarly concentrated in the Pennsylvania Dutch, as Germans in the area were called.

The racial logic informing Taylor's Schmidt example did not permeate all his writing, which often stressed the need to approach workers as individuals. Indeed his desire to uproot the arbitrary power of foremen and other petty bosses placed Taylor among those management experts least likely to express sympathy with everyday uses of antagonistic racial competition among workers to increase production. But the race-thinking that informed Taylor's presentation of his new system by introducing listeners and readers to the "Dutch" Schmidt comported with larger patterns that saw race management survive, and even expand, in the early years of the scientific management era. As David Montgomery has written of this period, "all managers seem[ed] to agree" with H. A. Worman, an expert working for the giant International Harvester farm implement manufacturing corporation, who held that "each race has aptitude for certain kinds of work." Montgomery further observed that the trend towards personnel management as a complement to Taylorism specifically "extended the purview of scientific management," a development that "flowed directly from the concern with recruiting from specific ethnic groups."

The Schmidt and Hoover examples, together with Montgomery's commentary, remind us that scientific management and race management coexisted because they were not so different after all. As Bernard Doray wrote two decades ago, Taylorist management, like Hoover's race management in the mines, was a "science" that could not escape "bear[ing] the scars of the social violence that characterized the society that gave birth to it." Replete with pro-management assumptions, this science selectively drew on folk knowledge and crude observations of existing work patterns in ways fully unearthed in Harry Braverman's dissection of Taylor's methods. Indeed Braverman shows that even in an "unskilled" task like the carrying of pig iron that Schmidt performed, Taylor began by watching the most productive workers in their most productive moments and boosting work norms by putting such knowledge into management's head. Scientific management was therefore broadly compatible with that other great scarring and scar-bearing "science" of the early twentieth century: the elaboration of racial hierarchies.

While true, this symmetry leaves us needing to account for the wide difference between the offhand tone in which Taylor discussed Schmidt's "race," the subject of cracker-barrel philosophizing, and the studied way that he treated Schmidt's labor as the subject of seeming mathematical precision. In such matters Taylor was typical. Even at their most ambitious, purportedly scientific connections between race and productivity remained crude in the extreme, both in the domestic US and in Hoover's international studies. When that towering figure in American sociology, E. A. Ross, urged slotting the Slavic "race" into filthy and unhealthy jobs because they were "immune" to dirt, he was offering an opinion, not a scientific conclusion. The chart ranking three dozen immigrant "races" according to their fitness for three dozen job types and conditions, posted at Pittsburgh Central Tube in 1925, assembled a much more impressive number of opinions. It served to systematize a huge factory and the peoples in it, in upwards of 1,000 multicolored squares. But it matched Ross' crudeness of judgment, gathering up managerial and professional folklore and summing up existing prejudices and practices. Italians allegedly excelled with pick and shovel but were unable to assist engineers. Armenians ranked "good" in none of the twenty-two job categories listed and rose to fair only once: wheelbarrow. "Americans, White" could do any job fairly well and excelled in most. Jews supposedly fitted well into no industrial jobs.

By the end of the Progressive era—that is, after the immigration restrictions of 1924 made race management able to operate only on a much smaller canvas—social scientists themselves ridiculed such systems as the irrational underside of a rational industrial society. Everitt C. Hughes and Helen M. Hughes observed that off-the-cuff opinions on racial difference so pervaded managerial choices and language, while hard data comparing racial performance remained so rare, that it was worth questioning whether "modern society is really guided by the impersonal concepts of the market and efficiency in choosing . . . its labor force." Commenting on US labor practices in the 1920s and 1930s, management experts Herman Feldman and T. J. Woofter rued the fact that manufacturers, so scrupulously careful in choosing raw materials, "rely on hearsay and rumor as to the grades of labor hired." Taylor had written that "Under scientific management arbitrary power . . . ceases; and every single subject . . . becomes the question for scientific investigation." But experts knew that where race was concerned, such a shift did not happen.

The deep historical roots of American race management as detailed above go some distance to explaining its impressive durability. But to emphasize only this history leaves us in danger of seeing management by race as a residual, even pre-modern, phenomenon—one at odds with the longer rational logic of capitalism. Instead it was central to such logic. Here, Commons's remarks are once again critical. As early as 1904, Commons had heard from an employment agent that the competition between the races—the term would have included various European nationalities—had been "systematized" in his factory. Such a system did not rest on the fixing of a scientific chart of hierarchy, however, but rather on the production of a series of contradictory and volatile managerial opinions—the sociologist Niles Carpenter found that workers thought lower management's racial prejudices and slights directly and devastatingly impacted the lives of immigrant labor, often by keeping all races productively on edge. In this way, the 1911 Immigration Commission report's conclusion of virtual unanimity among employers that Southern Italians were "the most inefficient of races," could comfortably coexist with Pittsburgh Steel's placing of Italians in the most efficient third, above Canadians, of all "racial" groups shortly thereafter. Nor did the fact that one steel manager might prefer "two Negroes" to "three Macedonians," even though most ranked the "alien white races" above African Americans, provoke any urgent desire to settle the question "scientifically." Even the basic questions of who was white and of who was black remained unanswered by managers who were nonetheless fixated on race. When a mine superintendent on the Iron Range in Minnesota told a government investigator prior to World War I that "The 'black races' cannot do the work in three days that a white man can do in one," the term "black" connoted Montenegrins, Serbs, Southern Italians, Greeks, and Croats; not African Americans.

So the system, brutally rational without being scientific, required that races be kept in competition with one another—often, in the case of African Americans, keeping them out of jobs altogether via color bars and using them as a reserve army of labor; the system quite deliberately avoided freezing them into a settled ranking. Historians have long known that Taylorism's revolutionary changes often supplemented, rather than supplanted, the "hurry and push" tactics in which lower management bullied and threatened workers, Taylor's wishes notwithstanding. But we have too often forgotten Commons's insistence that the hurrying and pushing were chronically affected by the playing of races against each other.

Such practices of management not only established racial, rather than abstract, labor as central to the logic of US capitalism; they also have broad implications for thinking about barriers to the development of a united workers' movement able to challenge hierarchies of both race and class. The same early twentieth-century Louisiana lumberjacks who read in the radical labor press that trees did not care who felled them, might also have laughed bitterly over a 1913 Mr. Block comic by the great Industrial

Workers of the World artist Ernest Riebe. In it, the stubbornly, stupidly anti-radical cartoon character Mr. Block performs back-breaking labor for a manager who circulates among Irish, German, Italian, Chinese, and black workers, threatening and cajoling them to greater competition and productivity. The black worker learns that the gang wants him off the job but the boss will protect him if he works "good and hard." In the last frame the manager reclines as all workers, drawn like the title character as blockheads, swap racial slurs.

Riebe's own faith that effective organization could overcome such divisive games is clear, but his strip also shows the formidable extent to which race contributed to management, both by creating competition for jobs and thereby lowering wages, and also by setting workers against each other every hour they were on the job. When the Irish worker responds to the boss by affirming "I can lick the whole bunch and I can make them work too," he shows at once the ways in which race management encouraged laborers to bring their cultural differences and stereotypes to work, the extent to which employers' appeals to race often overlapped with appeals to masculinity, and to the desire of some immigrant workers to ascend into the lower ranks of race management. Race management dragged workers towards narrow "caste and craft unionism," which often brought divided members together as whites and as "citizens," but less frequently challenged race-thinking by uniting all workers. Far from reducing labor to abstract and raceless inputs into the labor process, capital and management helped to reproduce racial differences over long stretches of US history and to divide workers in ways that compromised labor's efforts to address either race or class inequalities.

4

The Ends of Emancipation:
HOW RACE SURVIVED JUBILEE

In late 1861, with civil war raging and its outcome still in the balance, a newspaper in a Union-held part of South Carolina published a devastating satire of the advertisements from masters seeking escaped slaves that had so long disgraced the US press. Appearing over the signature of Sambo Rhett, an "ex-slave," it sent bounty hunters searching not for a slave, but for a slave master:

> $500 REWARD—Rund away from me . . . my massa Julian Rhett. Massa Rhett am five feet 'leven inches high, big shoulders, brack hair, curly, shaggy whiskers, low forehead an' dark face . . . Calls heself "Suddern gemmen," but I 'spose will try now to pass heself off as a black man or muletter. Massa Rhett has a deep scar on his shoulder, from a fight, scratch 'cross de left eye, made by Dinah when he tried to whip her.

The reward dipped to $100 if Rhett were returned alive with the apparent preference being for confirmation of his death.

Sambo Rhett's mocking pursuit of his "runaway master" signaled a world that had turned upside-down. If prewar notices of runaways had bespoken the absolute reduction of human beings to property, often noting for purposes of identification the physical marks masters had left on slave bodies, this one was written in a new era and could take pride in the fact that slaves had often landed some blows. By the time it appeared, blacks in coastal South Carolina had an impressive record of literally finding their own ways to freedom by seeking out the Union army even before it had asked for them or had beaten Confederate forces. That the world could change, and that they could change it, made anything seem possible, including the envisaging of such a profound change in the racial order that Massa Rhett would attempt to pass as nonwhite.

Even after the Civil War, with the Confederacy defeated and the end of slavery in the United States formally proclaimed, the portentous word "Reconstruction" did not suffice for freedpeople wanting to describe the period during which they seized their emancipation, as announced by Lincoln, and first lived. The official terminology settled too much for the physical remaking of war-torn places, for restoring a nation that had never included black people. Ex-slaves preferred to speak of "jubilee," describing the ecstasy of living in the moment of what W. E. B. Du Bois called "the coming of the Lord." But the term signaled more than simple jubilation. It hearkened to the Old Testament text of perfect liberation, reaching back, in a spectacular act of mass theology among a people long denied both Bibles and literacy, to the description in Leviticus of the year that slaves were to be emancipated and land redistributed. Thinking in terms of jubilee therefore implied both celebration and organization. Organization supporting land reform took shape around the slogan "forty acres and a mule," which first gained currency in the South Carolina sea islands a result of an early 1865 field order by General William Tecumseh Sherman temporarily provisioning freedpeople in this way. We know, with the advantage of hindsight, that this demand would not be won, and that regression towards slavery would take place. But the vision of jubilee that made ex-slaves confidently embrace such possibilities made them lead the nation in appreciating that a new society was possible.

To a great extent, the impossible had already happened, and ex-slaves were best positioned to know that, and how, it had. Their story, and that of the South, therefore structures much of this chapter. Before the Civil War, few demands had seemed more hopelessly utopian in the context of mainstream politics than that for the immediate, unplanned, and uncompensated abolition of slavery. Years of unsuccessful abolitionist agitation had shown how hopeless it was to gain votes on such a platform, with the result that many abolitionists themselves had moved tactically to the gradualist ranks of the Republican Party, which opposed the extension of slavery into new territories but lavishly professed respect for slaveholders' property rights where slavery existed. The war itself brought little initial change; even as the slave South showed itself to be a formidable enemy, and some Union commanders began to see, in slaves seeking refuge behind Yankee lines, the exposure of Confederacy's Achilles' heel. Early on in the war Frederick Douglass reflected black abolitionist disappointment when he bemoaned a conflict designed to "preserve slavery" on both sides, with the South of course standing for continued bondage, and with Lincoln unwilling to regard defecting slaves as anything but "contraband" property. Even in his warm memorial delivered a decade after Lincoln's assassination, Douglass recalled a leader elected as "pre-eminently the white man's President . . . willing at any time during the first years of his administration to deny, postpone and sacrifice the rights of humanity in the colored people to promote the welfare of the white people of this country."

But hundreds of thousands of slaves joined Douglass in believing that the war nonetheless was about freedom, and ensuring by their actions that it would be. What Du Bois called their "general strike" in leaving the plantations behind, combined with military and political necessities to force Lincoln into embracing the impossible. Lincoln's initial Emancipation Proclamation, taking effect on January 1, 1863, freed only the slaves of those in rebellion—that is, precisely those beyond the Union's ability to liberate. But a pattern of uncompensated, unplanned, and speedy emancipation was being set. By war's end, 200,000 African

American soldiers and sailors had served the Union cause, under-scoring the connections between sacrifice, self-emancipation, and citizenship, and at the same time gaining military experience and arms. When it became constitutional with the Thirteenth Amendment in 1865, the jubilee of emancipation was the largest uncompensated seizure of property—the ex-slaves themselves liberating their own persons—in the history of the world prior to the Russian Revolution. Further supposed "impossibilities" followed closely. A decade after the Dred Scott decision found all African Americans without any rights that the "white man" had to respect, the Fourteenth Amendment made their rights part of constitutional law. By 1870, the Constitution would specify that the right to vote was among those liberties.

Could an Anti-Racist Rainbow Rise?

Much of what has come before in this book connects the origins and reproduction of race-thinking to slavery, as well as to the casting of African Americans as "anti-citizens" whose presence served to convince "free, white men" of their own superior racial status and independence. The impact of the hitherto "impossible" transformation of slave property into citizens and citizen-soldiers was therefore bound to be considerable. Indeed, if there were a time when race might have disappeared in US history, it would have been precisely just after the Civil War. Full-blown scientific racism, for example, had taken hold in the US in the context of the pro-slavery argument and as a response to abolitionism. Many of its premises disappeared with emancipation, awaiting re-elaboration in a new society and on new grounds.

The possibility that an enduring politics of jubilee would replace a politics of race transcended even the remarkable individual transformations occurring among 4 million African Americans. The war, and in particular the general strike of the slaves and emancipation, unleashed broad dreams of freedom, making possible unprecedented coalitions. South and North, the

Civil War was called a "poor man's fight," so much so in the Confederacy that Georgia's governor, Joseph Emerson Brown, felt compelled to give an 1863 speech addressing the issue. Wartime demands for service, discipline and taxes in the South sparked significant disquiet and dissent, especially among farmers, hunters, and herders in areas holding relatively few slaves. Deserters in Alabama, often poor, found themselves chased down by the same dogs used to hunt runaway slaves. That the planter-dominated Confederate government led the region to disastrous defeat made poorer whites even more liable to challenge old elites. Since the newly enfranchised black male population neared a majority in many Southern areas, the possibility that even a minority of white voters might question the Democratic Party's protracted postwar attempts to restore planter dominance within a "white man's government" had great political implications. In a region where Lincoln did not even appear on ballots in 1860, Republicans could rule a decade later.

In the North, even as the fighting raged, the labor press asked what labor's "emancipation" would mean. The overwhelming answer, an eight-hour working day, came to be portrayed as the "nation's gift to workingmen in the army." When the gift was not forthcoming, massive agitation by trade unions and broad eight-hour leagues followed. The connections between this visionary demand—the ten-hour day remained a dream in much of the nation and the US quickly became the world's leader in eight-hour agitation—and the jubilation occurring among African Americans were both obvious and subtle. At the level of personnel, the movement quickly came to feature many leading abolitionists, including William Lloyd Garrison and, above all, Wendell Phillips. Its chief spokesperson, the machinist and theorist Ira Steward, was said to have fought alongside John Brown in Kansas antislavery battles. Steward called the eight-hour demand itself an "anti-slavery" measure, as well as a blow against "aristocracy . . . waste . . . Women's endless drudgery . . . and war."

The tenor of jubilee so pervaded the eight-hour campaign that Marx rightly spoke at the time of the "moral impetus" of the slaves' emancipation as central to labor's new direction. The rise of the short-lived National Labor Union (NLU) between the years 1866 and 1872 as the most important working-class organization in US history to that point reflected the new position of the white worker as nowhere having to compete with slave labor, and as no longer able to declare himself a "freeman," or herself a "freewoman," simply by virtue of not being enslaved. Marx's correspondence with NLU leader William Sylvis suggested that the slaves' emancipation set the stage for a larger jubilee in which "at last the working class shall enter upon the scene of history, no longer as a servile following but as an independent power."

Such power in turn had direct implications for the future of race-thinking. In 1869 the NLU made an unprecedented proclamation, that it "knew neither color nor sex on the question of the rights of labor," and in a similarly groundbreaking move invited black participation in its national meetings. The major black speaker at the 1869 NLU meeting, the waterfront worker Isaac Myers, lived a story of postwar transformation every bit as wondrous as Sambo Rhett's. A free black caulker before the war, in the same Baltimore port where Frederick Douglass had caulked as a slave, in 1865 Myers saw white workers mount a hate strike against black shipyard workers. He responded by organizing a cooperative—Douglass was among its first shareholders—in which those African Americans losing their jobs as a result of the white strike could work. So successful was the cooperative, and so broad its vision, that it came to include white workers by 1869, even as the NLU welcomed African American workers for the first time.

If there were an antebellum cause more apparently impossible than the immediate emancipation of slaves, it was the dream of women's suffrage. Like the rise of labor, this demand matured in the reflected glory of the slaves' jubilee, and invoked the idea of national "war debt," in this case to loyal and organized women who had concretely supported the Union cause. Historically far more organically tied to abolitionism than white labor had been, feminism promised to be a powerful ally in the post–Civil War struggle against racial injustice. Indeed, the emergence of voices for women's rights and the maturation of women's political skills in petition campaigns had taken shape from the late 1820s onwards in initiatives against slavery and the ethnic cleansing of Indians. Working women, particularly in the textile and shoe industries, supported abolitionism and balanced their own "slavery" and chattel slavery with a sophistication that lent itself to agitation against both.

Nonetheless when the US women most insistent on their own rights first met at an 1848 convention in the village of Seneca Falls (New York), the prospect of suffrage seemed sufficiently remote even to them that the meeting hesitated to include it in the list of priorities. Frederick Douglass's address to the convention helped embolden delegates on this front. The American orator most practiced at insisting the impossible be kept in play, he made the case for demanding what is necessary, not only what is immediately possible. In the changed conditions of the Reconstruction era, feminist leaders like Elizabeth Cady Stanton and Susan B. Anthony retained the sense that women's suffrage was a deeply radical demand—they called their publication *Revolution*—and also consolidated their ties with the black freedom movement: Stanton and Anthony's National Loyal Women's League gathered 400,000 signatures in a petition campaign that proved instrumental in securing emancipation through the 1865 Thirteenth Amendment.

However, any prospective rainbow of grassroots organizations comprising white workers, poor white Southerners, and women, inspired by and coalescing with freedpeople, would have had little real political force. It united those without the right to vote, those without prior political experience, and those unused to forwarding their own demands politically. To imagine the Republican Party as the possible vehicle for broadly radical and specifically anti-racist unity will require considerable suspension of disbelief on the reader's part; even in the short term, it proved to be a fundamentally flawed vehicle, and often enough an active enemy of freedom. Nevertheless for a time activists as diverse as Douglass and the white labor militant and martyr Albert Parsons regarded the Republicans as a "labor party," a view Du Bois later endorsed in regard to specific times and places in the Reconstruction South. The very fact that freedpeople realistically believed that "their" party might rule emboldened visions—planters were not wrong to believe, as John Rodrigue's study of Louisiana Reconstruction puts it, that "politics demoralized labor," making black workers restive and demanding. Even in the North, where its social base did not lie in the laboring classes, the party generated an avowedly radical wing.

Incorporating ex-abolitionists, and expressing popular revulsion with a former slaveholding class held responsible for a war that killed 600,000 Americans, Radical Republicans pressed for constitutional guarantees of black civil rights, which were also seen as blocking any attempts by conservative Southern elites to return to power. To the extent that the freedpeople's demand for "forty acres and a mule" found support among policymakers, it did so with Radical Republicans, some of who saw it as both just and expedient in breaking the power of white Southern landed elites. The greatest Radical Republican elected official, Massachusetts Senator Charles Sumner, strove for a time to include women's suffrage in the postwar amendments and, against perhaps still greater odds, tried—albeit unsuccessfully—to protect the rights of Chinese Americans in naturalization legislation. In such states as Massachusetts, Illinois, and Wisconsin, the Republicans, however rapidly they were becoming the party of big business, gave enthusiastic support to state laws making eight hours a legal day's work. Radical Republicans particularly championed the reform.

Why a Rainbow Could Not Reign

The tensions immediately appearing within this prospective post–Civil War rainbow remind us that, however useful we may find

Stuart Hall's admonition that racism is always (re)created in the present, not inherited from the past, the nightmarish weight of old habits does press down on movements for change. Despite all evidence to the contrary, the Reconstruction-era white labor movement proved unable to shed its deep-rooted associations of African Americans with degraded work and incapacity for citizenship. Accounts of the NLU's halting approach to cooperation with segregated black unions generally feature Sylvis as a heroic advocate of cooperation across the color line. They less often detail his extravagantly racist opposition to "social equality" between the races, or his ridiculing of the critically important working-class demand that freedpeople be able to serve on juries, or his denunciations of direct food aid to ex-slaves as a "swindle" serving "lazy loafers," or his wild assurances to readers that the Ku Klux Klan did not exist. In fact, Klan terror was very much part of the context in which black workers were hesitant to leave the imperfect protection provided by the Republican Party and to place their trust in "labor" politics. Since craft unions tended to organize around a "manly" defense of rights on the job, the question of who could be envisioned as a brother citizen-worker assumed great importance. The issue quickly arose within the rainbow in the most dramatic way possible, when bitter opposition and costly delays greeted the application of Frederick Douglass's son Lewis for membership in the International Typographical Union, and unions in other crafts began to scramble to add the word "white" to their membership requirements.

Among poor whites in the South the contradictory pulls of past and present were likewise strong. When freedpeople entered the fields after slavery, some white farmers worriedly responded by seeking to accentuate their continued difference from the region's new citizen-workers through a curious fashion choice. Shedding wide-brimmed straw hats of the traditional sort worn by ex-slaves, they opted for brimless wool hats in the scorching Southern sun. Unwise almost to the point of rehabilitating the crudest variants of Marxist analyses of racism that brand poor white commitments to racial hierarchies as "false consciousness," this choice of headwear created "rednecks" by virtue of sunburn. At the same time, "redneck" was also coming to signify the wearing of a kerchief or bandanna of that color, one common to laboring people and seen as a symbol of interracial cooperation: in this way did the term illustrate both paths available to poor whites.

In such a situation, any possible radical rainbow coalition paid dearly for failures and for partial successes that revealed the limits of jubilee. Despite Sumner's efforts, no viable amendment uniting black male suffrage and women's suffrage proved possible. Frederick Douglass's message to feminists, meanwhile, came to be very different than the one he had delivered in 1848. He began to underscore the historic postwar importance of the vote for African American men, and urged women to be patient during "the Negro's hour." The results were not utterly dire. As Elsa Barkley-Brown has shown, the spirit of jubilee kept freedwomen voting in vital community meetings, mandating actions by law-makers in parts of the South. Nor did long-established ties between abolitionism and feminism snap completely. Indeed Douglass would attend, with Susan B. Anthony, a pro-suffrage meeting on the day of his death in 1895. Nonetheless the previously intimate association of women's rights and African American freedom suffered severe strains. In her autobiography Anthony spoke of a sting that words could not express, and made it clear that this sting came not just from the denial of votes for women, but also from the franchise going to black men in 1870. The Constitution had "recognized as the political superiors of all the noble women of the nation the negro men just emerged from slavery, and not only totally illiterate, but also densely ignorant of every public question." Pragmatic dalliances with racist politicians by some suffragists followed in the short term and in the longer run white supremacist ideas came to compromise sections of feminism.

By far the weightiest contradictions within a prospective rain-bow of alliances occurred in the character of the political party that potentially glued such a coalition together. Du Bois introduces a key chapter of his masterful 1935 *Black Reconstruction in America* by musing on what divergent aspirations the Republicans gathered under one political tent, remarking on

> how two theories of the future of America clashed and blended just after the Civil War: the one was abolition-democracy based on freedom, intelligence and power for all men; the other was industry for private profit directed by an autocracy determined at any price to amass wealth and power.

The jarring of such ideals was bound to be dramatic; it was made more so by the fact that the two sets of priorities both found their sharpest expression inside the Republican Party.

Nor did that party simply divide into two clear factions on these matters. Individual Republicans, and particularly individual Radical Republicans, felt the powerful pulls of democracy and industrial development simultaneously. For a time, the greatest congressional friends of black freedom, men like the significantly nicknamed William "Pig Iron" Kelley, came from districts that had grown in the wake of pro-industrial legislation passed while the South was out of the Union, and which often shared in phenomenal postwar industrialization. Resolutely opposed to any reassertion of planters' power, and committed to black suffrage for partisan and moral reasons, such radicals also cherished deep commitments to capitalist market relations. At critical junctures the latter commitments held sway. For example, Republican legislators in Northern states could often be counted upon to support the demand for a legal working day of eight hours, but could also be relied on to honor the sanctity of contracts contravening such a standard, leaving loopholes that made the reformist legislation meaningless. While labor reformers were nevertheless often willing to settle for such symbolic legislation, intending to enforce the standard through mass action, Republican support of capital was likewise pronounced during struggles over the actual enforcement of eight-hour days, notably in the stormy Illinois strikes of 1867. Most importantly, commitments to the market and to capitalist work discipline led influential Republicans, including Freedmen's Bureau officials charged with administering to the welfare of ex-slaves, to oppose the demand for redistributing land to freedpeople. When black-influenced state governments then attempted to use taxes on land, both to fund social programs and to create opportunities for African Americans to buy land from large estates sold for taxes, they sometimes alienated precisely the cash-poor, small land-holding, anti-taxation whites who were critical to Republican electoral success. Thus the Republicans' refusal to address land reform at a national level reached to the heart of the possibility of meaningful interracial coalition-building.

White South Rising: Guerrillas and Great Compromisers

Given time, the fractures within the rainbow might have healed. Indeed, before the end of the nineteenth century significant alliances between black sharecroppers and poor whites emerged in some areas under the populist banner, with white "wool-hat boys" in Georgia responding with particular, if fragile, enthusiasm for interracialism. Founded in Philadelphia in 1869, the Knights of Labor had built similar, and likewise precarious, unity across the color line among workers by the 1880s. But rainbows are evanescent by nature. The very spirit of jubilee implied speedy, heady transformations. As Phillips wrote to Sumner near the end of the war, "These are no times for ordinary politics . . . The national purpose and thought grows and ripens in thirty days as much as ordinary years bring it forward." In such revolutionary times, each defeat, deferred promise, and division took on magnified proportions for coalition participants, as much as triumphs did. Moreover, time brought economic growth that made the pro-industrial capitalist and railroad forces in the Republican Party all the more powerful. Most importantly, time allowed racist forces in the South to organize, brutalize, and strategize. The religious language of their crusade for the "redemption" of the

South through the restoration of white supremacy mirrored the passions of jubilee but reversed its liberatory impulses, ultimately with great and horrible sophistication.

By far the most consequential Republican contribution to the end of jubilee lay in what it stopped doing, when it withdrew federal protection for black civil rights and suffrage in the face of political terror by white Southerners. According to its portrayal in D. W. Griffith's notorious 1915 film *The Birth of a Nation*, and to countless historical studies, such terror was a logical, even heroic, response to the alleged excesses of Radical Republican government in the South. A quote from one of those studies, President Woodrow Wilson's *History of the American People*, found a place as an intertitle in *The Birth of a Nation* itself: "The white men were roused by a mere instinct of self-preservation . . . until at last there had sprung into existence a great Ku Klux Klan, a veritable empire of the South, to protect the Southern country."

Little of such legend has withstood careful revisionist scholarship on the accomplishments of Reconstruction governments, but in appreciating such revisionist scholarship we must be wary of moving the focus of the story fully from purposeful terrorists to interracial legislatures. White terror, after all, is what helped to undermine the legislatures. The older view, that the white supremacist South fought a successful guerrilla war to take back control of the region, erred in its politics but not in its centering of critically important Klan-centered campaigns against democracy. Jubilee did not collapse under the weight of internal contradictions, but under extended assault. Moreover, the guerrilla campaign by the white South took studied care to extend an offer of ceasefire to Republican politicians, and to hold out the possibility of transfers of vast natural resources held by Southern states to outside capital, in exchange for white home rule, albeit in a semi-colonial economy.

In the 1873 Mississippi elections, the only elections in that state's Reconstruction history with more or less fully free African American voting, Republicans carried the day in one small constituency with just over 2,400 votes; two years later the same constituency polled just seven Republican votes. In Caddo, Louisiana, where no fewer than sixty Republican Party members were murdered during Reconstruction, the Republican vote in the 1868 election totaled exactly one. Such near-total suppressions of the vote flowed from persistent, varied, and targeted terror. One account of the 1875 Mississippi election refers to it as "civil war turned into massacre." In the well-studied case of Caddo, one black male in ten was murdered during Reconstruction. Political activism predicted death, with over half of the murders occurring in the two pivotal election years of 1868 and 1874. Of those murdered, 85 percent were black, with whites likely perpetrators in 84 percent of the cases. In an astonishing 70 percent of the murders, the killings were carried out by groups of whites. In Mississippi wholesale massacres killed scores when forcing out the elected governor and lieutenant governor prior to the 1875 elections.

Such events typified an extended pattern of evolving and resilient white supremacist terror. The war had hardly ended when the Ku Klux Klan, which came to be the best known of the white supremacist organizations, was founded in Tennessee in 1866. Its fortunes as a far-flung, and far from centralized, organization took off when the former planter, slave trader, and celebrated Confederate General Nathan Bedford Forrest associated himself with the group, becoming the first honorary "Grand Wizard" of an organization claiming hundreds of thousands of supporters. Regarded as tactically brilliant, beloved by troops, and popularly linked to the wartime Fort Pillow Massacre of black soldiers, he stood as a perfect symbol for white guerrilla campaigns. Forrest reportedly held that the goal of the Klan was to "keep the niggers in their place," and spoke of it as politically targeting Northern Republican "carpetbaggers" in the South, as well as homegrown white Republican "scalawags." If he envisioned a group with military discipline, he was bound to suffer disappointment. Local, uncoordinated acts of terror by disguised "night riders" were the rule, and the rise of similar white terror organizations like the Knights of the White Camellia made it difficult to know just who was responsible for what.

Nonetheless the Democratic Party's campaign to restore conservative white rule had, as Forrest more than hinted, acquired organized, armed support. Racist political terror broadly displayed a remarkably sure focus. One in ten participants in the 1867 and 1868 Southern constitutional conventions challenging white rule fell victim to political violence, despite the fact that politically acute and cautious guerrillas in the Klan tended to press their early activities mainly outside the "Black Belt" areas of large African American majorities. Republicans of both races came in for their share of the brutality: a white judge was among the victims in an 1870 South Carolina "negro chase" that killed thirteen in all. Forrest himself once held that he would "not shoot any negroes so long as I can see a white Radical to shoot," but this probably exemplified the "humor" for which the general was famed rather than characterizing precise patterns of terrorist actions.

A railroad executive and convict labor supervisor during Reconstruction, Forrest soon professed to think the Klan too indiscriminately violent and/or too little under the control of "gentlemen." He ordered it disbanded in 1869, an action somewhat at odds with his occasional claims that he had not actually been a member. Facing new anti-terror laws—ones with enough teeth to remain models for present-day legislation in that regard—but also reacting to its own successes in changing the electoral balance of forces in some areas, the Klan itself did dissolve in an uneven process completed by the early 1870s.

Since its first active incarnation did not exceed five years, the Klan is still sometimes seen as a historical curiosity rather than a monstrosity. But the centrality of terror to the whole project of "redeeming" the South for white supremacy cannot so easily be waved away. As we have seen, much of the fiercest anti-jubilee racist violence came between 1873 and 1876, well after the Klan had formally ended. As George Rable's exemplary research has shown, the more decentralized post-Klan wave of terror was no less bloody, or politically targeted and timed, than its predecessors. Indeed it took on bolder proportions, moving into Black Belt areas, and as more areas came to be "redeemed" or intimidated by terror, new organizations functioned more openly and in more transparent alliance with the Democratic Party. Louisiana's White League was functioning openly by 1874, becoming what Nicholas Lemann has called the "military arm" of the Democrats.

The fact that gentleman-terrorists like Forrest worried over the class composition of the organizations in which they were involved did not keep these groups from serving as important reassertions of white unity as well as of white power. As in the antebellum years when slave patrols had functioned to incorporate poorer whites into the defense of racial privileges that they scarcely shared, so too would postwar terror function both to dissuade white dissenters, and to give poor and wealthy whites a common project. Indeed the great anti-terrorist journalist and activist Ida B. Wells observed that emancipation had served to create material conditions for planter leadership in fully murderous attacks. During slavery capture of runaways followed by terrible punishment and renewed labor was the preferred order of things, but after emancipation "the vested interest of the white men in the Negro's body was lost," according to Wells. In Louisiana planters constituted a third of whites involved in Reconstruction-era murders of African Americans; if we add to that total the professionals, larger businessmen, and public officials involved in the terror, elites constituted half of the murderers. This still left more than a quarter of the deaths wrought at the hands of farmers, and an eighth at those of workers. Since whites committed so many of these crimes in groups, class lines were often crossed within individual conspiracies. Moreover, the necessity for terror to work through a combination of secrecy and publicity left many more non-participating whites knowing about, or even witnessing, murders.

The lynch law of the half-century after Reconstruction, which claimed over 3,000 individual African American victims and countless more in mass murders—Rosewood, Tulsa, Elaine, Chicago, Wilmington, Atlanta, Springfield, East Saint Louis, and so, tragically, on—even more jarringly combined spectacle and secrecy. Many lynchings were meticulously planned, with photographers called in not only to capture the violence but also [...]s. Excursion trains ran to [...]ed as many as 10,000 [...]es customarily displayed [...]s for years after the event, [...] and music composed for [...]s. At a very conservative [...]e Southerners, many of [...]nchings. Many millions [...] of the South's greatest [...]back to witnessing such [...]e that white witness—so [...]mes Baldwin and Ralph [...] or actively complicit. [...]white unity across sharp [...]variety of freedpeople's [...]reconstruction concerted [...]tical targets, but success-ful black trade-union activity, economic successes especially in acquiring land, petty-criminal behavior, "arrogance," and personal disputes provided other motives for attack. The defense of white women, though slow to mature as a "cause" of white violence and the impulse for only a minority of lynchings even at the height of post-Reconstruction violence, began to appear as a rationale. In Louisiana, of the almost 1,500 documented white-on-black homicides in Reconstruction, only eight involved even a charge of rape. Almost as many hinged on "laughing about a white woman," with questions of interracial cohabitation generating seven murders, and "protection" of a wife nine more. But even adding all of these categories, scarcely a victim in fifty was even allegedly connected to offenses regarding sex and gender. Nonetheless, symbolic arguments for the Klan and similar groups as defenders of white women proliferated. In one North Carolina county, the Klan's membership allegedly grew in response to a single attempt by a black man to "hug" interracially.

The power of such appeals matured into a multifaceted crisis in white Southern masculinity, now brilliantly studied by Laura Edwards, LeeAnn Whites, and others, that emerged out of the Civil War. With military and political defeat, with the end of slavery as a source of patriarchal authority, with poverty and landlessness increasingly undermining male roles as providers, with black women undercutting differences from white women by withdrawing from field labor, and with war-related disabilities rife, the white Southern gender system tottered, and the traditional definition of manhood was shaken to its foundations. Like their counterparts in the North, white Southern women could claim a heroic record of sacrifice for the war effort. They plausibly remembered shouldering greater responsibilities for production and management during the war than had Yankee women, only to be led by men to defeat. But if Northern claims of rights for women existed in troubled tandem with the rights of African Americans, Southern white women often saw their redemption as hitched to the rehabilitation of Southern white men and of white supremacy, connecting women's well-being more to protection than to equality. The Klan and other terrorist groups seized on such possibilities with alacrity, helping to create the stereotype of the black man as potential rapist, policing the behavior of white women in interracial relationships, and identifying free African American voting and speech with the impotence of white men and the peril of white women.

Forrest's own willingness to retreat as well as to attack, along with his business cooperation with Northern capital, typifies the range of actions central to the restoration of Southern white supremacy. At critical junctures, the terrible genius of white attacks on jubilee lay in the ability to alternate currents of brutality and conciliation. "Railroads," Forrest once observed, "had no politics." However overstated, his point had force. Surely building and running railroads did necessitate alliances of convenience with the local power of the Republicans and the seeking of capital from wherever it might come. Moreover, Forrest the railway man needed labor and proclaimed black labor the world's best, urging importation of workers from the African continent when he was not engineering schemes to bring in Chinese immigrants. While not ruling out white supremacist political violence altogether, such needs dictated that elite-sponsored terror would be targeted and timed rather than indiscriminate.

Since Northern politicians and capitalists wanted a stable South requiring little government expenditure and offering a predictable field for private investment, the white elite Southern strategies of terror and junior partnership made a perfect pair. As Klansmen pondered and slowly acted upon Forrest's 1869 call to dissolve the formal Klan organization, they could look to the uneven state-by-state patterns of ending military rule and to their own recent or upcoming re-entry into politics. Forrest himself was a delegate to the Democratic National Convention by 1868. In 1869 some Democrats in the South supported conservative Republicans at the state level, and highlighted the roles of former Whigs in their ranks, rather than frontally challenging for power. On the economic front, Republicans themselves pulled back from economic reform and reparation. Even black suffrage was paired with the end of significant direct aid to ex-slaves so that, as Du Bois wrote, "the Freedmen's Bureau died, and its child was the Fifteenth Amendment." In this context, "New Departure" Democrats temporarily accepted African American voting in and after 1869, though there would soon be new waves of political terror. Many Democrats urged patience, arguing that the Republicans nationally would lose enthusiasm for enforcing black civil rights in the South. They could point by the early 1870s to the national presence of so-called Liberal Republicans, a wing of the party counseling further retreats from active support for racial equality out of a combination of weariness and belief that a stable investment climate in the South was best secured by deeper compromises of civil rights. Such compromises would coexist with new atrocities.

The most famous of these concessions came with the Compromise of 1877, following the 1876 presidential election. Both the Democrat candidate, Samuel Tilden, and the Republican, Rutherford B. Hayes, claimed victory. Tilden clearly won the popular vote—if indeed such a term applies in an election with so much suppression of the black franchise. But the Republican Party still sufficiently functioned in South Carolina, Louisiana, and Florida to produce its own claims to victory in contested vote counts in those states, creating the possibility of a Republican victory if Hayes carried every electoral vote in those states. Looking back on fifteen years of war and guerrilla fighting, much of the nation's press predicted a renewed civil war.

The bargain that defused the crisis and installed Hayes as president reflected the aptitude of white redemption forces in the South for wielding the olive branch along with the sword. It reflected the climax of a pattern of interregional compromise at the expense of black civil rights. While sometimes portrayed as the product of dramatic back-room intrigues, snatching compromise from the jaws of renewed bloodshed, the terms of the 1877 bargain reflected established patterns. The Republicans got the White House in exchange for total withdrawal of the long-diminishing federal military protection of African American freedom in the South, for patronage concessions, and for the promise of significant investment in Southern infrastructure. The form of the negotiations was more significant. They unfolded in leisurely rhythm, based on earlier patterns in individual states. With the most enthusiastic supporters of local economic development in the US, a group of associated newspaper editors of the northern and southern Midwest, being given a central and moderating role in the negotiations, the compromise illustrated an already existing sense of mutual interest between anything-but-radical Republicans and Southern Democrats. Railroad entrepreneurs contributed their part to the construction of the bargain. With terror as a midwife, white supremacy and invest-ment had replaced jubilee, although African American voters and their organizations were strong enough to retain some power in certain areas of the South, such as Virginia, for two further decades.

Reflecting a deep commitment to compromise, recently in-stalled white supremacist "Redemption" governments of the white South immediately sold cheaply or gave away the region's natural wealth, in order to encourage outside capital investment. Although less conservative white men's governments would soon succeed the Redeemers in some states, this largesse to outside capital continued for more than a decade. Texas alone gave away to railroad entrepreneurs land equal in size to the state of Indiana. Florida sold 4 million acres of state land to one Philadelphia syndicate for a grand total of $1 million. Timber and mining concessions were equally lavish, with the best pine and cypress stands speedily going to Yankee and British investors. Such trends underscored economic desperation, to be sure, but also an eager-ness to stand as junior partners in a colonial economy where racial justice as a public issue had been buried.

Beyond Dixie: A White Nation

The theatre in which the drama and tragedy of jubilee played out lay overwhelmingly in the South. Indeed for thirty years and more after emancipation, the most heartening instances of interracial unity among workers, farmers, and voters almost all came in that region. But white supremacy remained a broad, far-reaching system. National and even transnational dynamics ultimately also accounted for the survival of race-thinking generally and, in important ways, for the failure of anti-racist struggles in the South itself. Northern and Midwestern racism, anti-Chinese agitation, energized settler colonialism and, by the century's turn, imperial war all contributed to a landscape in which white supremacy was shared across lines of political party and of region.

In his searching study of segregation's history, C. Vann Wood-ward observed that "The North was not in the best possible position to instruct the South, either by precedent and example, or by force of conviction . . . on racial equality." With slavery gone as a centerpiece of white supremacist racial control, Orville Vernon Burton has written, "southern whites took their cue from northern examples." In combining emancipation with paternalist control over black labor and a Jim Crow segregation system, the North had set an important, enduring, and very bad example. Segregated systematically from whites in virtually all forms of transportation long before they were in Dixie, Northern blacks also suffered exclusion from restaurants and hotels, segrega-tion in schools and housing, and seclusion in balconies and corners of theatres. "Negro pews" disgraced Yankee churches. Even the Fourteenth Amendment, ratified in 1868 and establishing impor-tant national protections for civil rights regardless of race, consciously and openly left intact state and local powers to make race and color distinctions. In doing so, lawmakers bowed more to existing Jim Crow education, transportation, and marriage laws and practices in the Northern and border states, than to Southern norms.

Alleged threats to jobs often constituted the crux of the problem. Even in his eagerness to praise free labor in the North, Frederick Douglass noted how color bars kept him from practicing his own trade on the New Bedford waterfront in the 1840s. As Lincoln was winning his first presidential victory, a black leader in Boston reckoned that it was ten times harder for a "colored mechanic" to work in that city than in Charleston (South Carolina). By the time Isaac Myers addressed the National Labor Union in 1869, little had changed. When Myers warned that "American citizenship is a complete failure if [the Negro] is proscribed from the workshops of this country," the North had the nation's worst record on that score. To the extent that policymakers addressing the postwar South looked to Northern precedents for implementing emancipation, they found patterns of surveillance, criminalization, and continuing dependency of freed-people in New England and the middle states.

Where racial atrocities were concerned the situation in the North differed little from that in the South. While the absence of black political power outside Dixie undoubtedly gave less incentive for partisan campaigns of terror, some of the worst racial violence occurred in Northern cities. In 1863 the anti-draft riots in New York City claimed at least 105 lives, most of them after rioters turned from fighting police to wholesale attacks on blacks. The slaughter included eleven or more lynchings, replete with sexual mutilation, and attacks on those in interracial relationships. The riots drew energy from, and advanced longstanding campaigns to create, an "all-white waterfront," pushing black workers out of jobs as well as from those neighborhoods where employment was to be found. Rioters burned the boardinghouse for "colored sailors" as well as a large asylum for African American orphans. In Philadelphia in 1871 rioting was more directly political, with four African Americans dying in widespread disturbances on election day as black voters helped create a Republican victory. Among the dead lay an activist schoolteacher who had helped lead a successful push for desegregation of the city's streetcars.

Before the Civil War the northern Midwest, in legal terms the region most closed to slavery, had proved in many ways even harsher where racism was concerned than the Northeast. The antebellum Midwest, much of it first called the Northwest, premised white supremacy on exclusion rather than segregation. Thus Alexis de Tocqueville found racial prejudice "stronger in the states where they have abolished slavery than where it still existed [and] nowhere stronger than in those states where servitude has never been known." Midwestern Republicans nevertheless led a transformation of law, and to some extent attitudes, in the Civil War years, with Iowa best exemplifying such change. Exclusionary and very hostile to fugitive slaves, that state's voters defeated by a record margin a prewar referendum regarding the enfranchisement of Iowa's tiny black potential electorate. By 1868, however, a similar referendum was passed, helping to make the state what historian Robert Dykstra has called the "bright radical star" in the period's civil rights history firmament. Yet Dykstra carefully added that what came to pass in Iowa ultimately amounted to only an "egalitarian moment."

Towards the end of the nineteenth century, there was a decided trend towards expulsions of small black populations from the Midwest towns where they had briefly found welcome in the period after the war. After 1890, with the drama of emancipation receding in memory, thousands of municipalities declared themselves "sundown towns," believing that they had law—and knowing that they had power and custom—on their side in barring blacks from being within city limits after sundown. Often such a declaration followed a lynching, a more general attack on the black population, or threats of the same. The leading student of "sundown towns," sociologist James Loewen, reckons that the majority of all incorporated municipalities in the US outside the South enforced "sundown" policies at one time or another. He identifies 475 such towns in Illinois alone, many being places that had welcomed blacks as the "patriotic" and Republican order of business after the Civil War, only to expel and bar them a generation later. By the early twentieth century, white racist urban riots erupted with particular ferocity in Springfield, Illinois, East St. Louis, and Chicago.

Similarly anti-Mexican, anti-Indian, and anti-Chinese racism and terror ensured that the Far West would not show Dixie how to transcend race. Although California had a relatively small nonwhite population, between 1850 and 1936 over half its 352 lynching victims were Mexican, Latin American, or American Indian. Providing one lynch victim in twelve, the Chinese in California also suffered out of all proportion to their number. In the sparsely populated state of Wyoming, white miners massacred at least twenty-eight Chinese immigrants in a single pogrom in 1885.

Indeed, violent postwar racism against the Chinese informed the politics of the Reconstruction as a whole. Given its role in the horrors of a secessionist war, and at times in countenancing disloyalty to the Union, the Democratic Party needed redemption outside Dixie as well as within it. This was especially the case in newer states where no longstanding base of support and party organization existed. In California the rehabilitation of the De-mocrats took its energy from anti-Chinese agitation. Winning the California governorship in 1867 as a Democrat, Henry Haight hailed his own victory as a triumph for those opposing "populating this fair state with a race of Asiatics—against sharing with the inferior races the Government of the country" and for those desiring that Southern states be "emancipated from negro dom-ination."

While there were only 63,000 Chinese in the American West in 1870, their presence held great importance in the development of politics and trade unionism. Over the following decades in California and other areas of the West, the Chinese acted as an "indispensable enemy," to use Alexander Saxton's apt term, shaping unions along lines of caste and craft rather than as a class movement incorporating Chinese workers. Democrats and "workingmen's" leaders warmed to attacks on the Chinese far more than to attacks on capital. At times such attacks centered on Chinese bodies and their alleged habits or diseases, as when California's racist, white, working-class leader Denis Kearney pressed for total expulsion of "almond-eyed lepers." At other junctures opponents of Chinese immigration fixed on the term "coolie" to connect the varied forms of labor recruitment from China to serfdom or slavery. Such conflations of race, disease, and subservience linked the Chinese with African Americans as sup-posedly emasculated anti-citizens whose very presence would endanger white republican freedoms. Substantial post–Civil War Chinese labor militancy in the West and in Louisiana did not shake the dominant white labor rhetoric branding "coolies" as "slavish." Indeed, if the possibility of jubilee and rainbow coalitions can be said to have had a definitive termination outside the South, it came in San Francisco in 1877, when the nationwide "July days" of railroad strikes and eight-hour day general strikes degenerated into a pogrom against Chinese workers.

The reaction to the threat of a phantom Chinese "invasion" of the Northeast US was perhaps more perversely impressive. When fierce protests arose in response to the importation of seventy-five Chinese laborers—they decidedly were not "coolies" contracted in China—to a Massachusetts shoe factory in 1870, there were only 305 Chinese people in the entire Eastern US. Given these demographics, and defenses of the Chinese by ex-abolitionists and labor leaders including Frederick Douglass and Wendell Phillips, anti-Chinese racism secured far less of a foothold in the East. But it was nonetheless remarkable that, in the virtual absence of any Chinese, anti-Chinese movements in the East could sustain themselves for well over a decade. After fueling the 1877 riots in San Francisco, the Workingmen's Party leader Kearney toured the East with considerable fanfare in 1878. He faced opposition—the great abolitionist William Lloyd Garrison pronounced Kearney more fit for a "lunatic asylum" than to be "running at large" – and suffered from an unfortunate tendency to discredit himself with drunken-sounding, overwrought speeches, but Kearney's reception still registered a measure of continuing anti-Chinese sentiment.

In the South, on the other hand, interest in the "coolie issue" had to some extent ebbed away. As Moon-Ho Jung's study of Louisiana's sugar industry shows, even those planters who pushed so hard for Chinese labor to be brought to the region after the Civil War gave up on the strategy in the depressed 1870s, when faced with the actual costs of imported labor. Moreover, as white conservative Democrats pushed for their own return to power in the middle 1870s, any aggressive campaign for importation of Chinese labor could have seemed overly divisive. Planters tended to suspend calls for such an importation when some white Southern opponents of the Chinese, and potential political rivals of plantation owners, claimed to better represent white unity and white supremacy by pushing instead for the encouragement of European immigration. Thus a temporary retreat from contemplating the importation of the Chinese occurred at the time of the restoration of white political supremacy in the South.

Where anti-Indian policies were concerned, the Civil War also ushered in new levels of atrocity and aggression, deeply connected to reconfigurations of party politics. Both North and South felt constrained not to alienate tribes, thereby creating allies for their enemy, while they fought with each other. Nonetheless the Civil War turned out to be an anti-Indian one in the long, and sometimes even the short, run. As whites brutalized each other in protracted and unprecedented ways, the war might have made it harder to think of Indians as savage and bloodthirsty. Instead comparisons with Indians became a way to indict the brutality of white enemies during the war and even after it. Following the war, labor radicals, or even simply striking workers, were branded as "savages" and "wild Indians." Such associative rhetoric emboldened the state and the army to take brutal action against white "enemies"; but when such enemies changed behavior or admitted defeat the whiteness of rebels and radicals could be reasserted, leaving savagery deeply connected to people of color. Moreover Union victory reconnected visions of liberty and nation, enlivening a messianic sense that the US was destined to strip away all impediments, including human ones, to the continent's rapid development. Such expansion would no longer be encumbered by interminable sectional angling over whether new states would be "slave" or "free." Anti-Indian racism also factored into debates over postwar civil rights legislation, including the specifics of the Fourteenth Amendment, limiting language against all race distinctions and for fully equal citizenship because there was no intent to empower Indians in terms of politics or self-defense.

The US experience of total war, connected to race, messianism, and powerful pro-development political forces, predicted tragedy for Indians. In welcoming the destruction of buffalo herds that sustained the lives and spirit of Indians on the plains, the veteran Civil War commander General Philip Sheridan emphasized in 1875 that extermination was, fortunately in his view, "destroying the Indians' commissary," making them less able to resist. Hearing that the Texas legislature was contemplating a measure to protect dwindling herds from hunters on the grounds of wildlife preservation, he hurried to Austin to tell lawmakers that the buffalo hunter—that is, the vast commercial enterprise of harvesting buffalo—had done more in two years to defeat Indian resistance than the regular army had in thirty. In language that also implied human eradication, Sheridan advocated total extermination of herds, which would cause Indians to "settle down," and would open the West to "speckled cattle and the festive cowboy . . . the forerunner of advanced civilization."

At the level of economic policy and technology, the Civil War brought pro-development innovations leading to speedier settlement of the lands on which Indians lived. The South's lack of representation in the Congress during the war enabled uncontested passage of legislation leading to the rapid construction of a transcontinental railroad on a non-Southern route. Lavish government aid to railroad companies set the pattern for a "great barbecue," in which the resources of the West and, later, the South were offered to corporations. Inevitably land grants provided much of the inducement, with 10 percent of the federal public domain ceded to railroads; individual states were in some cases still more generous. The railroad itself, along with refrigerated cars, and a boom in farm machinery production that took off as a response to wartime labor shortages, made possible a massive new trade in buffalo, beef, and grain. The trade in wheat generated for a time a vogue for giant bonanza farms on the plains. The Homestead Act of 1862 also hinged on Southern absence from Congress, as it encouraged Western settlement by non-slaveholding family farmers. Its fabled provision of 160 acres of "unappropriated public land" to those working the tract for five years ultimately proved to be the mechanism through which only a small proportion of lands came into settler hands. But state-sponsored homesteading did provide impetus for quick postwar movement onto "free land," often in fact Indian land, in the West.

The ill-fated General George C. Custer demonstrated a sophisticated grasp of rhetoric linking various postwar dreams for development of the West by praising the Black Hills as a place with "gold among the roots of the grass." He extolled the grass itself as a basis for pasturage and beef production, and held out the prospect of the mining and ranching to come when Indian tribes had been ethnically cleansed. As Custer led his men to their doom against a coalition of Cheyenne and Lakota forces at Little Big Horn in 1876, an article authored by him appeared in the journal *Galaxy* back East. In it he paused in his Western adventure story to praise land grants to the Northern Pacific, identifying railroads as, improbably enough, the best protection "from the horrors and devastations of . . . Indian depredations." Economic and military policy dovetailed in a Western rush that grew out of the Civil War.

Custer intrigued briefly with the Democratic Party in the middle 1870s, but his pro-railroad policies, like his support for herding of Indians onto reservations that would diminish in size, fitted well into Republican agendas. The association of Republican leadership with vigorous prosecution of settler colonial expansion began in earnest in the Civil War itself. In 1862 young Lakota tribesmen of the Santee groups in Minnesota, still in only its fourth year of statehood, conducted a series of raids against settlers over the failure of the US government to live up to 1850s treaties requiring payments in return for sharp limits on the extent of Indian territory. Clashes with settlers and federal troops left substantial casualties on both sides in the brief US–Lakota War. The hysterical response of the US press focused not on the treaty but in large measure on allegations of widespread sexual violence perpetrated by the Lakota fighters. Even as the charges of mass rape proved unsustainable the Lincoln administration ordered thirty-eight Lakotas to be hanged in late 1862. Minnesota's Republican governor, Alexander Ramsey, later President Hayes's secretary of war, held, "Our course is plain. The [Lakota] must be exterminated or driven forever beyond the borders of the state."

Less than two years later the Republican territorial governor of Colorado, John Evans, would echo the words of his Minnesota counterpart, pleading with a nearby commander to bring "all the forces you can then" to "pursue, kill and destroy" Indians. If there were doubts as to whether this death sentence applied only to potential aggressors, or to all Indians, the actions of Colonel John Chivington in leading Union troops at Sand Creek seemed to dispel them. Failing to engage with Cheyenne and Arapaho forces there, Chivington's soldiers and militia set upon a nearby Indian village which had been left largely unprotected as a result of US government promises of peace, their leaders being on one account "special friends of the white man." Almost all of the village's inhabitants, largely unarmed, were massacred. Evans quickly pronounced Sand Creek to be one of "the brilliant feats of arms of Indian warfare." He remained a defender of the massacre even when confronted by testimony that women and children con-stituted the majority of the dead, and that their corpses had in many cases been scalped and otherwise mutilated.

Evans himself displayed the combination of moral and business commitments common to many early Republicans, his career displaying, in Saxton's words, "an almost miraculous convergence of religious obligation and capital accumulation." A physician, a leader in the founding and nurturing of Northwestern University and Garrett Bible Institute, a speculator in the land north of Chicago around those two institutions, a veteran antislavery politician, and a railroad entrepreneur, he was far from unscru-pulous regarding the taking of life. But Evans represented the transition in Colorado from a time when Indian traders were the group most concerned with policy toward indigenous people to one when "industrial warriors," as Howard Lamar and Saxton term them, most shaped policy. Evans therefore rehearsed familiar arguments on the undesirability of Indians controlling land that they could not subdue. He insisted on a faster timetable for Indians getting out of the way of forces of progress that were now based on mines and rails, as well as on farms and trading posts.

Evans himself quickly retired from politics to devote himself to moneymaking, while Chivington was court-martialed and had to resign his post. Some Republicans, largely from New England, were sufficiently appalled by the events of Sand Creek that they began to experiment with alternative routes to ending tribal power by emphasizing individual citizenship and private property, a logic culminating in the Dawes Act of 1887. The creation of Massachusetts Republican Henry Dawes, the 1887 law sought to reform Indians by making them individual owners of largely unviable tracts of dwindling tribal lands. Such reformist logic remained deeply hostile to tribal autonomy. New England intellectual Francis Amasa Walker, a US commissioner of Indian affairs under Republican President Ulysses S. Grant, allowed as early as 1874 that seemingly liberal impulses regarding what he called the "Indian Question," in fact often bespoke a desire to "summarily dismiss the Indian as the subject of peculiar consideration," not necessarily from concern for "any good it may do" for native peoples. In any case, post–Civil War Republican policies toward Indians were far more characterized by moments of force than by attempts at reform.

Highly successful Republican electoral appeals, which allowed only one Democrat to win the presidency between 1860 and 1912, flowed far less from episodically attacking Southern racism against African Americans than from organizing occupation of Indian lands in the West with cold efficiency. The rapid expansion of the Indian reservation system, the subsequent shrinking of the size of those reservations, and the carnage in implementing such policies stood out as largely Republican initiatives. These were conceived during a Lincoln administration awash with reform-minded discourses of "humanity" and a "peace policy," but also in talk of "reclaim[ing] a barbarous and heathen race," a dialogue successively promulgated by President Grant and his Civil War generals, and by President Rutherford B. Hayes. California might be redeemed for Democratic white supremacy via anti-Chinese racism, but Republicans in Colorado, Minnesota, and much of the West constructed dominant coalitions of the wealthy, the aspiring, the fearful, and elements of the settler working class around a quickly won and tenaciously held status as the party of "protection" against Indians. As in the South, but with the parties reversed, the coalition offered the image of a common white manhood guarding ever-threatened women and children.

During Reconstruction, the Southern question intruded on events in the West, and vice versa. In May 1866, bloody white riots in Memphis targeted the freedpeople of that city and especially centered on the murder of black soldiers and the rape of black women. Believing that the presence of African American troops in the region provoked the violence, the federal authorities responded by withdrawing African American soldiers from the very areas where black citizens were under attack. The troops were redeployed to the West, where as "Buffalo Soldiers" they formed part of the rapidly downsizing federal army protecting the expansion of settler colonialism. Historians and monument-makers have managed to capture the institutional racism faced by the Buffalo Soldiers as well as their loyalty and sacrifice. But it remained for reggae artist Bob Marley to tell the larger story. His haunting song in tribute to the soldiers commemorates their bravery along with the tragedy of African Americans pressed into service for the forces of settler colonialism. Though usually recounted separately, the histories of emancipation, redemption, and Indian removal unfolded simultaneously. At Reconstruction's end, the Compromise of 1877 took shape in the wake of Custer's defeat at Little Big Horn and "freed" the diminished but significant number of white troops protecting civil rights in the South to join Buffalo Soldiers in fighting anti-Indian wars. While the potential rainbow of solidarity had failed to materialize, the various histories of the oppressed remained fully intertwined.

Coda: White Empire, Mississippi Plan

It was a familiar early 1870s story. White paramilitary organizations, loosely affiliated under the name Ku Klux Klan, conducted a series of sustained, bloody, and politically targeted raids, reaching right into the halls of the legally constituted government. Their leader, Mississippi-born James T. Proctor, was descended from a wealthy Louisiana slaveholding family and won celebrity fighting in the Civil War, losing a leg and gaining the picturesque nickname "Timber-Toes." By 1874, with no little help from Klan terror, regime change took place.

But this story unfolded in Fiji, with Proctor and other Klansmen enmeshed in British intrigues to penetrate that island economically and politically. The goal was to install a new regime based not on the Democratic Party but on the British Empire, which colonized Fiji in 1874. The "niggers" under attack were "indigenes" in Fiji, not ex-slaves. Proctor's peculiar tale intersects tellingly with the main stories of this chapter. His post–Civil War career in the Pacific centered on what Gerald Horne's fine account calls "blackbirding," a new slave trade moving island peoples to labor in the colonies of Queensland and Fiji. His enterprise, understudied but shared by many Southerners relocating to the Pacific after the Confederacy's defeat, capitalized on US reputation and experience regarding white management of other races. That figures like Proctor enslaved indigenous people in the Pacific reminds us that the forms of racial violence practiced against slaves in the US South and Indians in the US West were closely related. But most of all for present purposes, the peregrinations of the Klan force us to ask how the world of empire and the final extinguishing of jubilee coexisted.

In one of the most provocative passages produced by a US historian of his generation, C. Vann Woodward's 1951 *Origins of the New South* raised exactly this question. Vann Woodward reflected on the fact that in specific Southern US locales and coalitions Afro-Southerners continued to vote (whether under the aegis of paternalist white Democrats or dissenting forces) after the withdrawal of federal troops. He noted that it was only in the 1890s that the "Mississippi Plan" brought near-total disenfranchisement, and that it took further time for that brutal plan to become the "American Way": it was 1896 before *Plessy v. Ferguson* found the Supreme Court blessing the legality of Jim Crow. The three decades after 1890 witnessed a new "nadir" of racist terror and lynch law. Vann Woodward blamed this regression in large part on the reaction to black participation, potential and real, in populist electoral coalitions of the 1890s.

But Vann Woodward refused to treat the origins of this reaction as a wholly domestic matter. He insisted that turn of the century US imperial adventures in Cuba, Puerto Rico, Hawaii, and the Philippines conditioned how thoroughly the "Mississippi Plan became the American Way." Remaining Northern opponents of the worst Southern abuses of civil rights came as pro-imperialists to themselves embrace oppression and atrocity directed against people of color in occupied territories. So it was that the patrician Republican politician Henry Cabot Lodge of Massachusetts, who energetically supported a last major legislative effort to secure fair elections in the South in 1890, could a decade later be heard loudly justifying US imperial adventures in the Caribbean and Pacific. When one of Lodge's fellow Republican politicians from Massachusetts forcefully backed white American expansionist imperial adventures in 1899, a South Carolina senator tellingly if devilishly praised the Yankee colleague's "complete announcement of the divine right of Caucasians to govern the inferior races."

Vann Woodward's connection between white Republicans' embrace of empire and their retreat from even vestigial anti-racism has recently found support from the perceptive postcolonial scholar Amy Kaplan. Kaplan analyzes Theodore Roosevelt's denial of the heroism of black Spanish–American War troops under his command in the Caribbean. His suppression of the story of black valor was, for Kaplan, necessary to aggrandize fully and purely the national "white male subject." No racial subplot, reintroducing North/South divisions among white men, could be allowed to obtrude. Roosevelt's lies at the expense of black soldiers were thus part and parcel of "reuniting the nation," making the 1898 war the "final antidote to Reconstruction."

However provocative, Vann Woodward and Kaplan miss some of the extent to which the settler colonialism and anti-immigrant vitriol had compromised even the mildest Republican egalitarianism far before 1898. By the 1890s Lodge represented the cutting edge of racism against Eastern and Southern European immigrants to the US. His party defined the sort of hard racism against indigenous people in the US that presaged American brutality in the bloody occupation of the Philippines. Republican compromises with Southern white terror left not beachheads of black political strength in the South so much as vulnerable outposts comparable to the Indian reservations; already decimated, these outposts were destined to see their limited political influence eroded over time. In Fiji, Australia, Brazil, and elsewhere, the US had exported white supremacy and white supremacists well in advance of 1898.

The story told by Vann Woodward remains incomplete in another way as well. Reactionary "Mississippi Plan" Southern race politics did not always predict support for the "American way" in the Philippines or elsewhere. In some celebrated cases the racism of Southern Democratic politicians, and of many other Americans, carried such intensity that they actually opposed taking up the white man's burden of empire. One national journal asked the widow of the Confederacy's former president, Mississippi's own Jefferson Davis, to weigh in on the conquest of the Philippines in 1900. Mrs. Jefferson Davis, as she signed herself, professed astonishment that the nation would risk "add[ing] several millions of negroes to our population" through imperial conquest.

Even so, the connections of white imperial worlds of race to the nadir of post-emancipation black life in the US deserve emphasis. Far from bringing about a tolerant cosmopolitanism, increased US international presence intensified as well as reflected domestic white supremacy. Such patterns, which emerged well before the turn to formal US empire, could be seen in the international fairs and expositions of the mid-1890s. The 1893 Chicago World's Fair, named the Columbian Exposition in honor of European discovery and settlement of the Americas, closed itself to black participation in almost every possible way, as vehement protests from Ida B. Wells and Frederick Douglass made clear. Shortly thereafter, the African American educator Booker T. Washington announced the Atlanta Compromise, disavowing anti-racist protest at an 1895 international exhibition in that Georgia city, catapulting himself to a leadership position eventually recognized by black communities but especially by white opinion-makers. Displays of captive and commodified humans, especially Dahomeyans in Chicago and defeated Indians generally, drew crowds.

But even so the St. Louis World's Fair of 1904 constituted a qualitative leap: living Filipinos underwent display and judgment according to their "tribe" and "race." They were endlessly visited by those supervising the occupation of the Philippines, and much photographed and eroticized. Anthropologists assessed the specific uses to empire of the allegedly less degraded Filipino groups and reassuringly predicted the speedy dying-out of those at the bottom of the colonial racial ladder when in contact with civilization. Elite medical schools vied for the corpses of those whom it was presumed would die during the display. The occupation of the Philippines, amid fierce resistance, cost between 100,000 and 250,000 Filipino lives. Imperial carnage did not only reflect white supremacy; it also recreated such supremacy.

The war brought about even more insistent racializations of the enemy. The multi-purpose racial slur "gook," coined during the military occupation of the Philippines, followed US imperial adventures throughout the twentieth century, in Haiti and Nicaragua as well as all over Asia. White troops were less polite than Mrs. Jefferson Davis, referring to Filipinos as "niggers." When the studios of the inventor Thomas Edison used his "Wargraph" technology to produce a series of films on the Philippines—in fact, shot in New Jersey—the roles of Filipino resistance fighters went to African American performers. Though some race leaders effectively urged using the war to prove African American patriotism, significant black opposition to empire emerged in these contexts.

Nowhere was this resistance more importantly registered than among the Buffalo Soldier troops now serving in the Philippines. Life imitated Edison's art when some black soldiers, including the ultimately martyred David Fagen—a figure celebrated in the Philippines and to some extent in the African American press—crossed over to join the Filipino resistance. Others simply reported the facts to folks back home, with one gunnery sergeant ending his report, "I fear that the future of the Filipino is that of the Negro in the South." A new century was bringing new solidarities, and new problems for those using white supremacy to administer empire. But the grounds on which such struggles would be fought included hierarchies of race whose survival, and at times intensification, showed how tragically jubilation had been disarmed, and how many of the gains of emancipation had disappeared.

A Nation Stays White:

HOW RACE SURVIVED MASS IMMIGRATION

Paid to count, the economist Francis Amasa Walker threw in the fuss over the arrival of allegedly inferior immigrants in the US at no charge. Having superintended the federal census in 1870 and 1880, Walker today receives credit for modernizing its method and expanding its scope. A patrician New Englander, serving for many years as professor of political economy at Yale and then as the influential president of Massachusetts Institute of Technology, he symbolized the modern academic approach to social problems and the impact of an efficiency-based engineering ethos on the social life of the nation. He was also an Anglo-Saxon race man of the first order through much of his career, serving as United States commissioner of Indian affairs, and worrying loudly about Irish immigration in his official capacity as census director.

Walker developed and popularized the enduring notion that the immigration of allegedly inferior peoples such as the Irish brought with it a threat of racial degeneration in the US population. The sheer numbers in which they arrived contributed to the change Walker feared. Moreover, he argued that the very presence of the newcomers somehow shrunk Anglo-Saxon numbers by causing the native-born, supposedly dispirited by the presence of the immigrants, to limit their own family size. This idea underpinned the "race suicide" theories that issued from the presidency of Theodore Roosevelt, a sometime protégé of Walker's. Fond of making various projections of just when the national racial "stock" would be disastrously transformed, those terrified by the prospect of "race suicide" agreed that at some point a few decades hence the "alien" races of Southern and Eastern Europe would swamp the superior "English-speaking races," costing the nation its racial character.

Walker's distinctive place in the history of anti-immigrant racism stems in part from his ability to combine ultra-modern statistical methods with the basest racial and class-based bigotry, a pairing perhaps illustrating how the new and the old orders consistently combined to construct what Michel Foucault would later call biopolitics. Walker showed how racial nativism could rework itself, reacting to changing migrations in its choice of new threats. Before he died in 1897, just as the "new immigration" to the US from Southern and Eastern Europe began to outpace the arrival of newcomers from Northern and Western Europe, Walker had precociously registered and denounced the change. In the early post–Civil War years he projected census results to cast the Irish as a looming threat to US civilization and to Anglo-Saxon reproduction. As the century neared its end, he suddenly allowed that the Irish had instead magically assimilated into the "American race." The Anglo-Saxon fortress suddenly had a jerrybuilt Celtic wing.

In Walker's view the Irish challenge had been superseded by a new and more serious threat: "the ignorant and brutalized peasantry from . . . eastern and southern Europe." Branded as members of "races of . . . the very lowest stage of degradation," these new immigrants further earned Walker's contempt as individuals representing the very worst elements of those allegedly inferior races. They were, he wrote in a phrase destined to find its way into Roosevelt's pronouncements as well as the work of pioneering sociologist Edward A. Ross, "beaten men of beaten races." The connection between Walker's rehabilitation of the Irish and his denigration of Eastern and Southern Europeans became clear in the compressed and fractured natural history lesson he offered to the public and to policymakers. "Centuries are against them," he wrote of the latter groups, "just as centuries were on the side of those who formerly came to us"—those who presumably included in large proportion the very Irish immigrants he had formerly so feared and despised on racial and cultural grounds. Immigration of inferior peoples remained a "contact so foul and loathsome" that it had to be avoided, even as the Irish received a delayed pass into the white American race. A new focus for hate accompanied the process of inclusion.

Walker's venomous words remind us that in the nineteenth century, as in ours, race-thinking offered not only a spurious biology but also, as described in the key words of Alexander Saxton, a "theory of history," in which "habits of mind" supposedly calcified over centuries to become a force as intractable as genetics itself. Walker's grudging recognition of the malleability of racial position, as shown in the case of the Irish immigrants, signals the ways in which anti-immigrant racism responded to political and historical winds rather than only to dispassionate scientific investigation. That he used "race" to connote differing levels of ability, intelligence, and civilization among peoples originating within Europe, as much as to refer to supposed differences across the color line, reminds us that in the early twentieth century race and ethnicity were not firmly separated into distinct concepts, and indeed the latter term was scarcely used. Finally, his identification of putatively inferior Europeans with labor radicalism, though at times fanciful, predicted the decisive 1920s argument that led progressives and industrial employers to lose faith in relatively open immigration to the US; namely, that new immigrants could not be managed or controlled as a labor force. Since the mass strikes of 1877, Walker extravagantly argued, the "foreign element" dominated in all campaigns of labor militancy. By the time of the dramatic early 1890s strikes at Homestead, Pullman, and elsewhere, he alleged, no word of English, French, or German—somehow all these counted as the languages of the superior "English-speaking races"—could be heard when labor was on the move.

Most broadly, Walker's ideas and agitations remind us that the history of European immigration has a central place in the story of how race and white supremacy survived US history. In the standard American rose-tinted story of immigration, newcomers arrive overwhelmingly from Europe, "green" in their lack of urban and modern experiences but unproblematically white. They assimilate US habits and join the nation, often successfully competing with people of color for jobs as they do so. If race comes into the story of immigration history, it is generally around the subject of such job competition, or in telling the stories of Asian and Latino immigrants. But Walker was preoccupied by a racial threat from European immigrants. Coming to influence policy in a period spanning the first great wave of mass immigration, which began two decades before the Civil War, and the second, starting two decades before World War I, Walker found racial threats in each wave. In the first wave the threat was Irish. In the second, it was the Southern and Eastern European "new immigrant."

Yet the prognostications and projections of Walker and other experts—that by 1940 or so migration and reproduction of Eastern and Southern Europeans would have created a new racial majority undermining the US—fell flat, and we need to explain why this was so. How was it that white supremacy survived European immigrations which threatened either to divide the white race by the hierarchies it created, or to place large segments of Europeans outside of firm membership in that race? Why did the working poor, "largely Slavonic, Latin, or Negro in race," as one early twentieth-century account had it, not capture the potential of what W. E. B. Du Bois called an "anti-Nordic" coalition, uniting the disadvantaged across complex, blurred lines to challenge a white supremacy that exploited divisions among "superior" and "lesser" Europeans? How did the favored legal position of even those despised European immigrants as largely "white by law" contribute to their eventual acceptance into the dominant race, to their acceptance of its dominance, and therefore to the survival of race as a category?

A vigorous new historical scholarship has recently begun to examine precisely these critical questions, first by looking at whether a sea change in the racial position of European immigrants actually occurred and, if so, how to describe that change. Written in the shadow of dominant, race-minimizing narratives extolling the US as a "nation of immigrants," this new work has necessarily sought to challenge received wisdom through the construction of its own compelling story. The best alternative narrative available provided a stirring model. James Baldwin, the pre-eminent US writer of the late twentieth century, also stood as the thinker most aware of how pathological and in need of explanation was the enduring "lie of whiteness." He spent the last years of his life thinking through race and European immigration to the US in a series of linked essays. In Scandinavia, Baldwin observed, nobody sat around boasting of his or her whiteness. Baldwin portrayed the peculiar, US white supremacist order as the reason that it seemed a good idea at times for migrants to trade their Jewish names, their Italian cuisine, and their Irish brogue for white privilege. Certainly, such trading had no easy and direct relationship to achieving status as unassailably white, and indeed at times a secure place in the white race might allow public expression of ethnicity to flower. Nonetheless Baldwin's broad outline for a new narrative of race and European immigration was to inspire future explorations of how waves of immigrants, Irish, Jews, and Italians, "became white" in the US past, and of the costs of their doing so.

But the nature of what it meant for immigrants to learn a new racial system as a central part of "becoming American" has led to acute differences of opinion, even among historians agreeing that race mattered in the immigration history of European Americans. A host of phrases proposed by historians and sociologists to variously describe the racial experiences of immigrants from the poorer sections of Europe from the 1840s to the 1930s express the shadings of contending scholarly opinions: "becoming white," "white by law," "white on arrival," "white before coming," "conditionally white," "situationally white," "inbetween peoples," "probationary whites," "offwhiteness," or even, as the Southern writer John Dollard put it, "our temporary Negroes." Far more important than deciding which of these terms should always and everywhere apply is to imagine the process of acculturation into white America in supple and overlapping ways. Like Baldwin we ought to locate agency and moral choice among newcomers, who decided over time how to find and seek their places in the white supremacist US social order. But we ought also to follow him in seeing that such choices unfolded within terrifying systems of coercion—Baldwin once called them "factories" for the production of white identity— punishing those who did not identify with white Americanism. Such coercion came from the state, employers, earlier immigrants, law enforcement, schools, churches—indeed the very realities of life: those who witnessed dispossession, slavery, Jim Crow, and lynchings were made aware of the privileged safety that came with being white.

As the legal theorist Patricia Williams writes, changes in the racial positions of immigrants became matters of both "ascription," centering on coercion and categorization of immigrants, and "aspiration," focusing on their moral choice and ambition. Those embracing whiteness out of self-interest ended up paying what Baldwin wonderfully called "the price of the ticket" in alienation and lack of vision withal. The processes of choice and coercion never meshed into a single track. But the two sides always operated in relation to each other, a relation that consistently worked to ensure the survival and reproduction of race-thinking and racial oppression. It is impossible to capture all the complexity and drama of these processes here. However, I want to explore how changing political economic contexts shaped the experiences of those caught between full inclusion as members of the master race and exclusion as nonwhite. In doing so I will look at two very different waves of immigration: the arrival en masse of Irish

Catholics just before the Civil War, and the arrival of Southern and Eastern Europeans from the end of the nineteenth century until "race-based" immigration restriction came to apply to them in the early 1920s. These episodes highlight the critical, but contradictory, importance of being white by law. In the cases of both the Irish in the mid-nineteenth century and the Eastern and Southern Europeans in the early twentieth century, the presence of those fully racialized as nonwhite gave impulse and opportunity for the migrating European poor, though despised, to claim whiteness, or at least to see themselves as so different from nonwhites as to make unthinkable a broad anti-Anglo-Saxon or "anti-Nordic" front that could threaten white supremacy.

How the Irish Became White—Twice

As is sometimes pointed out by their admirers, the Founding Fathers managed to avoid using the term "white" (as well as "slave") in the Declaration of Independence and in the Constitution. However, the first Congress convened under the new Constitution wasted little time in clarifying these circumlocutions. Significantly, this Congress's most important and enduring connection of race to citizenship came in its fulfillment of the Constitution's mandate that they produce a "uniform rule of naturalization." The resulting 1790 statute set patterns for the development of traditions of liberality and of restriction where citizenship was concerned. The extremely swift and decentralized process of naturalization was available to "any alien," after just two years of residency—providing, it stipulated, that the immigrant was a "free white person." Although the statute nominally barred the declining numbers of white indentured servants from naturalization, later court decisions on the naturalization of Asian immigrants were likely correct in holding that the 1790 legislators had meant to emphasize that Indians and black migrants, the latter overwhelmingly enslaved, would not be eligible for citizenship. But since there were free black newcomers arriving in the major

US ports, and Indians crossing changing borders, the act must be counted as a precocious and portentous example of federal law drawing the color line, directly linking race and citizenship.

As critical as such negative precedents would prove, the "positive" guarantee of naturalization rights to all free "whites" had an equally enduring and consequential impact. As the 1790s wore on, the Federalists holding political power increasingly suspected that immigrant votes would elect their Jeffersonian opponents. In 1795 the stay in the US necessary before naturalization was possible was increased to five years. Three years later, in a reaction to party politics and international revolutions, it became fourteen years, a time frame reversed when Jeffersonians took power and passed new legislation in 1802. Despite British precedents imputing racial inferiority to the Irish, no US court ever doubted that even the politically radical "wild Irish" were eligible to naturalize as "free white persons." This is perhaps unsurprising, given that many of those under scrutiny were Protestants and therefore less susceptible to the racist English discourses regarding the Catholic Irish that permeated US elite culture. Moreover, the 1798 legislation was directed largely against the supposed threat of immigrant French radicals, who were, presumably, impeccably white.

The specific power of law and of precedent mattered greatly in a rapidly changing racial situation on both sides of the Atlantic. What Theodore Allen has called "religio-racist" oppression in Ireland, setting Catholics at the bottom of the social order, was decisively altering in the years after 1800, when Irish colonial rule increasingly relied on a layer of Catholic junior partners, even as the economic perils of colonialism gave rise to extreme social misery and eventually mass starvation. Only in the north of the island did a large Protestant settler population partially enforce patterns of a stark Catholic/Protestant "racial" split. But the ideology of anti–Irish Catholic racism had its uses in both Northern and Southern Ireland, as well as in England. Positing the Irish as intellectually inferior, religiously superstitious, physically ape-like, politically impossible, and chronically drunken, justified immiseration, dispossession, occupation, disfranchisement, and labor market discrimination.

Whether such racism could find powerful expression in the US was another question. The seepage of imagery—for example the transatlantic circulation of simian drawings of the brutalized Irish peasant—was perhaps inevitable. But the Irish in the US were securely white by law, positioned within the race of the settler, not as the victims of colonialism. Not only did the established precedent that all Irish were candidates for naturalization through whiteness continue to apply, but as late as the 1830s the heterogeneous Irish migration included equal numbers of Protestant and Catholic immigrants. Migrants included a substantial minority of Gaelic speakers, sometimes working as brutally bossed canal workers in the rural US, and a significant fraction of farmers who managed to secure land in the US, as well as immiserated weavers, Presbyterian, Methodist, and Catholic. Tending on the whole to come from groups with more means than the desperate Irish poor, the Irish Americans who arrived before the 1840s were slow to develop sharp differentiations among themselves on religious lines and sometimes cooperated in reform causes centering on Ireland.

The most brutal "anti-Irish" riots of the period, raging in the manufacturing enclave of Kensington and in Southwark in the Philadelphia area, in May and July of 1844, exemplify the difficulties of establishing "Irish Catholic" as a racial category in the US. The initial riot featured nativists, organized around questions of education and availability of alcohol, entering the neighborhood to attack a school and then to burn a church, rectory, and convent. Bloody and productive of political gains by nativist American Republican forces, the conflicts nonetheless suggest that it was initially easier to organize religious than "racial" hatred of the Irish. Kensington's overwhelmingly native-born and Protestant artisan population lived alongside a minority of Irish immigrants, mostly weavers. Though Catholics formed the majority of the immigrant weaving population, we cannot know their exact percentage, as the census did not consider the religious divide among Irish immigrants a weighty enough matter to enumerate by faith. In the decade before the riots, native-born artisans and Irish weavers found common cause in vibrant movements for the ten-hour working day and in trade unions generally. The depression of 1837 destroyed much of this cooperation, though Irish Protestant and Irish Catholic weavers apparently continued to band together and strike. Native-born workers' votes and cultural energy focused increasingly on divisive religious and cultural issues, especially alcohol consumption and a fierce contest over whether the Protestant Bible would be a centerpiece of public education. Disputes over whether political machines overcounted or suppressed the "Irish" vote likewise developed.

In this context the anti-Catholic movement gained sudden traction in Philadelphia politics and on Kensington streets. Identifying the Irish weavers' community as Catholic, nativists moved against it, indiscriminately destroying Protestant Irish property in the mayhem. For their part, Kensington's Irish Protestants did not act hastily on any religio-racial prejudices against Irish Catholics that they might have learned in the British context. They largely avoided fighting on either side, and Irish Protestant weavers' reluctant support of nativism was less a British import precipitating the violence, than a product of the riots. The eventual placing of American flags and nativist banners on Irish Protestant homes, in the hope of avoiding their destruction, signaled a highly coerced accommodation to US realities.

Indeed impressive cooperation among Catholic and dissenting Protestant weavers survived the Kensington riots, suggesting that religio-racial divisions are anything but intrinsic. Moreover, in the case of the Irish Catholics, the connections between religion and race proved formidable barriers to any doubt as to their whiteness on purely racial grounds. In order for British colonial notions of bestial Irish Catholics to be accepted in the US, and for Irish Protestants to be courted by nativists, it was necessary to spell out exactly how Irish Catholics could be identified. But, crucially, the distinguishing factor was identified as religion—Catholicism—rather than race. If such a view was to be harnessed in building a broad political movement against all Catholic newcomers (especially Germans), and in harnessing Protestant revivalist energies to electoral politics, anti-Irish Catholic animus in the US context had to be understood as turning on faith more than on race.

Nonetheless within a quarter century after Kensington, Irish Catholics in the United States would face bestial images of themselves, which weighed and questioned their racial status in counterpoint to blacks and to the Chinese, groups cast as clearly nonwhite and increasingly as the very antithesis of productive US citizens:

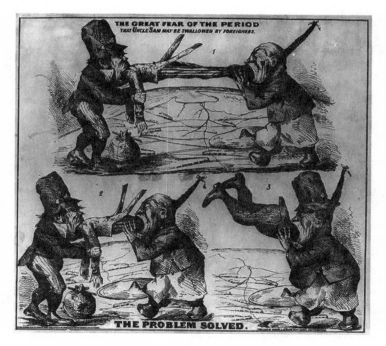

The Irish and Chinese threats to Uncle Sam, circa 1865

Thomas Nast, "The Ignorant Vote—Honors are Easy," *Harper's Weekly*, v. 20, no. 1041, New York: December 9, 1876. Courtesy of *HarpWeek*.

Such racialization of Irish Catholics as less than fully white set a pattern that would apply in very different ways to other nominally "white" groups that were not accepted as fully white, especially to those immigrating later from Southern and Eastern Europe. In all cases, the context of this racialization was one of high immigration in which a new, suspect group suddenly predominated. If immigration into the US was considerable in the 1840s, with 1.4 million arrivals, it nearly doubled in the following decade, with the Irish migrants—now largely Catholic—alone accounting for well over two newcomers in five. Far more importantly, Irish Catholic refugees from the colonially imposed famine were overwhelmingly "slotted," as the sociologist Richard Williams has argued, into the dirtiest and most despised urban US jobs. In New York City, for example, service had by 1855 slightly surpassed day laboring as the largest Irish job category, with the two together accounting for nearly half of all Irish–American workers. In Boston, laborers constituted 48 percent of Irish workers in 1850—as against 11 percent of German immigrants and a mere twentieth of native-born Americans. Service jobs were held by 15 percent of Irish Americans in Boston, who were generally described frankly as "servants," whereas 4 percent of the native-born served, usually under the title of "help." Indeed, one travel account of 1859 noted the euphemistic language with reference to native-born servants, but found US employers ready to "Let the negroes be servants and, if not negroes, let Irishmen."

Often working in jobs on which African Americans had previously secured a fragile hold made the Irish Catholic immigrants vulnerable to associations with racial inferiority, thereby fulfilling Frederick Douglass's prophecy that in taking "avocations" from African Americans the Irish also "assumed our degradation." Stories from the South told of Irish immigrants replacing slaves on the most dangerous jobs, as no capital was lost if they were injured or killed. In loading jobs, and especially in canal-digging, Irish workers were driven particularly brutally, though their resistance and exercise of the right to quit was also striking. Irish women increasingly predominated, both in service and in textile work, in the jobs most insistently identified with "white slavery." A bitter Irish-American joke from 1851 reported a black worker's complaint that his tyrannical master treated him like a "common Irishman." When slurs like "smoked Irishman" began to be used to describe African Americans, the racism had a double edge.

If the "ascription," to use Williams's apt term for one aspect of the race-making process, of status to the famine-era Irish was increasingly unclear and troublesome, the immigrants' own "aspirations" regarding racial identity seemed for a short time equally up for grabs. In a Civil War pamphlet, Democratic Party dirty tricksters falsely passed off the invention of the word "miscegenation" as the work of abolitionists and Republicans cheerfully predicting that Irish Americans and African Americans were about to amalgamate into one group. Their intentions were transparent. Appealed to as white racists, Irish voters were meant to be horrified that they were singled out as potential race-mixers, and therefore to hate all the more those with whom they had been identified as such. But the charge of Irish race-mixing rested on a far more complex history, in which the black and Irish poor in urban areas shared neighborhoods, workplaces, taverns, music, dances, families, and children. Such social realities, plus the tens of thousands of Irish in Ireland who had signed abolitionist petitions by the 1840s, and the deep links of Irish antislavery with the mass movements for temperance and self-rule, made abolitionists of the 1840s look forward eagerly to an Irish-American infusion into their egalitarian ranks. A year after its original US publication, Frederick Douglass's autobiography was already in its second Irish edition. In touring Ireland he emphasized unity among oppressed peoples, noting that he heard the same "wailing notes" in Irish music that he knew in the slaves'.

As pre-famine migration peaked in the early 1840s, radical abolitionists held a huge meeting in support of the "repeal" movement, which challenged the terms of British rule in Ireland and demanded the "repeal" of US slavery. Boston's historic

Faneuil Hall was packed with 5,000 people, with those radical abolitionists most eager to discuss class and race together taking the lead in crafting appeals to Irish Americans. But even before the height of famine immigration, abolitionist dreams quickly became nightmares. By 1843 the visiting British socialist John Finch could plausibly hold that "the poorer class of Irish immigrants," whose backwardness he linked to their support for the Democratic Party, were "greater enemies to the negro population . . . than any [other] part of the population in the free states." Daniel O'Connell, the charismatic, pro-abolitionist leader of the anti-colonial forces in Ireland, bitterly chided Irish Americans by charging that they had "learned this cruelty" of pro-slavery in the US, not Ireland. But the response of immigrants was not to move away from pro-slavery Democrats or the Catholic hierarchy that tolerated slavery, but instead to put clear distance between themselves and O'Connell. Irish Americans had in the 1830s largely stood aloof from the mobbing of free blacks and abolitionists, and at times had opposed such violence; by the 1850s and 1860s they were often at the center of such terror.

That the immiserated Irish immigrants of the 1840s and 1850s at times competed with free blacks for jobs has sometimes seemed sufficient to explain why they typically and tragically came to aspire to whiteness, rather than to participate in and create broad movements among the variously oppressed. But in fact the numbers of African Americans in Northern cities were so much fewer than Irish Americans, and the latter so quickly won competition for jobs that it is wrong to root Irish racism insistently in a struggle for employment. The deepest fears of job competition with African Americans remained hypothetical: when appealing to the Irish Americans as pro-slavery voters, Democratic politicians made much of the prospective possibility that emancipation of black slaves might flood the market with unskilled labor.

The powerful pull of whiteness certainly did connect itself to work, but not in a way easily summarized under the heading of job competition. The task before Irish Americans was not so much to best black workers in securing jobs as to separate themselves from the stigma of doing the service and hauling work historically associated with African Americans. The Irish-centered campaign for an "all-white waterfront" in antebellum New York City, for example, was surely meant to remove and exclude relatively small numbers of free black competitors. However this, and more general refusals to work alongside African Americans, tragically showed the Irish taking to heart Douglass's advice regarding the risks of assuming of the black worker's "degradation" along with his or her "avocations." Irish workers on the docks and elsewhere attempted to separate themselves from brutally bossed "nigger work," as degraded, racialized tasks were then called, by removing black workers.

Democratic politicians, who provided a bedrock of acceptance towards Irish Americans as white citizens, could be sure of a hearing in Irish-American communities. Their expressions of anti-black and anti-Mexican racism consistently coexisted with the embrace of the Irish and other European immigrants as full members of the white race. Massachusetts's Caleb Cushing averred that he did not "admit as my equals . . . the red man of America, or the yellow man of Asia, or the black man of Africa," but did count the "Celt of Ireland" as of "my blood and race." In Stephen A. Douglas's celebrated 1858 debates with Abraham Lincoln, the former counted the existence of the Mexican people as proof of the deleterious effects of "the amalgamation of white men, Indians, and negroes," while stressing that pure white Americans came from "every branch of the Caucasian race," including the Irish one. Missouri's leading Democrat, Thomas Hart Benton, conjured up a "Celtic-Anglo-Saxon race" As Reginald Horsman's magnificent research shows, politicians of Irish and Scotch-Irish heritage played no small role in popularizing the idea that a new white American race, decidedly inclusive of the Irish, had superseded the Anglo-Saxon "race" as the benchmark of fitness for white republican citizenship.

The distance between the ascribed "inbetween" racial position of Irish Americans—their legal claim to whiteness was secure but they remained subject to suspicions that they were less than full members of the dominant race—set them far apart from people of color, with whom they sometimes shared jobs and poverty. Even at their anti-Catholic worst, late antebellum anti-immigrant movements respected Irish migrants' rights to naturalization. They campaigned to delay, but not to deny on racial grounds, the ability of newcomers to become citizens. Indeed so important was the Irish vote, and so divided in party affiliation and religion was the similarly large German immigrant vote, that by the end of the national political party realignments of the 1850s even the Republicans muted nativist tendencies in their ranks, opting on balance to campaign for immigrant votes rather than against the ability of immigrants to vote. A decisive contrast was emerging between Irish Americans and African Americans, the latter being overwhelmingly enslaved and, after 1857, utterly without civil rights even outside of slavery.

Before the Civil War, courts had also clarified that the Chinese did not enjoy the protections extended to people with white identity. During Reconstruction, Congress specifically rejected extending naturalization to the Chinese. When Chinese exclusion laws began with the 1875 Page Act, women migrants in particular were targeted. Thereafter, as numbers of Chinese male immigrants outstripped those of females—even after the more general exclusion law of 1882—Chinese men were increasingly connected through racist popular imagery with interracial intimacy, seduction via drugs, and oral sex. By contrast, the Irish enjoyed almost a complete freedom to migrate throughout US history; for complex reasons, the numbers of Irish female and male settlers were almost equal. While Irish women in domestic work were seen as sexually vulnerable, the brutish, apelike caricatures of Irish men did not generally communicate hints of sexual menace. The Irish had reason to treasure, secure, and make demands based upon the claims on the whiteness that so powerfully differentiated them from those other races with which they shared the bottom rungs of society. Political power and patronage jobs unavailable to those racialized as nonwhite would play significant roles in propelling Irish Americans up the societal ladder and into a position from which even Francis Amasa Walker would recognize them as white and American.

New Immigrants, New Realities, and the Survival of Race

By the early twentieth century new waves of poor European immigrants would arrive in the US. Like the Irish, these new refugees often fled poverty and national oppression; equally, this huge, largely Eastern and Southern European wave of so-called "new immigrants" found themselves slotted massively into unskilled work, more often in industrial enterprises than in public works, domestic service, or transportation. The enormously varied new immigrant population arrived at a time when some experts counted a handful of races—generally the red, white, black, brown, and yellow—corresponding to their perception of broad divisions of humanity by color. But even such reductive lists of color-based races sometimes added a "dark white" category, thereby excluding some European ethnicities from full membership in the dominant race. Other experts identified dozens of races, enumerating endless hierarchical divisions among Europeans.

Within broad European categories, racial "excellence" allegedly descended from the favored Nordic racial group, through the Alpines, to the inferior Mediterraneans. Inside and across such categories, further racial distinctions appeared. Delineations of "Slavic races" in particular proliferated. The definitive US government report on immigration, issued in 1911, counted separate Northern and Southern Italian groups among the nearly four dozen races it named and judged. With the term "ethnicity" still largely absent from academic and popular parlance, definitions of race overlapped with nationality when applied to Europeans, and therefore incorporated both supposedly solidified cultural traits and biological elements. Speaking for industrialists wanting an open labor market, steel magnate Andrew Carnegie held the cheery view that language "makes race," with the implication being that simply learning English brought breathtaking transformations to even racially inferior European immigrants. The procession of immigrant workers into a giant pot at Ford English School graduation ceremonies, and their emergence from the cauldron as new American men, summed up self-interested industrial capitalist optimism about the transformative magic that a new language and a superior culture could work.

Dominant discourse and law regarding immigration persistently spoke of disability and disease in ways that were both distinct from and fully bound up with the supposed "racial" character of immigrant groups. Another aspect of this imprecision regarding whether the "new immigrants" carried biological or cultural "disabilities" lay in the identification of centuries of degradation as a source of potentially inherited deficient physical characteristics, as well as of bad habits. Experts spoke of race, as the literary scholar Walter Benn Michaels notes, as both "inherited" and "achieved." Sicilians were said to inherit "brutal natures . . . low receding foreheads, repulsive countenances and slovenly attire," in large measure from their supposedly horrific history as oppressed and feckless peasants in backward regions. The labor economist and reformer John R. Commons wrote of whole groups of immigrant peoples as "the product of serfdom." As Richard Weiss has aptly observed, "differences in language, the arts, social organization, and aspiration" were understood to reside in the " 'souls' of peoples," and were as much a part of "inherited propensities" as skin color. Moreover, migrants were often cast as the most desperate and unworthy representatives of already suspect races. Thus in dealing with migrants, both social scientists and Roosevelt cleaved to the "beaten men of beaten races" point of view, a characterization that swam in a sea of even less hospitable images: "scum," "trash," "dregs," "the offscourings of Europe." Even the hospitable Statue of Liberty, in Emma Lazarus's celebrated poem, welcomed immigrants as "wretched refuse."

Thus turn-of-the-century immigrants from Eastern and Southern Europe entered a racial order as daunting as, but vastly more complicated than, that encountered by the famine-era Irish. Arriving into a booming factory-based economy, but one also featuring cyclical recessions and seasonal unemployment, many new immigrants returned home to Europe, either with the money they hoped to save or in desperation and disillusionment. While the Irish had an exceptionally low rate of remigration, among Greeks return migration reached 63 percent of immigration in the period of peak immigration to the US, and for Italians return migration reached 58 percent. Highly unequal sex ratios among new immigrants were reflected in the largely male industrial jobs into which they would be slotted. As labor migrants were ready to come and go according to market forces, their free movement typically enjoyed considerable, decisive support from capital. But unlike the Irish case, no political party would unequivocally vouch for the fully white and manifestly "American" racial credentials of the new immigrants. Their contribution to the United States racial "stock"—a keyword connoting an alchemical mix of animal science, eugenic notions of racial hierarchy, and capitalist development—became the subject of scholarly, private, and especially political debate. New immigrant stock was on trial right up until the Congress passed immigration legislation aimed at restricting the entry of Southern and Eastern Europeans in the early 1920s on racial grounds. The Johnson-Reed Act of 1924 culminated and systematized such restrictions.

The multiplicity of new immigrant races identified by the government would be judged against each other by employers, sociologists, teachers, managers, settlement house reformers, potential marriage partners, and landlords, as well as by legislators. The now settled Irish-American population itself judged the newcomers, while providing them with a model to follow in negotiating the US racial system. Ubiquitous Irish politicians, priests, schoolteachers, police, foremen, contractors, and leaders of youth gangs stood as educators, guides, and as scourges for the new immigrants, showing how to navigate assimilation into white Americanism, and to a remarkably direct extent acting as on-the-ground arbiters of whether and how fast such a transition could occur. Irish-American foremen, for example, often picked out which of the immigrant workers who lined up seeking work would be paid and which would be jobless that day.

The slurs that new immigrants heard against themselves bespoke how subtle and how awful were the challenges and uncertainties they faced regarding their positioning within the United States racial order. Persistently denigrated as "guineas" or as "greasers," new immigrants were thereby connected to groups firmly recognized as nonwhite. "Guineas," an old marker for African Americans originally signaling their origins on the West African slaving coast, came to be applied widely and pejoratively to Italian Americans. As the term continued to apply to African Americans, and came to be applied to mixed-race Southerners, Pacific Islanders, and Puerto Ricans, it made multiple, volatile connections. Those associations carried weighty consequences. In 1924, attempting to capture the force of "guinea" as an epithet, the economist Robert F. Foerster made apt links between language and material conditions: "In a country where the distinction between white men and black is intended as a distinction of value . . . it is no compliment to the Italian to deny him his whiteness." Union organizers recognized that the use of "guinea" helped undermine efforts at labor unity, and Irish workers seeking to bar Italians from working alongside them used the term precisely to further such disunity.

"Greaser," already an "Americanism" identifying the most disfranchised Mexican Americans (in California, this was actually codified in an 1855 law called the Greaser Act), came also to be used against new immigrants, especially Italians and Greeks. Dictionary-makers recorded confusion about whether the term most applied to Mexicans or to Mediterraneans, but left no doubt that it was a fierce "fighting word." The supposedly natural greasiness of skin and hair among those groups led to the adoption of the term which shaded in all instances into reflections on hygiene, and into the supposed preference of the poor for cheap and greasy food.

"Hunky," which reflected a corruption of Hungarian, likewise singled out particular immigrants for abuse. It was a derivation of "Hun," a slur used indiscriminately against Eastern Europeans, although it would come to be directed against the German enemy in World War I. As such, "Hun" suggested a history of Asiatic hordes invading Europe's borderlands. As Erika Lee has shown, this persistent linkage of new immigrants to Asians, whether in direct comparison or in stories about their origins, was a ubiquitous way of questioning their full whiteness. Opponents of immigration argued that the nation faced a choice of "rice versus meat," framing immigration debates around standards of consumption in such a way that the alleged cheapness of Chinese workers' diets counted as a reason to bar their entry. Such invidious comparisons, as Gwendolyn Mink has shown, expanded to pose also a choice of "pasta versus meat," designed to ground a case against Italian immigration. In Kansas City after World War I, immigrant workers complained of bosses who refused to learn their names, instead resorting exclusively to "hunky" as a form of address.

Such racial slurs underlined the complexity of both new immigrants' categorization and their consciousness. Like the US Immigration Commission, Italians themselves recognized two Italian "races," North and South. The stereotyped and underdeveloped South was viewed as suffering from its proximity to, and miscegenation with, Africa. Thus Northern Italians in St. Louis might literally look down from The Hill neighborhood on those "little black fellows"—Southern Italians—living nearer the river. Italians in varying levels of assimilation might choose to ignore the slur "guinea," or even to attempt to rehabilitate it by using it internally and jokingly. Moreover, "guinea" came to denigrate not only Italians but also Spanish, Jewish, Greek, and Portuguese newcomers. "Greaser" likewise proved expansive, encompassing not only Southern Europeans generally, but also Filipinos and Russian Jews, and eventually the entire ethnic working class. The US Immigration Commission's fretting in 1911 over the "incorrect" application of "hunky" to "Slavs indiscriminately" did not prevent that epithet from being directed against not only Hungarians but also Russians, Tyroleans, Slavs, Serbians, Bohemians, and "allied races." It soon meant something as broad as "non-Latin foreigner" in the novelist John O'Hara's estimation. The great expert on the working class and slang in the twentieth century found "hunky" at times expansive enough to apply to any "foreign laborer."

The uneven, fluid targeting of various groups led at times to responses that would have given hope to a civil rights leader like Du Bois, who in the 1920s dreamed of building an "anti-Nordic" coalition of peoples racially oppressed in many different ways. When in 1909 Du Bois himself spoke to "Mediterranean immigrants" at Hull House, Jane Addams's settlement house in Chicago, Addams took note of the rapt attention of an audience, packed with Italians and Greeks, who were used to suffering indignities and assaults because of their origins. Addams concluded that the crowd was deeply and personally interested in "the advancement of colored people." Stirring "interracial" unity among new immigrants and people of color also occurred at times in the Southwest. In some Arizona mining towns, Italian immigrants chose to identify with, live among, and marry Mexicans, fellow members of a "Latin race." They learned Spanish and fielded sports teams of Mexican and Italian players. More modestly, as Josef Barton details, in Cleveland a broad "hunky" identity united Eastern Europeans across the same national lines that sometimes bespoke murderous division in Europe. Thus the terms "guinea," "greaser," and "hunky" each raised profound questions regarding the ascription of racial identity: was "guinea," at any given moment, a epithet directed against a particular Southern Italian subgroup, against Italians as a whole, against all "Mediterraneans," or against new immigrants generally? Did the use of "hunky" mean to slur some Poles or all foreign laborers? Equally profound were the questions of aspiration to racial identities: did confronting anti-immigrant racism require solidarity within a nationality, or among co-religionists, among groupings of European "races," among new immigrants more widely, among all working people, or among all "minorities" including the nonwhite? Or did such confrontation require a combination of all of these?

How White Supremacy Made
New Immigrants Excluded and Acceptable

The largest of many open questions regarding the ways in which immigration impacted on race-thinking and white supremacy centered on when, whether, and how immigrants responded when confronted by anti-immigrant racism. The reaction of new immigrants and their children was informed by encounters that fixed them somewhere between Northern and Western European full "whiteness" and the clear racial "disabilities" suffered by Asian Americans, African Americans, Mexicans, Puerto Ricans, and Native Americans. Judged constantly against each other, and as a whole, by a mixture of legislators, courts, employers, realtors, teachers, public health officials, IQ testers, and purity and temperance reformers, the new immigrant experienced biopolitical scrutiny that was more akin to that inflicted on post-1965 immigrants to the United States, than to the experiences of the Irish famine immigrants of the mid-nineteenth century.

The failure of corporations and progressives to defend Eastern and Southern European immigration to the US after World War I underscores how firmly even those with the greatest interest in immigrants nonetheless regarded newcomers as "on trial." After the start of the war, and especially after the relatively brief US entry into it in 1917, attitudes towards immigration grew harsher, at least in the short term. Poorly understood on every level, the proliferation of nationalities in US cities came to be seen as a security risk. Slavic immigrants, viewing the war through the perspective of their often nationally oppressed homelands, were subject to particular scrutiny years before their new nation joined the conflict. Before the outbreak of war, Henry Ford's Social Department functioned as a progressive, if coercive, agency of experts, whose programs and home visits insured that the company's high wages went to "moral" and "assimilating" workers. During the war years it quickly transformed itself into a security agency, ferreting out "disloyalty" among immigrant workers. Connections between significant numbers of immigrants and the antiwar Socialist Party predictably increased surveillance.

More generally, the imperative of "100 percent Americanism" became the object of a national campaign during the same period, with former reform advocates of a gentler pace of acculturation providing leadership. Progressive politics had long harbored a suspicion of enfranchised immigrants: as voters, they were seen as inclined to support political machines, and were therefore potential underminers of efficient, planned government. However, progressives' optimistic faith in reform and their ties to corporate interests favoring immigration held these impulses in check. With the war, progressive political leaders in both parties vied with each other in forcefully proclaiming that the hyphen allowing immigrants to proclaim a dual identity containing both a European and American nationality ought instead to be read as a minus sign and speedily discarded. With the bodily and mental fitness of those being drafted into the army an object of intense nationalist concern, military uses of culturally biased intelligence tests brought new opportunities to assess the immigrant "races." The resultant charting and ranking tapped into the worldview of progressive reformers as well as patrician conservatives concerned with "race betterment." H. H. Goddard, in an IQ test–based study begun in 1913, had concluded that as many as four-fifths of Jewish, Italian, Russian, and Hungarian newcomers were "feeble-minded." But links to the war effort and new claims of scientific accuracy gave the results of the military IQ testing greater currency than those of prewar studies. Experts ascribed the "disquietingly low" intelligence of new immigrants to their "Mediterranean race," and emphasized that the racial variation within Europe rivaled that "between negro and white." Italians and what one researcher called the "Slavish" [sic] races occupied the bottom of European hierarchies, standing in proximity to blacks and Mexican Americans.

Even so, the connection between war and race-based immigration restriction can explain only so much. While the huge German-American population attracted wide and deep hostility and suspicion as potential "enemies within" during World War I, anti-"Hun" rhetoric directed at Germans proved considerably easier to turn off than anti-"hunkie" suspicions. After the war, the Germans quickly resumed their place in the fold of the desirable English-speaking races, and enjoyed the preferential treatment accorded to other "Nordic" Europeans in the immigration legislation of 1924. Eastern and Southern Europeans, on the other hand, became even more suspect after the war, in large part because of their significant participation in postwar labor militancy. During this period virtually every major US industry saw vast upsurges in working class struggles as an unprecedentedly large and extended strike wave unfolded. Inspired both by the gains in unionization made during wartime and the example of the Russian Revolution, immigrant workers in steel, mining, textiles, packing, and clothing joined movements that pressed for radically reduced working days and higher pay, along with the recognition of unions and of the full humanity of industrial and immigrant workers. Following on from earlier mobilizations in the needle trades and Industrial Workers of the World-led strikes uniting dozens of nationalities, immigrants not only joined the postwar strike wave but made it theirs, insuring that the social basis of the most successful examples of "new unionism" would be new immigrants.

David Saposs, the sharpest analyst of the archetypical example of such unionism, the Great Steel Strike of 1919 and 1920, saw in it not just a labor action but an "immigrant rebellion." The strike, demanding an eight-hour working day and human dignity, shut down the nation's most important industry for weeks, idling hundreds of thousands of workers. It featured defiance of censorship, of company paternalism, of deportations, of corporation-hired spies, of police, and even of traditional religious leadership. New immigrants united around this defiance, showing solidarity that set them apart from the earlier-arriving immigrant groups, both in terms of their greater and enduring loyalty to the strike, and in their awareness of what was at stake in terms of full social citizenship. In that sense, the new immigrants did briefly support an immigrant rights movement, one that was powerfully lodged in working-class militancy and experience. But that movement proved deeply vulnerable to defeat, and to conservative union leaders' subsequent regression to craft unionism and opposition to immigration.

This heightened postwar immigrant-based union militancy precipitated the loss of industrial capitalist and progressive support for relatively unrestricted European immigration. In 1919 the Wilson administration so feared possible insurrections that it developed the draconian War Plan White as a set of repressive measures. The measures targeted African Americans and new immigrants, the latter suspect because they had been insufficiently "recast by the American 'Melting Pot'" and were therefore prone to follow "hostile leadership against Anglo-Saxon Institutions." This perverse paranoia regarding a possible "race" war came not during the World War, but in the context of the class war that matured after the armistice.

Support for open immigration by industrialists gave way to doubt and indecision. By 1919, Henry Ford's optimism regarding racial improvement via supervision, factory discipline, and migration had unraveled to the extent that his *Dearborn Independent* ran a series of anti-Jewish diatribes that would make it, and him, infamous. In 1923 when the National Industrial Conference Board tried to address immigration restriction, it allowed that the issue centered on a "race question," and that the "commercial purposes" that might have united its members in support of an open labor market could not withstand associations of class-based radicalism with the immigrant races. Herbert Hoover, the most sophisticated pro-business politician of the 1920s and in many ways the leading representative of that decade's style of progressive reform, completely avoided speaking to the immigration restriction issue. To quote the great defender of immigrants Horace Kallen, the idea that labor radicalism was "always an alien importation" disarmed progressive and corporate efforts to defend the immigration of workers and to champion the possibility of their Americanization. In the later 1920s, sectors of industry and agribusiness did still seek a more flexible immigration policy, but largely in the context of accepting the necessity of significant restrictions.

Abstentions from the race issue such as Hoover's, along with the labor movement's return to the anti-immigrant fold on openly racial grounds, ensured that the 1924 restrictions legislated in the Johnson-Reed Act would represent anti-Southern and Eastern racism at its unmitigated worst. As Ku Klux Klan membership soared into the millions, that organization enjoined "real whites" to defend the nation against "mongrelized" new immigrants. The act's main author was the Republican representative from Washington, Albert Johnson, who had been schooled in anti-Asian campaigns. It reflected his contacts with those whom John Higham's magisterial history calls "leading race-thinkers"—that is largely upper-class intellectuals such as Madison Grant, Harry Laughlin, and Prescott Hall—a group that popularized racist science, wrote sweeping alarmist histories, and advised politicians. The act, which enjoyed bipartisan support, reflected the general principle of using the makeup of US population in 1890 as the benchmark for setting 1920s immigration quotas, though it ultimately settled on a kindred solution using a different calculation. The idea was to define a national racial stock as it existed before the allegedly polluting influx of new immigrants and to return to that standard, literally writing the period of mass

Southern and Eastern European immigration out of national history. The early 1920s thus stood as the nadir of racial judgment directed against new immigrants. At that time, as the political scientist Gwendolyn Mink writes, race and nationality became the "new moral rachets of citizenship" in a process that left new immigrants sharing with African Americans poverty, dependency, and victimization by bigots.

Nonetheless in critical ways new immigrants' racial suffering as "inbetween people" differed from that endured by people of color. Indeed the 1920s turn out to be the key decade for understanding why such suffering did not give rise to an interracial movement of the poor that included the Slavic and Mediterranean "races." While Du Bois was right in noting that most of the nation had "anti-Nordic" grievances, those grievances took such different forms that they dictated disparate "racial" responses to a common enemy.

Two classic examples of such responses concerned Asian rather than European immigrants in the early 1920s. A Japanese American, Takao Ozawa, and a South Asian American, Bhagat Thind, went individually before the Supreme Court to seek naturalization, in 1922 and 1923 respectively. The law required a successful applicant for naturalized citizenship to be white or, as a result of Reconstruction-era reforms, African. Debates over naturalization law during Reconstruction spelled out that the immigrant Chinese were not intended to be eligible for citizenship. In both the Japanese and South Asian cases, litigants sought to establish scientifically that they were entitled to citizenship as whites, not Africans. Both therefore had to argue their difference from African Americans, and from the Chinese. After the Court had ruled against Japanese claims in the Ozawa case, Thind had to argue his racial difference from the Japanese. His claim to whiteness also failed, despite the presentation of strong scientific testimony that some South Asians were "Aryans." Indeed in Thind's case, his lawyers differentiated their client's "high-class Hindu" Aryan status from that of the "aboriginal Indian

Mongoloid" by saying that the former regarded the latter as "the American regards the negro."

While Mexican Americans could naturalize by virtue of treaty rights, they needed at times to establish distance from African Americans to try to dissociate themselves from the widespread segregation, lynching, and disfranchisement against both groups. Like African Americans who migrated so massively to Northern cities during and after World War I, they seemingly benefited from the increased job opportunities that resulted in part from the Johnson-Reed restrictions on Southern and Eastern European migration. But while the Mexican-American population trebled in the course of the 1920s, the surveillance and criminalization of immigrants fell heavily on them. Pursuit far beyond the border of immigrants who had entered illegally was introduced largely against arrivals from Mexico. As the historian Mae Ngai writes, " 'Illegal' [became] constitutive of 'Mexican' . . . a wholly negative racial category." When jobs dried up during the Depression, hundreds of thousands of Mexican Americans—including many born in the US and therefore holding citizenship—were repatriated to Mexico.

Ironically, the 1924 restrictions softened anti-immigrant racism against Eastern and Southern Europeans themselves. The historian Oscar Handlin once characterized the Johnson-Reed Act as both a "rejection of the foreign-born who desired to come" at the policy level and as a "condemnatory judgment" of new immigrants already settled in the US. The policy lingered into the 1960s, but the condemnation soon began, unevenly, to recede. Progressive reformers, who had so lost confidence in their ability to "ameliorate" any "flood" of new immigrants, could claim a surer ability to handle the post-1924 trickles allowed under the law. Following Johnson-Reed, as immigration expert Herman Feldman precisely observed in 1931, the assimilation of Italian immigrants involved "helping a maximum of 5802 new people" annually. Since the thrust of so much anti-immigrant rhetoric conjured up fears of an overwhelming mass of new arrivals "swamping" and "overrunning" the US, hysteria and dire predictions became harder to sustain after Johnson-Reed passed. Along with the sudden drop in newcomers, immigrants' reduced ability to travel between their original countries and the US meant that members of immigrant communities would increasingly be English-speaking. Sex ratios, too, became more equal. The new faces of the threatening urban subproletariat, often newcomers from the countryside allegedly unused to city life, were increasingly black, Mexican, Puerto Rican, and Filipino, as well as white: they included poor internal refugees from Appalachian poverty and from the Dust Bowl.

Even at the 1924 low point of racial condemnation of new immigrants, the differences between their "inbetween," less than fully white, racial status and the plights of those racialized as nonwhite remained clear. Given such realities, even as the 1924 legislation made their nationalities the victims of brutal race-thinking, it also encouraged some of the victimized to see the paltry but real advantages of whiteness more clearly, and to seek that status more energetically. Naturalization again provides an important example. With the stabilization of the immigrant population in the 1920s, naturalization rates advanced dramatically; despite considerable hurdles, new immigrant women in particular pursued citizenship with unexpected zeal. So, even as the numbers of migrants decreased, the political weight of the new immigrant vote did not. The vote, available to Eastern and Southern Europeans as it generally was not to people of color, gave new immigrants a resilient political power that even anti-immigration politicians could not ignore. In the debates over the 1924 act itself, a small group of congressmen, often from heavily new immigrant districts, offered some opposition to the Johnson-Reed legislation. Their attempts to change the subject in debates over the law to immigration by Asians and "Mexican peons," and to claim superior status for all Europeans, could not stem the anti-new immigrant tide. Nevertheless, the act did treat "inferior" Europeans differently from Asians, offering small quotas to the

latter and exclusion to the former. Such a scant difference doubt-
less provided small consolation at the moment of the 1924 defeat.
But as attitudes to new immigrants softened, and new scapegoats
for urban misery appeared, distinctions between those with fragile
claims to whiteness and those with none became clearer. Access to
political power enabled new immigrants, although victims of
"Nordic" supremacy, to become in time also the beneficiaries
of white supremacy.

Indeed at the very moment of immigration restriction, a
different story was unfolding on the ground in US cities. The
realty industry promulgated racial hierarchies ranking neighbors in
terms of their desirability. Russian Jews and South Italians took the
bottom spots in Charles Male's influential 1932 study of urban
land values and "race," with debates sometimes centering on
whether the "invasion" of a neighborhood by the "Negro" or by
the "new immigrant" most imperiled property values. But in
practice the Great Migration of hundreds of thousands of African
American Southerners to cities, beginning with World War I and
continuing into the 1920s, made the exclusion of this group the
overwhelming priority. Since a 1917 Supreme Court decision had
outlawed the open use of Jim Crow zoning laws to maintain
residential segregation, the preferred mechanism to exclude African Americans became the "restrictive covenant" in which
neighbors promised to sell homes only to "Caucasians." New
immigrants, as homeowners and potential buyers in those urban
neighborhoods being "defended" from integration were accepted
as Caucasians, however suspect. Indeed at times they played a key
role in movement for restrictive covenants. New immigrants were
thus simultaneously the objects of housing discrimination in
certain suburbs and enclaves and the agents of restriction in many
cities; in this way their stories exemplified how white supremacy
variously incorporated and victimized, empowered and embarrassed, Eastern and Southern Europeans.

By the 1930s, the political power of new immigrants, along
with their central participation in a more successful industrial

union movement that once more embodied a quest for immigrants' dignity, helped Eastern and Southern Europeans approach full, white social citizenship. But for the most part the achievement of such citizenship marked a triumph only of the immigrant communities themselves, not necessarily implying a critique of racism generally. Moreover, anti-immigrant racism gave ground in the context of immigration restriction, not of liberal successes in arguing for a nation open to new waves of diverse migrants. Such realities framed the story of how race survived modern liberalism, to which we turn next.

6

Colorblind Inequalities:

HOW RACE SURVIVED MODERN LIBERALISM

In 1937 a remarkable New Deal federal project hired an African American researcher to interview Susan Hamlin, a poor ex-slave in South Carolina who claimed to be over one hundred years old. The interviewer, Augustus Ladson, paid Hamlin a dime for her testimony, a detailed, unsparing account of her witness to the brutalizing atrocities of slavery, and to what she described as the "brazenness" of the white race. By the end of the project nearly one ex-slave in fifty had been interviewed by the ambitious Federal Writers Project initiative, whose leading figures included the great African American poet and literary critic Sterling Brown. For all the problems inherent in their being gathered so long after emancipation, the interviews stand among the most important sources on the history of slavery from the slave's point of view. Moreover, gathering them created temporary work for many young African American intellectuals and artists at the depth of the Depression.

Shortly after Hamlin's indictment of slavery, a second interviewer approached her, a white woman who allowed the interviewee to think that her visitor was a welfare agent. This second interview, which featured questions and interjections from the editor leading to a favorable view of slavery, produced an account of Hamlin's youth bathed in moonlight and magnolias, with her love for old master central to a story that mixed history with pleas for welfare payments. Because the tone of the second account is so at odds with that of the first, and because her age was listed as 101 in one interview and 104 in the other, the texts read as if they come from two different ex-slaves.

Nonetheless these two differing interviews come from the same source, a black woman caught in the crosscurrents and the contradictions of race at the New Deal beginnings of modern US liberalism. The interviewing project itself, the gathering of ex-slaves' truths, would have been unthinkable a decade before. But the presence of the second interviewer, and that she had the last word, typified the continuing and overwhelming power over politics and patronage held by white supremacist members of the Democratic Party in the South. Southern Democrats kept Susan Hamlin and other African Americans from resources and indeed from voting. Hamlin's performance in pleasing the second inter-viewer, mistaken for a welfare official, reflected the fact that the New Deal provided unheard-of levels of direct emergency aid to African Americans, and some old-age assistance. However, in doing so the same New Deal empowered functionaries of the whites-only Democratic Party in the South to administer such aid or to withhold it. And Susan Hamlin knew as much.

Hamlin negotiated, at nearly its foundational moment, a tension that opponents of white supremacy would continue to face through the New Deal's successors, Truman's postwar Fair Deal, the reforms of the 1960s, and arguably up to the present. Electorally, legislatively, and even emotionally, a liberalism tied to the Democratic Party provided unprecedented opportunities for relief through access to welfare benefits from the state. By the 1960s, this liberalism, pressured wonderfully by freedom move-ments at home and abroad, helped to usher in the achievement of formal legal equality and the possibility of what Lyndon Johnson called a Great Society, an expanded welfare state promising to empower poor people of color. But liberalism remained anchored to a base of voters, and to assumptions and interests, that not only slowed but also at times decisively opposed a change in the racial order, and which helped to create new realities that ensured the continuation of race-thinking and racism.

The most straightforward accounts of the tensions contained within the Democratic Party from the 1930s through the 1960s have centered on the evocative phrase "strange bedfellows." It was a term used to describe the coexistence in the party's ranks of those Northern liberals apt to bemoan inequality, and those Southern "Dixiecrats" who most insistently enforced discrimination and led what they called "massive resistance" to efforts for change. On this view, the New Deal and its successors could go only so far in challenging Jim Crow and the other structures of daily life and economic inequality that made it logical, even imperative, to see society in racial terms. The paths of least resistance to Southern racism had clear appeals: emphasizing relief for all rather than racial justice; backing the cause of labor abstractly, but seldom championing the dismantling of color bars in the workplace; symbolically consulting a New Deal "Black Cabinet" instead of supporting anti-lynching legislation, and so on. Persistent concessions to the Democrats' Southern wing produced, in Ira Katznelson's memorable phrase, a long period in which "affirmative action was white," even as African American voters moved to the Democrats' ranks.

If seen as strange, the coalitions inside the Democratic Party are also portrayed as having an air of inevitability. African Americans themselves seemingly found the best political shelter, and prospects for avoiding starvation, in a party whose liberal leaders could not embrace equal citizenship without losing the long-established white Southern politicians who guaranteed it victory and committee chairs in Congress. When the Democratic Party finally did give partial support for the Civil Rights Act of 1964 and the Voting Rights Act of 1965, the power of the Southern conservatives to reshape US politics was tragically highlighted. Diehard Southern Democratic leaders opposed the reforms, with some leading a long march of the white South into the

Republican Party. Despite adding millions of newly enfranchised voters of color, the Democrats lost decisive white support. From the election of 1932 to that of 1968, the Democrats had lost the White House to only one Republican, Eisenhower, who ran as a military hero as much as a party politician, and attracted black votes. After 1968, despite their membership being boosted with potential black voters, the Democrats provided only two presidents—both Southern centrists—in four decades.

However, this chapter argues that the idea that Southern Democrats constituted the bulwark of reaction inside of the Democratic Party before the mid-1960s, and a bulwark of reaction in the Republican Party in the more recent past, gives us at best a partial truth. It misses powerful tendencies toward conservatism in the entire Democratic Party, expressed in conciliation of the South before the 1960s and in profound retreats from the pursuit of racial justice in recent decades. Indeed, in the entire post–New Deal period a Democrat from a non-slaveholding Civil War-era state has held the White House less than three years, and one credential of the border-south and Southern Democratic presidents who served twenty-seven of those years has consistently been a supposed ability to keep racially conservative Democrats, Southern and suburban, in the party's ranks. In many ways it is thus more useful to interrogate the racial politics of all Democrats than to simply imagine a small group of Southern racists holding back larger anti-racist impulses of the party and the nation. Liberalism failed, and was not merely held back, where race was concerned.

The legislation of the mid-1960s did mark a break with the old color-obsessed Jim Crow legal system that administered white supremacy, and helped consolidate a system that its advocates have increasingly praised as "colorblind." But continuities with the earlier status quo are also striking, in that stark inequalities persisted in the post–civil rights era. As this chapter emphasizes, color-blindness itself had roots inside of liberalism dating back to the New Deal. Such an avowedly race-neutral stance has contradictorily influenced policy not just for the last forty years but for the last seventy-five. It has worked to advance an insistence on present and future fairness, on the one hand. But on the other hand it has excused a tendency to refuse to engage with questions regarding the effects of past white supremacist practices and of broad, ingrained preferences given to whites institutionally in the present. Such patterns imply that liberalism's complicity with the persistence of race has been sufficiently deep and abiding to require more than an explanation based on North/South differences. If Malcolm X was deliberately being provocative when he declared that everything south of Canada was South, or that every Democrat was a Dixiecrat, his words remind us that the Democratic coalition growing out of the New Deal contained consenting bedfellows. The racial landscape had strangenesses far more complex than what Ralph Ellison called the "morality play explanation in which the North is given the role of good and the South that of evil."

A New Deal: Dreams, and Dreams Deferred, in a White Security State

Around the time that Susan Hamlin testified to the horrors of slavery, the great African American intellectual Ralph Bunche wrote of seeing a deep rebirth of hope among African Americans in the same region. Making contacts with friendly forces in New Deal agencies, black Southerners organized around the need to appeal for relief, and around the public displays of support for civil rights and sharecroppers' labor rights by First Lady Eleanor Roosevelt, in the process actively pushing for transformations towards which the New Deal at best only gestured. While President Roosevelt episodically consulted a "cabinet" of black leaders, even as he accepted African American disfranchisement in the South, African Americans in several cities elected their own "mayors" to underline their sense of grievance, their organization, and their hope. Lawsuits and educational campaigns seeking to prepare the ground for the expansion of voting rights in the South unfolded as the Democrats openly and unprecedentedly appealed for black support in areas outside the South. Most of all, Bunche and others argued, Afro-Southerners were talking and acting in the context of a New Deal. As Peter Epps, working in South Carolina in the federal Works Progress Administration (WPA), put it when describing African Americans on a particular South Carolina farm, "since Mistah Roosevelt been in . . . the Negro . . . has been talkin' 'bout politics."

Bunche's energetic documentation of such optimism reflected two converging and mutually reinforcing hopes regarding change. The first involved intellectuals and activists like himself who, swept up in a wave of enthusiasm for the possibilities of an activist state committed to the redistribution of wealth, were dedicated to loosening the hold of Southern Democrats on national politics, and to encouraging a new and growing political centrality for integrated industrial unions. Even the black and white organizers of farm labor, who knew first-hand better than anyone the tendency of the New Deal to bend policies in favor of planters, petitioned the Roosevelt administration, again appealing particularly to Eleanor Roosevelt.

Secondly, below this leadership level, Bunche was chronicling a hope born of desperation, at times literally of starvation. In both the countryside and the urban South, African American family income averaged about a third that of white Southerners, who were themselves immiserated but hardly united with blacks in degree of poverty, let alone in politics. Average white incomes substantially exceeded the "poverty line," a minimum set by experts as necessary to maintain a family. African Americans typically fell well short of even an "emergency budget" on which a family might survive unhealthily on a restricted diet. W. E. B. Du Bois, a rare black leadership voice of caution regarding the New Deal, nonetheless realized that any relief mattered greatly in such desperate times, and that the New Deal provided such aid federally in ways unheard of before the 1930s. He wrote, "Any time people are out of work, in poverty . . . any kind of deal that helps them is going to be favored. Large numbers of colored people in the United States would have starved to death if it had not been for the Roosevelt policies."

But help and hope came with a price, and not only one exacted by racist Southern Democrats. Modern liberalism was formed by compromising with the worst practices of Jim Crow and embracing, if not inventing, the grossest illusions of colorblindness. In another moment and mood, Du Bois commented very differently on New Deal reform. Writing in 1935, he held that African Americans had never faced a more critical moment, even in slavery or civil war: "More than ever the appeal of the Negro for elementary justice falls on deaf ears. Three-fourths of us are disfranchised; yet no writer on democratic reform says a word about Negroes." In some cases, the strange Southern bedfellow of liberalism bore clear responsibility for such powerlessness and peril. This was evident in the Democratic Party's election campaigns, as it sought black ballots in the North while enforcing bars against such voting in the South.

When lynching, for a time in decline, again spiked during the Depression, the National Association for the Advancement of Colored People (NAACP) built significant support among whites as well as blacks for federal anti-lynching legislation. Although the Southern Democrats represented a dwindling proportion of Democratic voters, and realized as much, their strategic position nonetheless imbued them with confidence, or at least bluster. In 1940 Mississippi representative John Rankin urged Democrats from the North to "remember that southern Democrats hold the balance of power in both Houses of Congress" as they voted on the "vicious," in his view, anti-lynching measure. He charged that Republicans were only supporting the bill to split Democrats, and threatened that if the bill passed and Roosevelt signed it, the president would be "ruined" in the South. The failed bill did not get administration support. This sort of coercion from Southern Democrats occurred repeatedly, a particularly striking example being the passage of the Fair Labor Standards Act (FLSA) in 1938.

That bill began by serving Southern planter interests in laying out wages and hours provisions, which, it stipulated, would not apply to agricultural workers—who in the South and Southwest were overwhelmingly black and Mexican. As the legislation proceeded, Dixiecrats wanted and won still more, forcing no fewer than five Senate roll calls to expand exemptions to those trucking farm produce or packaging and preparing fresh fruits and vegetables; in each case, they held Northern liberals' feet to the fire, and the whole law hostage.

That proponents of the New Deal credited it for achievements in aiding African Americans even though it did not challenge Dixiecrat power or racial oppression or set dangerous, lasting precedents for liberalism at the level of language as well as policy. The reformers often claimed to be administering race-neutral or colorblind programs, even as their deference to local racist practices left Jim Crow intact. Liberalism's appeals to race neutrality were twofold. First job growth, union organization, and relief could be said to benefit all of the poor, thereby justifying a strategy of progressing on economic fronts without emphasizing racial justice. Secondly, even the most glaring omissions of people of color from economic reform programs took on race-neutral forms. The centerpiece of the first New Deal, the National Industrial Recovery Administration (NIRA) of 1933, refused to eliminate racial wage differentials and in fact enshrined them out of respect for Southern practices and labor markets. Unwilling to legislate specifically for racial justice, NIRA's drafters refused to prohibit selective layoffs of black workers. The law's exclusion of agricultural and domestic service occupations from many of its codes accomplished racial exclusion without mention of race. That practice continued in the National Labor Relations Act and the Social Security Act of 1935 and the FLSA of 1938, all of which used what political scientist Robert Lieberman aptly calls "race-laden" job categories, rather than specific racial language, to leave out the large majority of black and Mexican workers. Insistence on the exclusion of the latter group came from beyond the South, with the economist Paul Douglas noting the key role of "Congressmen from other sections of the country where there were unpopular racial and cultural minorities" in shaping the policy.

Susan Hamlin's concern that her interviewer might be a welfare agent poised to give or take away relief payments made perfect sense in terms of the wide latitude in distributing aid that the New Deal left to white supremacist Democrats at the state and at local level. While the New Deal brought unprecedented levels of federal relief to the South, it did so through state-based administrations, even though at times 80 percent of the resources to Southern relief efforts came from federal funds. The levels of aid were unprecedented and unequal, varying widely from race to race and place to place. Despite overwhelmingly greater need among Afro-Southerners, by 1935 rates of relief payments to whites exceeded those to blacks in ten Southern states. In Mississippi, less than 1 percent of African Americans received relief payments, and in some Georgia counties none at all. Perversely, because workers of color had such lower standards of living they could be assumed to have fewer "needs"; when they were made, aid payments were often racially tiered to the further disadvantage of black Southerners.

In 1935, the jerrybuilt system of direct federal aid, usually discriminatingly distributed by the counties, gave way to a system based on the Social Security Act. However, the act excluded occupationally most black, Indian and Mexican workers from its social insurance and unemployment plans. Wage discrimination and other factors left over two in five African Americans who were working in occupational categories covered by the act nevertheless excluded by the system, twice the proportion of whites. Unemployment insurance institutionalized colorblind discrimination by profiling the eligible and worthy worker as possessing a wage and employment history that workers of color were far less likely to have. Moreover, differences in life expectancy, together with the vastly higher percentage of African Americans who continued working well into old age, left social security a thoroughly racialized benefit. Because social security and, by 1938, fairness in wages, were systematized under federal auspices in ways that left Jim Crow intact, social citizenship was marked yet again as the province of whites.

While social security marked out new areas of entitlement for most (although by no means all) whites, it left workers of color scrambling for locally administered relief. Indeed the policy, begun under Herbert Hoover's presidency, of encouraging the mass deportation and repatriation of Mexicans, continued during the New Deal, though amidst some new protections and fuelled more by local than by federal energies. The numbers deported reached the hundreds of thousands, including many native-born US citizens. Mexicans were therefore doubly marginalized in the new welfare state, excluded by job category from benefits and often by "race" from the nation itself. For black Southerners, Social Security Act-based aid came mainly in the form of Aid to Dependent Children (ADC) and old age assistance, administered—and withheld—by the same Dixiecrat local powers that had overseen emergency relief through 1935. As in the earlier period, the results were unprecedented, if still meager, federal benefits, disproportionately directed to white Southerners. In Georgia in 1935, eligible whites were about ten times more likely than eligible blacks to receive ADC payments. As for aid to the elderly who were not covered by social insurance, the Social Security Board somewhat coyly summarized its own failures in 1940 when it concluded that the "number of Negroes to whom aid was granted . . . was low in proportion to the number who needed assistance."

Even so, the tragic irony was that race so structured rates of poverty that African Americans could be both severely discriminated against and slightly overrepresented on the recipient rolls of certain types of welfare. Such was true at times of WPA jobs and, especially in Northern cities, direct relief. Increased aid energized the transition of African Americans from the Republican to the

Democratic Party. Patterns of welfare distribution also had the far more sinister impact of implying that the aid African Americans received was the result of their peculiar indigence—and in the view of white racists, their indolence. Such aid could then be construed as a handout or a make-work scheme, while federal benefits to most white workers could seem the result of their paying in to the system—of their responsible labor and full citizenship. It was particularly around ADC that the myth that the absent black father caused African American poverty coalesced and was at times made a self-fulfilling prophecy by channeling benefits to single-parent households. By 1939, one ADC recipient in six was black, not nearly enough to meet the dire needs of African Americans, but four times the rate at which blacks had accessed pre–New Deal mothers' pensions, and more than plenty to associate the program with race and illegitimacy. Access to even separate and unequal levels of aid opened African Americans to the charge of being the undeserving poor, chiseling away at benefits.

The political scientist Linda Faye Williams has aptly described the New Deal's creation of a "white security state," a situation in which the majority population could claim entitlements while working poor people of color chased arbitrary and episodic welfare payments. A central virtue of Williams's work on the "New (White) Deal," lies in a sure grasp of the fact that such dynamics unfolded on a national scale, not simply as a result of the machinations of Southern conservatives. Williams forces us to realize that an illusion of safety, which James Baldwin puts at the very heart of modern white identity, took shape around who was included and who was excluded in social security at the federal level. She insists that the white security state emerged out of appeals to New Deal constituencies beyond the South.

Nowhere was this more emphatically the case than in labor law reform. While Southern Democrats could plausibly charge that Republicans at times injected racial non-discrimination provisions into reform proposals in order to see them defeated, such was not the case where sponsorship of the National Labor Relations Act

(NLRA) in 1935 was concerned. The progressive Republican senators who joined with New York Democrat Robert Wagner in forwarding the law, wanted it to pass as it stood, containing language that made racial discrimination by unions an unfair labor practice. The NAACP championed the anti-discrimination provision and black organizations broadly warned that enhancing labor's power without addressing the existing and looming racist misuse of power by unions steered a dangerous course.

However, Congress and the Roosevelt administration produced a final version of the NLRA that confirmed the worst fears of civil rights activists. Closed shop contracts, requiring individual union membership in workplaces where workers had voted for a union, received legal protection under Section 9 in the bill. Nothing in the act prevented these closed shops from clandestine, and sometimes open and strident, Jim Crow rules, closed by unions to all but white workers. With the American Federation of Labor (AFL) decisively opposing the act's anti-discriminatory language, the Roosevelt administration agreed to a bill that empowered the National Labor Relations Board to "take . . . affirmative action including reinstatement of employees with or without back pay" when employers breached the law. This colorblind language offered no protection against racial discrimination for workers of color regarding union-based unfair labor practices. Debates over how to structure a seniority system to address past practices of discrimination, or how to open skilled trades to workers of color, would not become a part of union culture even in the more inclusive Congress of Industrial Organizations (CIO) unions that emerged when industrial unions split from craft-based unions after 1935. Indeed a proud boast of the CIO was that it organized "regardless of race"—that is, in a colorblind manner—in industries where white supremacy firmly dominated the status quo. The law asked no more of the unions.

Such colorblind refusals to address discrimination, in the name of passing the most "progressive" legislation possible or of avoiding divisiveness in the union, contributed to huge unemployment among African American workers in the 1930s. In a fascinating mid-1960s speech at Howard University, President Lyndon Johnson retrospectively acknowledged that thirty-five years previously "the rate of unemployment for Negroes and whites was about the same." He continued, "Tonight the Negro rate is twice as high." Johnson might have added that the origins of this pattern lay in the New Deal, during which black women suffered especially great losses in job opportunities, and reformers either ignored or contributed to the problem. Such differentials in employment solidified the notion that African Americans sought handouts rather than work. That notion, developing decisively outside as well as within the South, was driven by racist fantasies but also by specific national policies contributing to job loss and to discrimination in the provision of welfare. In much of the North, where African Americans voted and could successfully demand access to welfare but not to good jobs, ADC payments, in the words of the historian of welfare Michael Brown "coercively substitute[d] relief for jobs." Denied training, the black poor could get a measure of cash relief, fueling yet again the notion that they were among the undeserving poor. When a Connecticut Federal Writers Project worker glossed oral histories in that state he wrote, "The Slovak people as much as the people from other ethnic groups on the block, feel the negro people are treated better by . . . welfare than any other group of people." But such a pattern, when and if it existed, reflected the New Deal's colorblind and white supremacist failures at least as much as its successes.

New Deal housing policy similarly showed that national failures to address racial justice stemmed from more than simply Southern racism. The post–World War I campaigns to enforce residential segregation through the mass signing of restrictive covenants by whites had left the real estate industry, and many homeowners, convinced that stable property values required Jim Crow practices everywhere. While the New Deal never began to budget enough money for housing to address the needs of the third of all Americans whom Roosevelt counted as "ill-housed," its housing policies did manage to set pernicious precedents where race was concerned. Initiatives took place on two tracks.

One set of programs funded highly unequal, overwhelmingly segregated, public housing: the very shoddiness of the structures and crowding of the units could unfairly identify residents as undeserving recipients of welfare. The other track of federal housing policy subsidized and stabilized private homebuyers' loans, the overwhelmingly white recipients of which were cast as embodiments of an American Dream based on individualism, rather than as welfare recipients. Using realty industry guidelines on the quality of neighborhoods, the Home Owners Loan Corporation (HOLC) from 1933 to 1935 and the Federal Housing Administration (FHA) set up in 1934 developed metrics to "grade" the desirability of neighborhoods partly based on their racial composition. The color-coding of FHA maps of the neighborhoods outlined the often African American and/or diverse neighborhoods graded as least desirable in red. Since the lowest grade meant the denial of loans, the term "redline" came into the language to mean the identifying of a neighborhood for unfavorable treatment. The "color line" defined the state-sponsored "redline" more than any other factor. "Segregation," fair housing activist Charles Abrams wrote in 1955, "was not only practiced . . . but openly exhorted" in the federal home loan programs. Rating neighborhoods, the FHA grouped "racial occupancy alongside pollutants like smoke and odors." It offered a model restrictive covenant enforcing segregation and extolled such devices as the "surest possible protection against undesirable encroachment."

Housing, social security, fair labor standards, and labor reform raise critical issues of racial inclusion as well as of exclusion. The Eastern and Southern European workers, whose place in the nation was made so brutally insecure by the race-based immigration restriction campaigns of the mid-1920s, found acceptance as social citizens in the reform and entitlements programs of the following decade. Having massively exercised the right to naturalize as whites, they anchored the New Deal electoral coalition.

The CIO's drive for industrial unions was understood in many places as a "hunky" rebellion, which decisively claimed dignity for recent Eastern European immigrants, and offered new opportunities to exercise union leadership and to secure more skilled jobs. Now the new immigrant woman, a voter, could claim social security and widow's benefits based on marriage to a citizen-worker, at the very moment when the female black or Latino worker could claim no such entitlement based on either the husband's labor or on her own. Across the board, the New Deal state laid down racial guidelines about who was fit for citizenship and who for exclusion. In the realm of housing, although "mixed" city neighborhoods in which varied European immigrant "races" resided together typically received low HOLC and FHA ratings, those groups generally came to have far more access to federal subsidies if they moved beyond the heterogeneous inner cities to suburbs that planners regarded simply as white. The government imprimatur on race-based loans could leave homebuyers believing that they were making federally approved investments in white neighborhoods.

Similarly, CIO practice, unchallenged by the New Deal state and only sporadically confronted even by communist leaders in the unions, was to emphasize organizing interracially mainly at those workplaces that were already relatively integrated. The unions further followed colorblindness by countenancing (and sometimes institutionalizing) covert color bars keeping African Americans out of plants, and out of the best-paid, safest, and cleanest jobs in industries where they could find work. If the industrial unions were to live up to their sometimes glowing egalitarian rhetoric, it was evident that they would do so only in the very long run. The seeds of colorblind inequality, of disunity between "white ethnics" and workers of color, and of what Martin Luther King would call the "tranquilizing drug of gradualism," were present in the very foundations of the New Deal. It can and has been argued that such realities represented as much hope as could be wrung out of the sorry voting and disenfranchising patterns of the 1930s. But the problem for such a sanguine view is that New Deal liberalism not only failed to dismantle connections between government and white supremacy but also reforged those connections in new, modern, mass-based, and enduring forms.

All Deliberate Speed: Race and Liberalism in Wars and Peace

In 1938 the Carnegie Corporation employed the Swedish economist Gunnar Myrdal to begin his massive study of race in the United States. His general thesis that the American Creed of equality might soon be applied across the color line was more grounded in hope than history. Moreover, the prospects for his particular argument, shared with the great American sociologist Robert Park, that the acculturation and acceptance of the immigrant "races" from Europe could predict a similar advance for African Americans, were equally faint: recent New Deal history had afforded yet another example of how such progress was achieved specifically at the expense of African Americans. Ralph Ellison's astringent review of Myrdal's work thus rightly pointed to its tendency to view history as "simply background and not as a functioning force in current society."

But in 1944, when Myrdal's study appeared under the title *An American Dilemma*, the possibility of a new beginning of anti-racism less burdened by history itself seemed somehow plausible. Nazi atrocities against Jews helped call forth widespread usage of the word "racism" for the first time; more limited terms like "bias," "prejudice," or "discrimination" failed to convey the systemic horror involved in that persecution, or the urgent need to oppose bigotry. Many opponents of Hitlerism came to question race supremacy in unprecedented ways while carrying an anti-Nazi war forward. After the defeat of Nazism, with a decolonizing world and a Soviet Cold War enemy watching for US failures to live up to the American Creed, open embraces of racism came to be potentially seen as international embarrassments. World War II saw the Roosevelt administration support what the New Deal would not. The president's 1941 Executive Order 8802 banned discrimination in defense work, and set up the Fair Employment Practices Committee (FEPC) to provide at least some means of enforcing equal treatment in the workplace. During the war a combination of FEPC actions, worker militancy, migration from the South, and acute labor shortages helped to increase black trade union membership to ten times the 1935 figures. In 1943, partly to counter Japanese references to Asian exclusion by the US in anti-American appeals, Congress reversed a tradition of Chinese exclusion that stretched back over seventy years. Such exclusion, President Roosevelt made clear, had been both an "injustice" and an "historic mistake."

Within three years of the armistice, President Harry Truman had set up a committee on Civil Rights and begun the process of desegregating the armed forces. Six years later, when the Court found in *Brown v. Board* that "separate but equal" education was both unconstitutional and impossible within the US racial system, the State Department quickly announced the decision worldwide in planned press releases in multiple languages. The same desire not to be seen as a white supremacist nation—and not to provide grist for Soviet propaganda—animated some provisions of the Immigration and Naturalization Act of 1952, which at long last provided what Mae Ngai has called "colorblind citizenship," extending the possibility for naturalization to Asian groups generally.

In distancing itself from the race supremacy of its Nazi opponents, and then from the charges of racism directed against it by Communist enemies, the US government took wholly unprecedented actions calling white supremacy into question. Cold War liberals developed a new capacity to press their Southern bedfellows for change, on the grounds that ending the worst abuses of Jim Crow was a patriotic move. But although liberalism helped to bring about change, it did so in ways that failed to challenge the fundamentals of white supremacy. Indeed a desire for Cold War national unity could actually lead to further conciliation of white racism, North and South. The ongoing expansion of the welfare state continued to direct benefits overwhelmingly to whites, who often continued to see what they received as earned, and to view aid for people of color as handouts.

Even the FEPC, the greatest war measure for racial justice, was a half-measure. Its record of enforcement was uneven. The inherited New Deal reflex of tailoring programs in the South to the needs of the elite's vision of a low-wage, white supremacist political economy left the pattern of significant African American wage gains during the FEPC years not applying to the region in which most black Americans still lived. Finally, the "war measure" rationale of the FEPC left it vulnerable to demobilization and its existence ended in 1946. The committee itself emerged only after intense wartime pressure from African American trade-union leader A. Philip Randolph, who threatened to mobilize the March on Washington Movement in highly visible wartime protests. Roosevelt's administration had needed no such mass pressure to address the issue of discrimination against white ethnic workers on government jobs, taking action on that issue even before US entry into the war. In the words of historian Richard Steele, the Roosevelt administration viewed anti-black racism as a "complex sociological problem" to be remedied over a lengthy period of time, while anti-ethnic bias was seen as needing to be changed immediately.

When black demands involved getting African Americans into more skilled work, the same logic of unity that undergirded the FEPC could generate caution and gradualism. "Hate strikes" by white workers could stall enforcement of equal treatment by federal officials who feared disrupting the war effort. The 1944 hate strikes that greeted Philadelphia's employment of black workers in motorman jobs, driving vehicles in the public transport system, did produce a case in which a local black movement made gains, forcefully pointing out that "HIROHITO'S BULLETS DRAW NO COLOR LINE," and calling upon the help of the

FEPC, of a radical union, and of intervention by federal troops. But the opposition to black motormen by white, often Irish and new immigrant, workers was intense. Their stance reflected that such workers thought that they lived under a Democratic government committed to white neighborhoods—motormen often lived near the barns they worked out of—and that they had joined unions committed to organizing "regardless of race," not to breaking bars against black skilled employment.

To invoke patriotism as a reason for racial change meant that the issue of race took a back seat to a larger purpose, and had to be fit, gradually, into a national imagination burdened by symbols and social relations that remained anything but transformative. In this way, while the FEPC to some degree protected employment rights of workers of color, the great image of the anti-fascist war worker became Rosie the Riveter, whose name announced her race. Rosie's well-paying wartime industrial job could be portrayed—falsely since women sought good jobs in industry before and after the war—as a sacrifice by a white female anxious to return to the domestic sphere after victory. In a cosmetics advertisement of the period, Rosie appears in blackface, happy though begrimed by work. Her good cheer points towards the product, a cold cream that would remove the dirt and return her to an accustomed white femininity, much as she was seen as awaiting defeat of fascist forces in order to get back to more traditional gender arrangements. But the black worker, veteran of long struggles to secure industrial work, could not symbolize the war worker without bringing up divisive issues: he or she clearly did not want to return to a romanticized normalcy after the war's end.

Despite the limited reforms symbolized by the FEPC, the Roosevelt administration chose to fight an anti-fascist war with a Jim Crow army and navy. The situation on the ground forced black troops into labor battalions, hounded by discriminatory military disciplinary and dishonorable discharge procedures, and suffering systematic abuse in training camps and garrison towns in and beyond the South. "Who wants to fight," NAACP leader Roy Wilkins asked during the war, "for the kind of 'democracy' embodied in the hair-trigger pistols, and the clubs of the Negro-hating hoodlums in the uniforms of military police?" The massive Southern Californian Zoot Suit Riots of 1943, in which white servicemen attacked young people of color for wearing extra-vagant "unpatriotic" clothing, showed that this violence extended to Mexican-American youth, with the first victims being two boys aged twelve and thirteen years. Stirring campaigns for "double victory"—against both Hitlerism abroad and racism at home— were met by official responses stressing progress and telling African Americans that their "future, like the future of all freedom lovers, depends upon the triumph of democracy." Anti-racism, on this view, should wait for gradual future progress.

Such a perspective would continue to hold sway in the Cold War. In 1955 the Supreme Court revisited *Brown v. Board* in a *Brown II* case focusing on determining appropriate measures to relieve the segregation made illegal under the earlier ruling. In deciding to send cases back to lower courts, the justices added the proviso that desegregation should proceed "with all deliberate speed." Even speed, in this important phrasing, could be, and was, slowed to a gradualist crawl. Such contradictory language broke from a long tradition in which, as NAACP General Counsel Robert Carter observed, constitutional law conceived protected rights as "personal and present." Instead, legal theorist Cheryl Harris writes, the Court predicated the pace and scope of relief "not on the nature of the injury to Black children," but on the "level of white resistance" anticipated. Harris makes the important case that the Court's wording stemmed from an inability to break with a long line of decisions and realities that recognized "white-ness as property." But in adopting "an approach that invited defiance and delay," the Court also reflected the limits of logic tethering civil rights to Cold War nationalism. Since resistance by racists would lay bare national disunity regarding race, change had to occur at a deliberate pace. Du Bois was undoubtedly correct in his assessment that the "world pressure of communism" decisively contributed to the first *Brown v. Board* decision; however, the imperative of national unity and the habit of white supremacy in the Cold War equally structured the ways in which *Brown II* made "the tranquilizing drug of gradualism" into the law of the land.

The logic of pressing for racial justice by emphasizing wartime sacrifices and Cold War goals not only underwrote gradualist approaches to addressing old injustices but also produced new arenas for race-thinking and oppression. In World War II, the fate of anti-Asian racism included far more than the reversal of Chinese exclusion: at the same time, the US government forced 120,000 Japanese Americans—only 40,000 of whom were classed as enemy aliens—into incarceration camps. Although Italian Americans made up two-thirds of all those bureaucratically classified as enemy aliens, they managed to deflect the blanket punishment that language implied, furnishing only a seventh of those put in camps. An NAACP publication at the time found the disparity in rates of incarceration between Japanese Americans and Italian Americans to result from "barbarous treatment" caused by a drawing of the "color line" against the Japanese.

In the series of low-intensity conflicts taking place in Asia during the Cold War period, militarism, empire and the re-production of anti-Asian racism were intertwined. The sneering, dehumanizing epithet "gook," with its roots in the early twentieth-century US occupation of the Philippines, was used by US troops during various invasions in Asia and elsewhere, slurring Haitians and Nicaraguans, for example, before World War II. In the Korean War, the wholesale use of "gook" to describe the enemy, and Asians generally, proved embarrassing enough for General Douglas MacArthur to hold that the term gave "aid and comfort to the enemy" and to forbid its use. The opposite was to happen in Vietnam, with one celebrated veteran, Senator John McCain, defending his own continued reliance on "gook" until well into his 2000 campaign for the

Republican presidential nomination. It applied, he held, to bad Asians but not to good ones.

While the 1952 Immigration and Naturalization Act broke the US from a 160-year tradition tying naturalized citizenship to race, its origins and content perfectly illustrate Mae Ngai's point that the Cold War simultaneously both opened and closed space where anti-immigrant racism was concerned. Immediately after the war, with the costs of US refusals to accept Jewish immigrants still fresh in the nation's memory, anti-communism and a lingering commitment to the 1924 immigration restrictions targeting Eastern and Southern Europeans stopped the US from adopting a substantially more open immigration policy towards those fleeing what was increasingly called totalitarianism. The 1948 Displaced Persons Act proved so limited in scope, and so intent on counting the migrants from Eastern and Southern Europe displaced by war against the discriminatory quotas established for their groups after 1924, that Truman signed it only "with very great reluctance." Portentously, the bill also foregrounded nationalist needs: 30 percent of Displaced Persons were required to be agricultural workers and preferences for professionals and the highly skilled also obtained. Efforts to bring Estonian, Latvian, and Lithuanian anti-communist refugees to the US initially ran up against such strong opposition, in the form of "Nordic" supremacists and media-driven fears of Communist spies, as to necessitate educational efforts to portray Baltic peoples as among the world's whitest and most freedom-loving. Unsurprisingly, those fleeing the Chinese Revolution fared worse, unable to receive such a makeover.

The 1952 act's cosponsors, Pat McCarran and Francis Walter, stood among the most conservative Democrats in Congress, the former being an ardent admirer of the Spanish dictator Franco, and the latter heading the Pioneer Fund, sponsor of much suspect eugenics research on race, nationality, and IQ. Both divided their passions between pursuing "un-Americans" in the US and regulating immigrants. McCarran had sponsored the infamous

Internal Security Act of 1950, which included provisions for radicals to be detained in concentration camps. But in 1952 they were both aware enough of a watching world to explicitly stress that their cosponsorship of the act was not motivated by "any theory of Nordic superiority," citing instead the need for a national "similarity of cultural background." This implied the continuation of discriminatory quotas where Eastern and Southern Europeans were concerned, and near-exclusion of those in the Asian Pacific Triangle, who were awarded tiny annual quotas of one hundred people per Asian country. Fully half of all places went to those with specialized skills that were sought after in the US.

The 1952 act passed only over the veto of Truman, who sought a more liberal bill. In response the president created the Commission on Immigration and Naturalization, which in 1953 began to serve as a focus for the powerful ongoing critique of what Truman had called the "dead hand" of old immigration policies. The critique, put forward by a coalition led by the Harvard historian Oscar Handlin, produced compelling research and impressive political action, but its central mission was to refight the battles of the 1920s. With mainstream organizations of white ethnic groups energizing the coalition, the critique emphasized removing the stigma of past and present quotas from Eastern and Southern European groups that had come to be seen far more solidly as white since 1924. Trying to ensure that the nation be seen as more than Nordic in its heritage, the immigration reformers of the 1950s and 1960s had their sights much set on intra-European matters. The eventual 1965 legislative reforms thus paid little attention to the bill's possible effects on immigration from Latin America, the West Indies, and Asia. The openings created for additional entry from those areas were more a result of miscalculations about potential immigrants' facility to relocate than a mark of considered and dramatic liberalization of immigration policy as it applied to migrants from beyond Europe.

Indeed in the key case of Mexican immigration in the 1950s and 1960s liberals were, as today, deeply split over possible regulations.

From 1948 until its termination in 1964, the Bracero Program institutionalized much of the importation of Mexican immigrant labor under the auspices of the US government in cooperation with the Mexican state. The program brought to the US an annual average of 200,000 Mexicans as temporary workers designed to meet the perceived need of agribusiness for what Ngai calls a "steady oversupply of cheap farm labor"—that is, a level acting to depress wage rates. Championed by Truman's liberal Fair Deal administration as an alternative to illegal "wetback" immigration—the racist term implied swimming or wading to the US without authorization, identifying the body itself as unlawful—the Bracero initiative had its roots in early 1940s war production. Involving nominal civil rights and contract protections for the incoming workers, but no prospect of citizenship, the program might be seen as expressing some priorities of Cold War liberalism, but bringing in Braceros was firmly opposed by liberal labor groups in the US, who viewed it as a roadblock to organizing agricultural workers, and by many mainstream liberals, reacting to highly publicized abuses.

Moreover, the Bracero Program did not prevent illegal immigration or the victimization of Mexican-American citizens. Growers preferred utterly rightless labor to Braceros, or they preferred to have mixtures of the two compete for work. McCarran, so fretful about security and threats to civilization in general, spoke up for the farmer's right to "get a wetback." In fact, the distinction between Bracero workers, defined as legal but without citizenship, and illegal immigrants became increasingly blurred. Braceros, former Braceros who had become illegal because of overstaying, and illegal "wetbacks" worked in the same places and sometimes lived in the same households. Adding to the confusion, immigration officials occasionally affected on-the-ground amnesties, forcing "illegal" workers back across the border briefly, and then processing their entry as legal to stabilize the supply of legal labor in an area. But despite attempts at the time by organizations of often long-settled and middle-class Mexican

Americans to draw firm lines between themselves and newcomers, repression against "wetbacks" reflected and increased a more generalized anti-Mexican racism combining biology, nationality, and legality. By 1954, the policy acquired a harder edge in "Operation Wetback," in which General Joseph Swing deployed military methods and technology to deport over 800,000 Mexicans in two years. At the time, the general's proposal for a border fence to keep out Mexican immigrants seemed a bad idea to the State Department, which saw it as a likely target of Soviet propaganda.

Although Cold War liberalism's insistence that the US not be embarrassed as racist in the eyes of the world opened up ways of moving beyond capitulations to Southern racists, anticommunism also greatly impoverished anti-racist freedom movements at the levels of ideas and of leadership. To say this is not to endorse the sometimes extravagant claims by historians that Cold War hysteria stopped in its tracks a happy process in which the CIO unions stood on the verge of unifying the labor and civil rights movements. Such a view not only mistakes a few swallows for spring, but denies the considerable presence of chickenhawks in the union movement where labor and antiracism were concerned. Only infrequently had CIO unions broken from the "regardless of race" organizing on which they were premised. Their failed postwar effort to unionize the South, Operation Dixie, which ran from 1946 to 1953, showed little appetite for raising questions of racial justice, choosing instead to focus on the nearly all-white textile industry. Operation Dixie largely excluded left-wing organizers, who in certain times and places, especially in packing, tobacco processing, and the Southern steel industry, did push more strongly and even heroically against Jim Crow. However even the left-led unions—by 1950 eleven of them would be expelled from the CIO for communist ties—had a mixed record on anti-racism. Union leaders in the Communist Party had seen their organization abstain, in the name of national unity, from more militant phases of the "double victory" campaign during the war. The communists opposed the wartime March on Washington Movement as divisive, and failed to speak and organize against incarceration of Japanese Americans.

The possibility—energized by the massive entry into the NAACP of workers who got well-paying unionized industrial jobs in the war and of black veterans who had traveled and fought internationally—of strong, direct solidarity between African American labor and anti-colonial movements was specifically undermined by Cold War anti-communism. Prosecuting and persecuting the African American leaders most able to speak to the intersections of labor and race, the Cold War state isolated the very leaders most able to articulate intellectually why colorblind, "regardless of race" policies would not eliminate white supremacy. Those victimized leaders, some communists and others not, included C. L. R. James, Paul Robeson, Alphaeus Hunton, and, above all, Claudia Jones and W. E. B. Du Bois. They were likewise the activists best positioned to put US anti-racism in dialogue with wider anti-imperial struggles, and to develop ties among racialized groups in the US.

Contradictions abounded as the Cold War simultaneously created and curtailed space for freedom movements. Even as the post–World War II Supreme Court undermined restrictive covenants, the FHA nonetheless continued to hope for ways to use them, and the federal government vastly increased its subsidizing of new and overwhelmingly segregated suburbs to which millions moved. The FHA's work, as one NAACP official wrote as early as 1948, did "more than any other instrumentality to force nonwhite citizens into substandard housing and neighborhoods." One FHA underwriting manual counted as "equally objectionable" the presence in white neighborhoods of "pigpens" and of "unwelcome races." As Myrdal himself came to realize, all reforms based on allegedly colorblind "ordinary business principles" would reproduce inequalities already in place. Housing policy bent much further in the direction of white supremacy, with its subsidies providing a basis for inherited wealth subsequently passed from generation to generation among white Americans but denied to nonwhites.

Nor did African Americans' armed service against the Nazis or in the Cold War produce relief from discrimination. The general provisions of the GI Bill providing benefits to veterans from its original passage in 1944 followed New Deal precedents: its colorblindness inhered in its omission of language requiring nondiscrimination. Thus the law's nation-changing provision of educational aid to former servicemen was funneled into a system of Jim Crow education in the South, and one of only meager inclusion of students of color in the leading institutions of higher learning throughout the country. While trade schools may have been more open to students of color, union jobs in the trades seldom were. After World War II, new Veterans Administration-approved home loan packages followed HOLC and FHA precedents in racially grading and redlining practices that extended existing equality and gave racial preferences a connection to patriotic military service. As the President's Committee on Civil Rights reported in 1947, prevailing practices brought together "interlocking" barriers founded in federal policy, "business customs," and "public agitation," all arrayed against fair housing.

The dream suburban house—typically subsidized and often seen as a reward for whites' military service, while being off-limits to nonwhites—came to symbolize what was being fought for in the Cold War and what was said to produce security for families. Thus when Vice-President Richard Nixon confronted the Soviet leader Nikita Khrushchev regarding the inevitability of US triumph he chose to do so most stridently precisely in a manufacturer's display of an American dream kitchen, the very incarnation of US superiority. One developer of suburban housing subdivisions told *Time* in 1947 that children raised in this environment "will go out and fight Communism." In 1954, the Civil Defense Administration made the connections among home, security, and patriotism explicit and bizarre. Its film, *The House in the Middle*, staged a nuclear test with three small display houses located as if they were "on the outer fringe of an attack directed against a nearby city"—that is, in a suburb. The well-kept, freshly painted house withstood attack; the others were destroyed. The defense administrator's voiceover closed by driving the point home: "The white house in the middle survived."

The suburban home also enclosed so much else, from the empty lives of housewives to the sad conformity that the "free world" too often generated. Frequently an attraction to black culture gave some direction to the flight from such homes and such conformity, with beatniks, hippies, rock and rollers, and women liberationists as noteworthy examples. But as a national symbol the suburban white house remained the privileged place to be a consuming, entitled, and white Cold War citizen, leaving those excluded on racial grounds as less-than-citizens yet again, even as some of the old exclusions began to give way.

Cold War military spending meanwhile stimulated the Southern economy in a way that gave racist Democratic leaders there a new lease on life. The rapid economic development of the South following World War II featured Democratic leadership in securing military appropriations, locating bases and war industries in the region. The most effective advocates of the region were congressmen from one-party Southern states, elected again and again. They commanded influence, particularly on the Armed Services Committees, based on seniority. The backwardness of such figures regarding race was tied in the 1930s to their representation of a failing sharecropping system, but in the Cold War white supremacist Democrats stood for a kind of regional economic progress.

After 1964 and 1965:
Liberal Anti-Racism's Apex and its Wake

In the 2008 Democratic primary campaign between Barack Obama and Hillary Clinton the candidates quarreled over who should gain credit for the civil rights legislation of the mid-1960s. Obama praised the visionary leadership of Martin Luther King, while Clinton foregrounded President Lyndon Johnson, casting him as the political stalwart who transformed "dreams" into public policy. Unsurprisingly, both fixed on the mid-1960s as the apogee of racial liberalism. Responding to freedom struggles, the passing of the 1964 Civil Rights Act and the Voting Rights Act of 1965 signified the high-water mark of civil rights legislation. Subsequently, only the Fair Housing Act of 1968, passed after King's murder, bears comparison to these dramatic legislative milestones against racism. The Cold War state much more typically took its moderate anti-racist actions through courts and bureaucracies than through open debates by lawmakers. The 1964 and 1965 laws themselves were principally expressions of colorblind policies, prescribing equal treatment in public facilities, in jobs, and in voting. But they passed as Johnson announced a War on Poverty that invited participation by the minority poor. Thus for a time Congress and the president seemed ready to implement both colorblind fairness and positive action to remedy past effects of discrimination.

Many deserved credit for bringing about the sharp breaks with the national history of white supremacy that occurred in the mid-1960s. Some Republicans today rightly applaud their party for providing decisive support for civil rights and voting rights since votes from within their ranks made up for the continued hardcore opposition of Southern Democrats to passing the measures. Johnson's substantial contribution lay not only in providing leadership to those who, like himself, were on the margins of the white Solid South and ready to break with Jim Crow, but also in his dexterous management of the Democratic Party's break with its long-term attempts to reconcile Cold War liberalism and "strange bedfellows" in the Deep South. More than any politician of his time, Johnson knew the risks of losing "white votes" involved, and he took them.

Johnson's response to the prospect of losing the South as a base of Democratic support was to offer something for everyone, coupling 1964 civil rights and anti-poverty measures with what are now called "business Keynesian" or "supply-side" tax cuts, an inherited Kennedy policy designed to stimulate growth and to attract corporate support and conservative voters. Johnson's Great Society initiatives also included health programs for the aged and poor with benefits cutting across class and race lines. In the short term, the tax cuts coincided with an economic boom generating unprecedented revenues that funded reforms. The idea that social programs could be paid for out of economic growth rather than redistributions of wealth became a bipartisan article of faith, even as war-related deficits fed inflationary pressures and as business leaders by the early 1970s clarified their unwillingness to finance rising social and infrastructural expenses. If new entitlements, conservative tax policy, and the common purpose of imperial war seemed able to make the risks of political realignment around race manageable for the Democrats in the very short term, such factors conspired to compound the problems of Johnson and his party in the longer run.

To say that Johnson took great risks in pursuit of racial justice does not, however, mitigate the implausibility and moral obtuseness of Clinton's comments, insofar as she tended to make Johnson a roughly equal partner with King in producing the triumph of civil rights legislation. While Johnson was, to borrow Lerone Bennett's phrase, "forced into glory," it was the civil rights strugglers, symbolized by Dr. King, who did the forcing. As has already been made clear, the logic of New Deal liberalism, and its evolution in the Cold War period, fell well short of challenging the tranquilizing drug of gradualism. Between 1941 and 1964, the great majority of African Americans who gained voting rights and access to more equal schools and welfare benefits did so by themselves moving north or west, not by seeing liberalism move against Southern racism. The furious pace of Johnson-era civil rights legislation reflected not a natural evolution of liberalism but a sharp, brief break from gradualism. The willingness to face jails and mob violence by numberless sit-in civil rights protesters and Freedom Riders brought about that break.

Since the first stirrings of postwar decolonization, civil rights movement activists in the US had thought long and hard about the success of Third World nations such as Ghana in emphasizing the simple word "NOW" in their demands to end imperial rule. The US slogan "FREEDOM NOW," popularized by Dr. King and others, dramatically challenged approaches urging African Americans to wait for justice to unfold gradually. Liberal Democrats at times allied themselves with such an urgent stance, but also acted as a brake on it, most notoriously in their refusal to seat the full Mississippi Freedom Democratic slate of delegates at the 1964 Democratic convention, opting instead for recognizing the whites-only slate chosen through traditional Jim Crow practices. King was then threatened with loss of financial support from union and liberal funders should he act strongly in solidarity with the Freedom Democrats.

Sometimes the central civil rights slogans broke decisively with Cold War racial liberalism, with the spectacular 1963 March on Washington demanding both jobs and freedom now. Dr. King's celebrated speech at the march outlined the "dream" that African Americans might redeem the "bad check" of US government promises, materially as well as legally. Even before the ghetto rebellions and Black Power later in the 1960s, Malcolm X was thus only one among many voices raised to make racial justice focus on much more than demands for desegregated access to public spaces such as lunch counters. As the pro-freedom struggle *Southern Patriot* put it in 1960, reflecting on the words of the great African American organizer Ella Baker, the movement was about "much more than a hamburger or even a giant-sized Coke."

The weight of such protests forced into existence a dramatic new set of policies that began what anti-poverty expert Michael Harrington called a "social war" against want, a campaign that forced liberalism itself to briefly move beyond colorblindness. Writing as both a participant in, and moderate socialist critic of, Democratic Party efforts at anti-poverty reform, Harrington documented the changes that for a time made Johnson's War on Poverty real. In his 1962 exposé *The Other America*, Harrington poignantly captured the extent of poverty and what it meant to live below the poverty line in the US. But in keeping with New Deal precedents, the book foregrounded the white, especially Appalachian, poor. It included scant descriptions and even less analysis of black poverty. In post-1964 editions of the book Harrington registered the change wrought by the freedom movement, portraying in his new introduction an anti-poverty energy emerging out of Chicano and Filipino farm-workers' struggles and African American civil rights campaigns.

Having launched the War on Poverty with his first State of the Union address in January of 1964, Johnson used his commencement address at Howard University the following year to spell out why such a war had to include a comprehensive reckoning with the racial past of liberalism. He listed many indices showing that New Deal and Cold War reforms had failed to address racial inequality and had often deepened it. Democratic leaders well understood how local control had been used to undermine African American interests. When Johnson signed a 1964 act creating the Office of Economic Opportunity (OEO) as the centerpiece of the War on Poverty, the language of the legislation acted to foster change, requiring "maximum feasible participation" by the poor themselves. Given the contours of social movements at the time, and the racial distribution of poverty, such a provision opened dramatic possibilities for poor people of color. As urban African American-led rebellions increased in and after 1964, most famously in places like Watts, Detroit, and Newark, the OEO's short-lived turn towards incorporating community and movement organizations into economic opportunity programs matured, especially in the more than 1,000 Community Action Agencies it funded locally. The policy seemed to some an essential strategy for offering an alternative to militant protest and to others an empowerment of the rebels themselves.

Given these cross-pressures, OEO would not last a decade. The idea of "maximum feasible participation" challenged not only the white supremacist Democratic patronage systems in the Deep South but also those of liberal Democratic machines in big Northern cities. By late 1965, Chicago Mayor Richard Daley was complaining that agitation by community groups over War on Poverty resources was "kicking the hell out of us," even as he absolutely controlled distribution of the federal funds. As *Time* nicely observed, "it took the Watts riots" to make Los Angeles Mayor Sam Yorty add just seven members from minority community organizations to his thirty-five person poverty board. In Syracuse, OEO was scarcely a year old when, under pressure from the White House, it reigned in a Syracuse program using federal funds to bail protesters out of jail. "As early as 1966," journalist Roger Morris has written, OEO critics "began trooping in numbers through the Old Executive Office Building—liberal and conservative but uniformly self-preserving, the single party of incumbent power." OEO head Sargent Shriver unsuccessfully struggled under such increasing pressures to preserve something of "maximum feasible participation."

When Richard Nixon became president in 1969, he trained extraordinary firepower on OEO. Three future secretaries of defense presided over its burial. Donald Rumsfeld left Congress to head the OEO. His aides, Dick Cheney and Frank Carlucci, worked in an office in which Rumsfeld was called "The Undertaker" of the very agency he headed. Cheney, then a young intern, wrote a decisive planning memo outlining a strategy of gutting the individual OEO programs. Carlucci, who eventually succeeded Rumsfeld at the helm of the sinking OEO, brought experience in fomenting coups, most notably and infamously in the early 1960s in the Congo. This extraordinary overkill of OEO, and the absence of energetic liberal Democratic defense of the agency, suggests that the War on Poverty's reach beyond colorblind formal equality touched raw nerves across political divides.

As a whole, the War on Poverty could claim some successes, but not in severing the links of race and inequality. In the decade after

OEO began, the poverty rate fell from 22.4 percent of the population to 11.1 percent. Since 1973, poverty figures have ranged up from one American in nine to nearly one in six, but they have not approached levels from the 1950s and early 1960s. During the OEO years and after, poverty remained starkly tied to race. From 1966 until 1973, the black poverty rate fell more slowly than that of the general population—indeed, there was actually an increase in black poverty in relative terms. In 1959, black Americans were three times as likely to be in poverty as whites; they were 3.7 times as likely in 1966 and four times as likely in 1973. The gulf in unemployment rates across racial lines, which had opened up during the Great Depression, also failed to erode in the wake of the War on Poverty. Indeed as capital was reinvested in worker-displacing technologies, in nonunion areas in the US, and in plants abroad, good industrial jobs began disappearing just as they were partially opening up to workers of color. Meanwhile, some of the newly activist liberal states' actions—encouraging movement of jobs to suburbs, and financing urban renewal schemes that destroyed minority communities—served to reproduce and extend patterns of inequality. A 1969 presidential report reminded readers that, to date, government policies "had destroyed more housing for the poor than [they have] built."

The historical roots of such failures were global as well as national. Johnson's war-making actions in 1964 and 1965 deeply compromised any possibility of effective liberal anti-racism. In 1964, his administration fabricated the Gulf of Tonkin incident, an alleged attack on two US Navy destroyers by North Vietnamese forces, as a pretext to acquire a blank check for full funding for a much-expanded war in Vietnam. In the middle of 1964, the US had just over 21,000 troops in Vietnam, a figure that would increase six-fold by the end of 1965, and triple again by the end of 1968, reaching almost 600,000 soldiers before Johnson left office. Johnson's 1967 budget request for all anti-poverty programs totaled $1.75 billion. By 1975, the Vietnam War had cost 100 times that amount. "Tens of billions of dollars," Harrington wrote, "were not channeled into the right war at home but the wrong one in Southeast Asia."

Acute as was Harrington's indictment of Johnson's choice of "guns over butter," that choice was less a betrayal of liberalism than an expression of its dominant Cold War forms and priorities. The policies of prioritizing immediatism for funding anti-communism abroad and of settling for gradualism in anti-poverty and anti-racism at home bespoke liberal commitments to US economic hegemony. Guns—that is, the massive military spending widely believed at the time to stimulate the economy—promised to deliver unity among the various trade-union, African American, Southern and corporate Democrats around an agenda of full employment and economic growth. Tax cuts and increases in military spending—business and military Keynesianism—had emerged as the key ways to plan growth. Johnson's aides relied on such mechanisms in their assumption that guns and butter could coexist. The unions, advised by the leading US military Keynesian policy expert, Leon Keyserling, joined the Democratic presidential candidate Hubert Humphrey in foregrounding full employment as the central issue of the 1968 presidential campaign. Indeed even while Harrington sharply denounced the war, describing how it had undermined 1960s liberalism, he took care to point out not only that most white Northern workers voted for Humphrey in 1968, but also that the war itself had staved off social crisis, creating a million defense-industry jobs and 700,000 more in the military.

Nixon's "Southern Strategy," developed in and after the 1968 campaign in concert with the young political strategist Kevin Phillips, actually had ambitions far beyond the region for which it was named. That strategy—like the reactionary populist presidential campaigns of the famously segregationist Alabama Governor George Wallace inside and outside the Democratic Party in 1964, 1968, and 1972—appealed in all regions to voters said to be influenced by what was increasingly being called a "white backlash" against anti-racist initiatives and militant protest.

Robert Kennedy had written that his brother's administration, in considering early versions of voting rights legislation, feared losing two conservative votes for each African American and progressive one gained, and particularly projected losses in Northern suburbs and cities. Nixon, Phillips, and Wallace tried to insure that such losses for liberals materialized. Even within the South the focus was as much on metropolitan areas as the countryside. Indeed, as the historian Matthew Lassiter has demonstrated, growing government-subsidized suburbs in the South and West were among the key battlegrounds and seedbeds of a newly powerful national conservative movement. Southern suburban voters articulated "an exclusionary brand of homeowner populism grounded in class privileges and racial barriers" that resonated in the North. Once again the South was not simply the strange bedfellow of a racially progressive North. Indeed frequently enough Dixie became a bellwether for the national forms that retreats from racial justice would take.

The Wallace candidacies of 1968 and 1972, like Nixon's victorious campaigns in those years, played successfully on racially laden fears embedded in broader issues. These included urban crime, "forced" busing to integrate schools, and the presence of allegedly irresponsible "welfare mothers." Welfare had particular appeals as an object of conservative attack because it could be tethered to the issue of taxation, in ways implying that butter for the poor cost taxpayers money, whereas guns for the military did not. Such sentiments echoed popularly in the 1970s, a decade when middle-class tax revolts raged, culminating with the passage of California's anti-tax Proposition 13 in 1978. Resort to such racial "code words" as crime, busing, welfare, and taxes, rather than to open expression of racial hostilities, showed how thoroughly the moral high ground of debate had been captured by the civil rights movement. But the code words worked, ushering in a long period in which the feints and signals by both major parties as they made indirect appeals to white voters rendered it difficult to have real and open political debate addressing racial inequality.

The Republicans, it must be said, knew the codes better than the Democrats. Reagan opened his 1980 campaign in Philadelphia, Mississippi without a word of the infamous murders of civil rights workers there in the 1960s, and obsessively retailed crafted tales of "welfare queens," who allegedly grew rich by defrauding the system. George Herbert Walker Bush's 1988 campaign advertisements featured Willie Horton, a convict who committed crimes while furloughed from a Massachusetts prison in a program approved by Democratic presidential candidate Michael Dukakis. Lee Atwater, the publicist behind the promotion, set out to make Horton, the personification of black crime and menace to white womanhood, seem like Dukakis's "running mate." But the Democrats also had their own moments of attempted appeals to racially coded issues, from Jimmy Carter's 1976 homage to the importance of "ethnic purity," to Bill Clinton's gratuitous attack on the rapper Sister Souljah, and his hectoring speeches on personal morality to black audiences in 1992. More serious than such rhetorical and symbolic ventures have been Democratic attempts to wrest racially laden issues from Republicans by adopting conservative positions, so that Clinton's administrations became the instruments for "ending welfare as we know it" and, despite overwhelming evidence of racism in sentencing, for the "effective death penalty" legislation of 1996.

Affirmative action, the main "wedge issue" dividing voters over race since 1969, took shape during a moment when the Nixon administration posed itself as a liberalizing force. Indeed when Nixon died in 1994, *Fortune* remembered the "incredible but true" story of his administration giving the nation "employment quotas" regarding race. The truth was somewhat more complicated, in that "quotas" themselves had already been found legally untenable in a series of rulings growing out of the language on "preferential treatment" in Title 7 Section J of the 1964 Civil Rights Act. So strong was the wording of that passage, and so explicit the denial of any intent of racial preferences by Democratic leader Senator Hubert Humphrey in debates on the bill, that those in the Johnson administration wanting to attach firm numbers to plans to desegregate the skilled construction trades had to abandon such plans in cities like St. Louis, Cleveland, and Philadelphia. With many of the black leaders, from King to Fred Hampton, then placing their energy in organizing broad multi-racial movements as vehicles to empower the poor and to then address both white supremacy and class injustices, the immediate fate of "quotas" seemed a secondary issue.

But Nixon, on taking office in 1969, subverted the OEO even as he resurrected Johnson's abandoned Philadelphia Plan to desegregate the building trades in that city, finding language to circumvent explicit reference to quotas. Although applying to just hundreds of jobs initially, the plan had great symbolic impact—the building trades so expressed craft-union racism as to make James Baldwin doubt that there was a labor movement in the US at all—and effectively divided trade-union and African American Democratic constituencies. Some Nixon scholars find evidence that the Philadelphia Plan expressed a longstanding and continuing commitment by the president to a dying strain of moderate Republican anti-racism. This certainly was the case with Arthur Fletcher, the dynamic black liberal Republican who provided much of the plan's language and who spoke of it as a continuation of Dr. King's work. But the larger truth is that Nixonian affirmative action matured in the thrall of a presidency committed to a Southern strategy of coded racism and to dividing and conquering his enemies. Moreover, by 1970, Nixon's Democratic adviser, Daniel Patrick Moynihan, urged a period of "benign neglect" of supposedly overly polarizing questions of racial justice. When New York City construction workers staged a 1970 "hardhat" demonstration in support of hawkish Vietnam War policies, the subsequent federal agreement covering their labor required no Philadelphia-style affirmative action. The Philadelphia Plan and Fletcher were both gone by 1973. Affirmative action thus implied at best a return to a gradualist approach to racial justice and an atmosphere of partisan angling for advantage.

Liberal Democrats soon became the reluctant custodians of affirmative action, as Republicans turned increasingly against the initiatives that Nixon had helped to instigate, branding them forms of "reverse racism." Reagan was an especially effective and insistent enemy of largely non-existent "quotas." Indeed it was in opposition to affirmative action that Republicans, who had devised the close-mouthed Nixon strategy of appealing to white voters by using coded rather than direct language and by deploying the notion of a "Silent Majority" of conservative whites opposed to noisy civil rights advocates, now started to emerge as the party more openly discussing race and policy. Conservatives claimed for themselves the mantle of colorblindness. They won important referenda against affirmative action in California in 1996, Washington in 1998, and Michigan in 2006 by identifying their proposals as race-transcending "civil rights initiatives," implausibly but confidently implying that the same Dr. King, who had insisted that the bad check of US faithlessness towards black Americans be redeemed, would have supported right-wing attacks on affirmative action.

That the appeals of Ronald Reagan attracted large numbers of white working-class and even unionized voters brought urgent soul-searching and focus-group polling among Democratic strategists. Reagan's sure command of divisive code words such as "state's rights," "welfare moms," "quotas," and "reverse racism" came to be seen as key to his success at winning over "Reagan Democrats" via racial appeals. The center-right Democratic Leadership Council and its political strategist Stanley Greenberg argued, especially in the context of the 1992 presidential campaign, that among disaffected white workers progressive symbols had been thoroughly "redefined in racial and pejorative terms." Thus only a return to "universal" rather than "race specific" policies could win them back into the Democratic column. Assurances, on this view, had to be offered that the Democrats would not again stray past colorblind formal equality where race was concerned.

Significantly, Greenberg defined the problem as being the racial terms in which programs were understood by whites, rather than the programs' actual content. The most backward, ungrounded, and self-defeating assumptions of Reagan Democrats thus became arenas not for education—the sort of ambitious, egalitarian, class-based policies that would have invited a more open discussion of race with white workers were well buried—but for accommodation. Thus Clinton waited until 1995 to give a major speech on affirmative action and then offered a tepid "mend, don't end" defense of a scaled-down version of a policy already greatly constrained by judicial rulings. Central to the problem of the speech, to the Clinton administration's policies in the area, and to the unwillingness of the Democratic Party to respond vigorously to right-wing anti-affirmative referenda in the late 1990s, was the acceptance of the notion that affirmative action was a race-based program, because some Reagan supporters saw it that way. In fact, white women were the largest single class of its beneficiaries, and veterans also benefited from affirmative action. Similarly, ending "welfare as we know it" became another Clinton priority, in large measure because Aid to Dependent Children was widely seen as a race-based policy, although it of course applied to all groups and its benefits were widely accessed by whites.

While the Clinton-Greenberg strategy strove to answer charges that the Democratic Party was elitist and meddlesome regarding race, in practice it risked having the opposite effect. The Democrats left whatever weak defense of affirmative action did occur, beyond efforts by civil rights organizations themselves, to corporations, elite universities, and military brass. They made the federal courts the focus of affirmative action controversies, with Democrats often campaigning for office on promises to keep conservatives out of positions of judicial authority rather than by proposing any clearly articulated anti-racist agenda. While the right wing branded court decisions on race, and particularly on desegregation of some urban schools, as the leading edge of a liberal conspiracy, the Democratic reliance on litigation by the Department of Justice, other government agencies, and private civil rights groups as the central anti-racist strategy actually signaled and exacerbated the weakness of commitments to building a broad movement addressing inequality. Liberal anti-racism lost its residual moral force by not clearly speaking out in efforts to win the public to anti-racist positions.

Moreover, the reliance on the courts made meaningful coalitions, and even intelligent descriptions of problems, difficult to achieve because of the ways that the legal system required plaintiff groups to be constituted. The production of a "class" with standing in lawsuits focused matters starkly on oversimplified categories—"Women," "African Americans," and "Hispanics." These groups could be represented as a side in a lawsuit, but only if they marched alone in isolation from other groups. Courts therefore proved poor venues for articulating black-Latino unity, for example, and worse ones for considering how oppressions intersected in the real lives, for example, of Afro-Puerto Rican women. Of course social class could play no role in structuring how a "class" with standing in court was constituted. Addressing what feminists of color call the "intersectionality" of oppressions was out of bounds.

Democratic eagerness to rely on the courts, and the party's attempts to disarm racially laden issues by moving towards conservative positions, had especially dire consequences where crime and incarceration were concerned. Indeed in no other arenas of race and public policy has the terrible impact of what is unspoken by liberals, and of what is spoken and suggested by conservatives, been more clear. Between 1976 and 2000, the highly publicized anti-crime initiatives pioneered by Barry Goldwater and Nixon in the 1960s became fully bipartisan. Incarceration rates skyrocketed and highly racialized anti-crime political appeals, Democratic and Republican, proliferated precisely during the last quarter of the twentieth century, a period when Democrats held the presidency half the time and had overwhelming power in Congress and the states. In 1975, incarceration rates stood nationally at about 1 per

1,000 people; by 2005 they had reached over 7 per 1,000. The rise in the black inmate population was especially catastrophic. At the time of the 1954 *Brown v. Board* decision, only 98,000 African Americans were in prison, and for twenty years this number grew only in rough parity to the population. But between 1975 and 2004 a nearly six-fold increase occurred. Today 60 percent of the prison population consists of people of color, with African American men seven times more likely to be imprisoned than white men, and Hispanic men three times more likely.

A perfect storm of racism, highly publicized crime increases, political demagoguery, illusions that economically failing small towns could rebound through hosting prisons, prison industry lobbying, and general corporate support for spending on prison building as an alternative to welfare spending, led to the astonishing boom in prison construction that sets the US apart from the rest of the overdeveloped world. This boom rested critically on bipartisan support for harsher and more inflexible sentences, especially for petty drug crimes that people of color commit at about the same rate as whites, but for which the former are far more likely to be incarcerated. Again President Clinton and the Democrats played a key role, although the crime rate itself had actually entered a long period of decline just before he took office. His *Between Hope and History* bragged about the force of his 1994 crime bill and his 1996 Anti-Terrorism and Effective Death Penalty Act. Such laws made a "three strikes and you're out" policy apply federally so that a third felony conviction inevitably led to a life sentence, and generally mandated that 85 percent of the time of a sentence be served before possibility of parole.

Clinton also kept in place the Reagan-era disparities in sentencing for crack cocaine as opposed to powdered cocaine offenses. The law equated 1 gram of crack, the form of cocaine more used in communities of color, with 100 grams of powder for sentencing purposes. Only crack cocaine possession carried a mandatory prison sentence on first offense. These disparities were a source of much of the pattern of racial inequality in incarcerating drug offenders. In a recent semi-apology for refusing to challenge the disparity, Clinton described the policy that he supported as a "cancer," and then explained that it was politically necessary to support it. That sense of necessity, and the policy that resulted from it, summarize only too well the long and deep-rooted inabilities of modern liberalism to develop anti-racist strategies and to confront its own complicity in the reproduction of race.

Afterword:

WILL RACE SURVIVE?

Possibilities and Impossibilities of the Obama Phenomenon

The idea of race, this book has argued, emerged and continued to have meaning amid evolving processes in which government, economy, and society sorted peoples into very different relationships to property, to management, to punishment, and to citizenship, according to fictive biological categories. Great struggles, peaking in the 1860s and 1870s and again a century later, forced important changes where race and citizenship were concerned. But those struggles lost momentum and unity before effecting other political economic changes that might have decisively disconnected color from degradation and suspicion. These failures left even formal, legal equality fragile. They also allowed room for the development of new forms of state-centered race-making processes around incarceration and deportation.

With whites today having on average more than nine times the household wealth of African Americans and Latinos, and with white male incarceration rates at less than one-seventh those of African American males, desires to claim white identity and to defend the relative advantages attached to it will persist unless dramatic changes occur, even in the wake of post–civil rights gains for sections of communities of color. This is so not only because the past of slavery and racial discrimination lingers on, but also because since the civil rights movement, deep racial inequalities have now been recreated across two generations. Only a tiny remnant of the always inadequate palliative of affirmative action remains as legal recourse to address racial inequality, and that remnant is seldom defended out loud by political leaders.

And yet, we hear often that race is almost spent as a social force in the US, eliminated by symbolic advances, demographic change, and private choice, if not by structural transformations or political struggles. Nowhere is this line of argument more forcefully, or more contradictorily, made than in analyses of Barack Obama's 2008 campaign for US president. At times the divergent responses reflect campaign strategies, as for example when the Hillary Clinton camp attempted to deflate Obama's South Carolina primary win by attributing it to a black vote, and Obama supporters replied by chanting "Race doesn't matter" at their victory party. But to see what Obama can and cannot be where race is concerned requires placing him in newly imagined worlds of race and racelessness as well as in tragically familiar patterns of racial inequality.

"Race Over" was the headline of Harvard-based sociologist Orlando Patterson's recent prognostications in the *New Republic*. In 2050, Patterson assured readers, the United States "will have problems aplenty. But no racial problem whatsoever." By this time, "the social virus of race will have gone the way of smallpox." Inconsistencies littered his predictions. Blacks in the new raceless US would use new technologies to change their appearance. In the Northeast and Midwest "murderous racial gang fights" would persist—allegedly without any involvement of race. In the Southeast, the racial divisions of the "Old Confederacy" would continue, but would somehow make no difference in the national picture. A still more glaring contradiction obtruded when Patterson added another set of futurological observations in a *New York Times* article, which contested the common view of demographers that whites would become a minority in the US in the twenty-first century. Arguing that "nearly half of the Hispanic population is white in every social sense," Patterson forecast that the "white population will remain a substantial majority and possibly even grow as a portion of the population." Patterson's point—that some of the children of white/Hispanic intermarriages will identify as, and be identified as, simply "white"—is not implausible, but the contrast between the two articles is jarring. Race will vanish—but whiteness will persist.

In 2008, for good measure, Patterson was back in the *Times*, analyzing Hillary Clinton's "red phone" campaign advertisement. In it, Clinton answers an emergency 3 a.m. phone call with an assurance that Barack Obama, her chief rival for the Democratic presidential nomination, could not provide, according to the advertisement. Patterson observed that the commercial had Clinton defending white children (and perhaps some Latino children) in a way that implied the nebulous danger might in fact be a black man. Not only did the advertisement cast Obama as unfit to be the reassuring solution; its subtext associated him with the menace itself. Patterson drew a straight line between the vicious racist classic 1915 film *Birth of a Nation* and the "red phone" promotion. In his view these were the same old appeals recycled for a contemporary audience. Race, over or almost done, still saturated public discourse.

Patterson is by no means alone in his vacillations. We are often told popularly that race and racism are on predictable tracks to extinction. But we are seldom told clear or consistent stories about why white supremacy will give way and how race will become a "social virus" of the past. Often multiracial identities and immigration take center stage as examples of factors making race obsolete. To take one example, the special 1993 issue of *Time* on the "New Face of America" used a computer to morph into existence a new "Eve," created out of images of those migrating to and mingling in the US. As the cover girl Eve typified a future America in which the white majority would give way to "cross-breeding," she presented an obsession with race, types, and genes, even as she ostensibly undermined the old order. The result of feeding variously "raced" faces into a computer program, Eve looked possibly Latina, possibly white—and strikingly beautiful. Her image conjured up a nation "beyond race," one no longer divided into black and white. Surrounding articles and advertisements concentrated on transnational US business and the proliferating consumption of things ethnic, which were also loosely connected to an undermining of race.

The extinction of race by a fixed date acquired legal weight in the 2003 Supreme Court decisions on the Grutter case, in which Justice Sandra Day O'Connor's majority opinion upheld the affirmative action admissions policy at the University of Michigan. Outlining the reasoning behind the justices' ruling, O'Connor emphasized the benefits of diversity for majority students, but added that the Court "expects that twenty-five years from now" no preferences will be needed to further even that limited goal. The research group on inequalities of wealth, United for a Fair Economy, reached a quite different and much better grounded conclusion in its annual "State of the Dream" report assessing racial justice for 2008. The report estimated that the "parity date," when existing trends would equalize black and white median household wealth, is not in fact 2028, but more than half a millennium away. On some measures, the report adds, equality is several thousand years in the future, given existing trends.

The attack on the World Trade Center and the Pentagon on September 11, 2001 solidified the perception that race is almost over as the fear of a common enemy was said to erase divisions among Americans. Indeed in the wake of 9/11, politicians, editorialists, and even comedians repeatedly emphasized the essential unity of everyone in the US, regardless of race. The War on Terror, and in particular the 2003 invasion and subsequent occupation of Iraq, offered a spectacular display of "black (and brown) faces in high places," as policymakers and military leaders on the transnational stage. However, the longer aftermath of 9/11 has strongly challenged the idea that participation in the wider world dissolves racial divisions at home. From the outset of the War on Terror, the racial profiling of Arab Americans and of Arab and Islamic travelers became a concern. Initially, jokes from black standup comics played on their relief at getting to take a rest from being the subjects of such suspicion and profiling. But such lines proved less funny as the broadcast faces of terror often resembled those of South Asians, African Americans, and Latinos, not only the imagined Arab stereotype. The possibility of an Obama presidential campaign matured in a post-9/11 moment, but that moment also created the dynamic leading some conservatives to make political use of the candidate's full name, Barack Hussein Obama, hoping to cast suspicion on him.

Postracial Possibilities and Obama's Hopes

The Obama campaign itself became alleged proof that the US had so quickly moved beyond race that even Justice O'Connor was pessimistic in her timetable. However, that campaign has also illustrated the tenacity of old racial divisions, and the force of new ones. The conservative *Wall Street Journal* greeted the earliest of Obama's primary triumphs as proof that the nation had transcended the bad old days of racism. The misnamed, conservative American Civil Rights Institute somehow parlayed Obama's primary successes into proof of the absence of institutional racism, and of any need for affirmative action. At the same time, the "color-blind" press combined such assertions of racelessness with strikingly reductionist resorts to race to "explain" voting patterns. Early in the campaign, for example, African Americans were said to support Clinton because of an atavistic questioning of whether Obama was "black enough," as *Time* headlined in February 2007. The *Levee*, an acute New Orleans satirical newspaper, greeted Republican candidate Mike Huckabee's success in the Louisiana primary as proof that conservatives there found John McCain "not white enough."

When Obama proved to do very well among black voters, these arguments were immediately cast aside, although there was no acknowledgment in the press that its earlier reasoning had been egregious. Nor did the media stop to notice that African Americans massively supported in Obama a mixed-race candidate with a foreign-born father, making them perhaps the most cosmopolitan sector of the electorate. As the campaign progressed, the candidates were said to grapple over who would get the Hispanic vote, and/or to appeal for the "white male" vote, with the press assuming simple equations between identity and voting. Crude race-profiling of voters jostled for space with extravagant claims regarding the transcendence of race.

Such careening representations of the Obama campaign reflect an overwhelming desire to transcend race without transcending racial inequality, as well as the impossibility of doing so. Obama embodies many of the powerful changes that Patterson and others regard as dissolving the old racial categories. First, as Obama seldom tires of saying, he is the product of Kenya on his father's side and Kansas on his mother's. Thus he evokes the promise that a greatly increased number of interracial marriages will register and further the breakdown of color lines. He presents, in the words of columnist Maureen Dowd, an "exquisitely cosmopolitan self" to the electorate. His youth, spent in Indonesia and Hawaii, underscores these associations with the transnational and the multiracial. If his second-generation immigrant success story has so far resonated only a little with the recent immigrant population of the US, it is nonetheless a part of his broader appeal. His elite education typifies a stratum of a new black middle class that has matured as segregated education has partially given way. Above all, his political attractiveness to a substantial minority of white voters is unprecedented and momentous, with the support of young white voters at times especially impressive. Among much else it indexes how much African American protest traditions, however hesitantly embraced by Obama, are associated with the possibility of change in the US. The seeming impossibility of a black US president also connects his election with the idea of big and dramatic, if unspecified in policy terms, transformations.

When Obama has deflected difficult questions regarding race with the charming response that, given his parentage, he could not be on any one side, he also reflects an increasing experience of the nation, especially its youth, with what cultural studies scholars call "hybridity." Moreover, he appeals to a widespread sense that race is now, more than ever before, about choice, and less about status ascribed by the state. With Jim Crow illegal, with science firmly declaring against the biological import of race, with racial status on the census having for decades been determined by self-identification, and with the 2000 census offering an array of mixed-race choices for such self-identification, race is today a far more fluid category, both popularly and at law.

The dramatic recent rise in American Indian population recorded by the census signals how thoroughly new imaginations of selves and reclamations of family heritage can conspire to change racial choices. In 1960, the American Indian and Alaskan Native/Aleut population was 552,000. It would roughly quadruple by 1990 and reach almost 2.5 million in 2000, when an additional group of nearly 2 million Americans identified as native, mixed with another race. Much more generally, a huge share of the "white" population now regards itself as identifying with "nonwhite" peoples or culture in some way that they regard as central to their lives. These identifications range from living and loving interracially, to parenting interracial children or adopted children of color, to devotion to Buddhism, to intense reggae, salsa, jazz, hip-hop, blues, gospel, or world-music fandom, to idolization and emulation of Michael Jordan or Tiger Woods. They are often powerfully and at times superficially connected with, to borrow from Paul Gilroy, wanting to be free and to be seen as free. A mixture of the exalted, the everyday and the fanciful—of the intimate and the commercial—informs the ways that whites identify with "nonwhite" cultures, figures, and products. Support for Obama matures among a broad spectrum of political, personal, and consumer choices regarding race.

Black/Latino/Immigrant Unity: Imperative and Impossibility

Fluidity and choice therefore exist within the very structures of deep contemporary inequality. Such inequality especially afflicts those readily identifiable as black and poor, or as Latino, poor, and "illegal," and as Indians on or off reservations. Possibility and tragedy coexist while two desirable changes remain impossible both for Obama and for the larger society. The first impossibility centers on the achievement of meaningful black-immigrant unity, the second on speaking out in mainstream politics against the existence, persistence, and continued reproduction of racial hier-archies. Both of these impossibilities spawn endless discussion in the media coverage of Obama's campaign. Nonetheless the full import of each remains almost fully hidden, while the extent of the problems they raise for all who seriously want to live beyond race goes largely unacknowledged.

It is possible, of course, that the growth of a mixed-race population and of immigrant communities divided more by nationality than race might someday simply overwhelm attempts to repackage what James Baldwin called "the lie of whiteness." But history should make us wary of predictions that demographic changes will cause race to disappear, rather than simply to mutate. In any case, we are at this moment very far from such a reality, and are not on a road that leads in any sure direction. Experts estimate that about 8 percent of Americans are "mixed-race"—the term itself is anything but post-racial—although less than a third of that percentage claimed mixed-race identity on the 2000 census.

If we project the recent increase in births of mixed-race children over a long stretch of time, new patterns do emerge. However, such patterns remain contradictory, and compatible with either a decline or a continuation in race-thinking. A recent study by population specialists Sharon Lee, Barry Edmonston, and Jeffrey Passel, uses computer modeling to project the population in 2100, and concludes that in that year the "pure" (both parents of the same "race") and the mixed-race populations of the US would be

almost exactly equal. But this hybridity would be greatly concentrated among Latinos, a group in which the "pure" would
constitute 30 percent of the total population while the Latino/
mixed would total 70 percent. Among whites, on the other hand,
65 percent would be "pure" and 35 percent white and mixed.
Sixty-three percent of African Americans would have two African
American parents and 57 percent of Asian Americans would have
only Asian-American parents.

Interracialism, therefore, might well vary dramatically by race.
Indeed, if present patterns of inequality persist the projected 2100
population will contain 66 million "unmixed" African Americans as
well as new generations of desperately poor immigrants whose
"race," class, and illegality are linked in popular perceptions. Those
groups would almost certainly be racially despised. Offered as a
serious effort at estimates, not an iron guide to what is a fully
unpredictable future, these figures also remind us that no one knows
what the racial identification of Latino mixed-race people, the largest
single category projected, will be in 2100. It is entirely possible to
imagine a white majority continuing for centuries based on choices
that mixed-race people make. As Lee, Edmonston, and Passel
themselves wisely point out, the racial future is a political question,
just as it was a century ago when sometimes dire and sometimes
celebratory predictions, that a new racial order would form out of
mass immigration and multicultural blending, failed to materialize.

In particular, the ways in which those whom the Chicana
feminist Cherrie Moraga called "Twenty-first-century mestizos"
unite with other people of color, both in voting patterns and in
struggles to end the material bases of race-thinking, will be key to
whether the idea of race can survive. But it is precisely on this
point that Obama's candidacy has so far failed to offer hope for
even symbolic change. Although he can win over voters as an
African American candidate, a mixed-race candidate, and an
exemplar of racelessness, Obama has not been able to gain support
as a second-generation immigrant candidate appealing to recent
immigrants to the US and to their children. In the California

primary he lost, despite his great successes among black and even white voters, because of Latino and Asian-American support for Clinton. Like most children of African and Afro-Caribbean immigrants, Obama is seen within the US racial order as black. Therefore, the punditry has exhaustively repeated, Obama loses Latino votes to Clinton, with this pattern hurting him badly in states like California, Nevada, and Texas. Indeed in the twenty-two Super Tuesday primaries combined, Clinton defeated Obama by nearly a two-to-one margin among Latino voters.

The press's drumbeat of emphasis on the oversimplified analysis of voting by people of color says both too much and too little about "race" in an election in which Obama lost Latino voters for reasons of politics far more than for reasons of color. It is manifestly false that black candidates cannot win significant majorities of Latino votes: Harold Washington did so in Chicago's mayoral election in 1983 as did David Dinkins in New York City in 1989 and 1993. In the 2005 Los Angeles mayoral election the turn of black voters to Antonio Villaraigosa was pivotal. In most presidential elections big majorities of African Americans and Latino voters unite behind white Democrats. Up against a Clinton machine very experienced in turning out Latino voters, Obama ran a relatively poor campaign among Spanish-speaking voters, only producing bilingual materials late in the day. In March 2008, when Obama for a time began to discuss race, he forced complex divisions onto an African American/white axis. As the political scientist Michael Dawson astutely remarked of the fullest Obama speech on race, "Most surprising, perhaps, was the minimal acknowledgment given to the recognition that the racial landscape has fundamentally changed with the large-scale immigration of particularly, but not exclusively, Latino and Asian populations into the United States." That the estimated 12 million "illegals" are overwhelmingly disfranchised contributes to such oversimplifications by those devising electoral strategies.

With neither candidate forwarding ambitious plans for immigrant rights nor concrete proposals for immigration reform, exit polls in Texas showed that over half of Latino voters counted the economy to be the dominant issue. The votes of this large block of economically concerned, Democratic Latinos are what overwhelmingly went to Clinton, although some in her camp joined the press in turning a particular trend into a universal truth about Hispanic hostility to black candidates. Clinton operative Sergio Bendixen, for example, told the *New Yorker* that "The Hispanic voter—and I want to say this very carefully—has not shown a lot of willingness . . . to support black candidates."

While the existence, and the "racial" character, of a black/ Latino electoral divide has been inflated and inflamed by the media, the fact remains that anti-racist forces face significant legislative and structural hurdles in attempting to forge an impactful black/immigrant coalition. Perhaps least noticed are the difficulties in creating unity among immigrants and the descendents of immigrants themselves. The 1965 immigration reform passed with negligible input from people of color. Its framers paid little attention to the reform's potential impact on patterns of immigration among, and racial hatred towards, Latin American, Asian, and African migrants. Statutory openings to those advantaged by their professional, medical, or technical occupational status, or by family networks able to negotiate bureaucracies and secure passage to the US, separated immigration and poverty somewhat for certain layers of newcomers, but imperial wars and neoliberal trade policies ensured that other sectors of the immigrant and refugee populations would be desperately poor.

At the same time, in its desire to rectify slights towards Eastern and Southern European nationalities victimized by discriminatory immigration quotas since 1924, the 1965 act featured an abstract and unworkable emphasis on formal equality among nations. It therefore applied quotas to the immigration from the Americas and refused to adjust universal limits on legal immigration to acknowledge that Mexico, a large and adjoining nation, was bound to furnish a number of immigrants far exceeding its quota. By 1976 the tiny 20,000-immigrant annual quota for Mexico was particularly unmoored from reality. The government-sponsored Bracero program to temporarily admit Mexican agricultural workers, discontinued in the early 1960s, had admitted ten times as many Mexicans a year at times. Results were predictable: 781,000 immigrants from Mexico suffered expulsion from the US in 1976 alone. Although "illegal aliens" have come from many nations—the Irish influx was handled with particular speed and liberality by Congress in the 1980s—this continuing pattern made "Mexican" yet again what the anthropologist Nicholas De Genova calls "the distinctive nation/racialized name for migrant 'illegality.'" If legal status has been yet another source of division among immigrants, it has more tragically also served as the rallying point for overwhelmingly white anti-immigrant vigilante groups along the border, and for political mobilizations purporting to defend the nation's racial character.

Divided as they are by class, immigration category, language, legal status, nation, and race, migrants are very far from a unitary category. The massive 2006 immigrant rights demonstrations in Los Angeles, the largest working-class mobilizations in US history, relied on the combination of an energized Mexican-American base and grassroots leadership by many experienced in activism prior to their arrival in the US. They succeeded in reaching across different immigrant nationalities, in uniting the undocumented minority with the "legal" majority of immigrants, giving immigrants common purpose and eliciting solidarity from those longer established in the US. This unity rested in no small measure on the extent to which people of color are subject to attacks based on both recognition and misrecognition: Sikhs were among those targeted in the post-9/11 "anti-Arab" attacks in the US; while Vincent Chin, whose 1982 murder came to symbolize violence connected to resentment against Japanese inroads into the US auto market, was in fact Chinese. The South Asian-American children most likely to distance themselves from model minority stereotypes, the ethnographer Sunaina Maira shows, are likely not only to be from working-class backgrounds, but to have suffered because they are thought to look like other racialized groups. It is patterns like these that make opposition to anti-immigrant racism, often expressed as a demand for dignity, central to the immigrant rights movement. Dramatic differences between, for example, the treatment of incarcerated Haitian refugees and Irish undocumented workers have likewise helped to make race a central part of some immigration policy debates.

But so far these struggles against anti-immigrant racism have not coalesced to produce enduring alliances that can challenge a situation in which it is easier, as the "Keep on Crossin'" art project maintains, for toxic waste than human workers to traverse the US/Mexico border unmolested. The labor movement, impressed by immigrant heroism in organizing campaigns and aware of the threat of deportation used against union supporters by employers, has belatedly adopted more humane positions on immigration at the national level, although in some unions the impulse to exclude immigrant workers remains strong. Moreover, the unions are currently so weak that their insistence on immigrant rights, or on prosecuting employers of undocumented labor, tends to be ignored. To change the many decades of increasingly ingrained reliance on a combination of illegal and legal immigration to do many of the hardest, dirtiest, and lowest-paid US jobs, and of the importation of skilled professional and technical labor from the global South, worldwide patterns of inequality and power would have to change dramatically in ways neither Democratic nor Republican policymakers are prepared to consider. Sidestepping these fundamental considerations, the immigration debate centers instead on border fences, harsh judgments, serial amnesties, and new guest-worker projects, which are almost certain to coexist with "illegal" immigration and to reproduce racial division.

The question of what could anchor meaningful black/immigrant unity—in tough local situations where competition over space is intense and fights over jobs and politics and confrontations in small stores owned by immigrants and patronized by African

Americans leave scars—goes largely unexamined amidst all of the talk about racial voting blocs. Even the insight that labor lies at the heart of the question is too easily oversimplified into the question of whether "Americans" (in this context, usually meaning jobless African Americans) "want to work" in backbreaking, sub-minimum-wage jobs far from their homes. The structure of the debate continues to allow African Americans to be damned as degraded if they do want these jobs and as lazy if they do not.

A more fruitful approach might begin with the work of De Genova, whose recent study of Mexican Chicago shows how management in factories constructs a divide between immigrant unskilled labor and African Americans, with Mexican workers told they have been employed as a result of their being more tractable and less union-minded than their black predecessors in the plants. As De Genova says, "the refined legal vulnerability of undocumented migrant labor—above all, materialized in its deportability—evidently serves to radically enhance the preconditions for its routinized subordination within the inherently despotic order of the workplace." In urban hotels and in packing houses in smaller Midwestern cities, the recrudescence of management by race and nationality (and now by legality) is ever more apparent, with the poor of the world vying to keep jobs and avoid immigration service raids. To bring these concrete realities into dialogue with the demands of black communities is critical, but so far it has proven fully impossible within national presidential campaigns and largely impossible outside of them.

Will (Not) Talking About Race Undermine Racism?

When Obama's primary campaign seemed to be heading for victory in early March 2008, he came under sharp attack from conservatives in the media and from the Clinton campaign for his relationship with Reverend Jeremiah Wright, the former pastor of the church Obama attends. Influenced by black liberation theology, Wright's jeremiads indicted American racism in ways reminiscent of Malcolm X and Martin Luther King. After two weeks of calls to "denounce" Wright, Obama delivered a Philadelphia speech in which he sharply separated himself from the minister's message, but did not abandon the man. The "Cradle of Liberty" setting of the speech—one quickly heralded as the most honest and perhaps important on race by a viable presidential candidate—evoked the "stain" of race on the founding of the US. However, Obama found that an end to that stain was "already embedded within" the Constitution, so that, in his view, long struggles for equality were bound to win and in many ways already had.

Wright's "offending sermons" were therefore not "simply controversial" but deeply "wrong" and "divisive" by virtue of their "profoundly distorted view of this country—a view that sees white racism as endemic." Whatever sympathy Obama professed for Wright stemmed from the latter's specific experience with the frustrations of Jim Crow, which left many in Wright's generation refusing to see that the nation had changed, and apt "to simplify and stereotype and amplify the negative to the point that it distorts reality" where white American practices are concerned. While Obama did call for expanded discussion of race and vigorous civil rights enforcement, the speech lacked concrete proposals for producing equality. It managed to be vague to the point of indecipherability on affirmative action, broached as a source of understandable "white resentment" rather than as a policy worth defending. By April 2008 Obama denounced Wright more stridently, reckoning his former pastor as the polar opposite of the unifying figure that Obama himself worked to be. He attributed his angry opposition to Wright's divisiveness to something written in his own "DNA," presumably as a mixed-race person, in a perfect illustration of how biology-based conceptions of race persist in the post-racial US.

The point here is not to expect that Obama or any mainstream politician will take risks to defend aggressively the last fragments of affirmative action still permitted by the courts and not yet outlawed by state referenda. His reticence on the issue is widely shared. When pressed he has vaguely suggested that affirmative action be based less on race and more on poverty, allowing that his daughters should not benefit from the policy. In making the case for "class-based" affirmative action he follows the impractical but high-sounding path of some conservative opponents of "race preferences" and of John Kerry and other Democrats. Such a policy is not challenged by Hillary Clinton. Indeed many activists are tempted to give up the affirmative action ghost, as even Reverend Wright himself has perhaps signaled in advocating more far-reaching measures like reparations for slavery and for racism. But it is nonetheless worth stressing that Obama does not represent the triumph of an advancing anti-racist movement but rather the necessity, at the highly refracted level of electoral politics, of abandoning old agendas, largely by not mentioning them.

However, it will not be easy after the primaries to avoid taking strong public positions on "divisive" racial issues, such as affirmative action, as Republicans will aggressively raise "wedge" issues to split Democrats along racial lines. The political scientist Darren Davis observes, "On every racial issue Barack Obama is walking the tightrope." Conservatives will surely test his balance as he stands as candidate in the general election. Indeed they have already organized four anti–affirmative–action referenda to coincide with the presidential election in pivotal states. "The more he supports traditional black issues like affirmative action, the more that will eat into his white base of support," Davis writes; equally, open retreats from these issues will decrease enthusiasm among parts of his base.

Adroitly responsive to polling data, Obama's maneuverings nonetheless serve to distort how we conceptualize and address white supremacy, past and present. He moves from the casting of race as "divisive," to terming it a diversion from "real" issues affecting all Americans—the environment, war, housing, jobs, and healthcare. However, the problem with settling for that partial truth is that racial inequality itself remains a fundamental problem, both in coalition-building and in everyday life. When Obama waxes nostalgic for the good old days of economic progress and calls for a focus on pocketbook issues like job training, trade policies, or gas prices, his narrative breaks faith with remembering the bitter days when Reverend Wright was growing up and likewise underplays the impact of the past on us. In critiquing race politics in his Philadelphia speech, Obama proposed a new departure based on too-easy appeals to economic unity: "This time we want to talk about the shuttered mills that once provided a decent life for men and women of every race, and the homes for sale that once belonged to Americans from every religion, every region, every walk of life."

Not only is such a departure not new—ironically it was a staple of Bill Clinton's strategies to appeal to win back conservative "Reagan Democrats"—but it posits as objects of its nostalgia the two historical arenas most responsible for present inequalities. The closed mills Obama refers to were presumably the Southern textile factories that were long the embodiment of Jim Crow employ-ment practices, and the steel factories in which limited, much-resisted attempts to undertake affirmative action were so long delayed that their eventual implementation coincided with the industry's decline. Moreover, the overwhelming channeling of federal subsidies to home loans for white families, and to the construction of infrastructure for segregated suburbs, has served decisively to create and increase the tremendous racial gaps in wealth that exist in the contemporary USA.

Such a blind spot has far more than mere historical importance, as it calls into question the very way that Obama portrays today's issues as simply cutting across racial lines. Nowhere is this more apparent than in the subprime mortgage crisis, the seriousness of which became clear as the primaries progressed. The wholesale foreclosures accompanying that crisis fall in distinct racial patterns, reflecting the lack of resources black and Latino homebuyers bring to the market because of past discrimination, and the ways that they are still steered and preyed upon by lenders. As the National Association for the Advancement of Colored People (NAACP) entered a lawsuit against the lenders' role in the subprime crisis, United for a Fair Economy titled its 2008 "State of the Dream" report "Foreclosed." The report warned that the loss of as much as $200 billion in wealth for people of color arising from the last eight years of subprime loans would be the greatest such loss in modern US history. Federal data shows people of color to be over three times more likely to have subprime loans, with a substantial majority of African American borrowers in that category as against one white loan recipient in six.

The lack of an aggressive response by Obama to the subprime crisis through much of the campaign has led some critics to propose that this issue best marks the limit of his economic populism, reflecting instead his close ties to banking and investment capital. Such critics are not wrong, but race has also mattered in the evasion of the full gravity of the crisis in home mortgages. The absence of any racial and historical framing of the subprime issue, a deficiency shared by Obama with Clinton and McCain, strengthens the tendency to rely for a cure on the very banks and investment firms that caused the problem. The subprime catastrophe was poised to serve either as a perfect vehicle to show how issues capable of dragging down much of the whole economy are about both race and class, or as occasion for generalities, pro-mortgage industry policy changes, and wishful thinking. The latter road is the one taken by Obama and all of his major competitors.

To expect more that is concrete, forthright, and policy-oriented regarding race from Obama in the context of a presidential campaign is apparently fruitless. Eloquently summing up the ways in which the idea of race has and has not changed, the most important aspect of his campaign has been to show how much and how many people desire peace, and want to find a way to move beyond race. To make their hopes and their commitments match up will require new, even unforeseeable, considerations of the role of white supremacy. It will require new alliances, especially of African Americans with immigrants, and of feminist and working-class organizations with anti-racist forces, in movements seeking not only to be represented within a highly unequal order, but also to transform that order. The alternative is that race-thinking will survive in new and destructive permutations, and will continue to serve not simply as a diversion from other brutalities, but also as a prop on which they rest.

Sources, Inspirations and Suggested Further Reading

This book attempts to synthesize a large and varied secondary literature to produce a short, accessible general historical interpretation for lay readers. Where possible, it calls on my earlier, more detailed publications, and where necessary it adds new archival research, for example on race and management. What follows is therefore meant to identify important, often relatively overlooked, works from which I have learned as suggestions for further reading, not to exhaust the list of all the books from which I have drawn. For my own more expansive and academically styled treatments of the future of race, see *Colored White: Transcending the Racial Past* (Berkeley: University of California Press, 2003). On race and immigration, see my *Working toward Whiteness: How America's Immigrants Became White* (New York: Basic Books, 2005) and on free labor, capitalism, immigration, and race, *The Wages of Whiteness: Race and the Making of the American Working Class* (New York: Verso, 2007).

Acuña, Rodolpo. *Occupied America: A History of Chicanos*. White Plains, NY: Longman, 2006.

Baldwin, James. *The Price of the Ticket: Collected Nonfiction, 1948–1985*. New York: St. Martin's Press, 1985.

Baron, Harold. *The Demand for Black Labor: Historical Notes on the Political Economy of Racism*. Somerville, MA: New England Free Press, 1971.

Blackburn, Robin, "Emancipation and Empire: From Cromwell to Karl Rove." *Daedalus*, 134 (Spring, 2005): 72–87.

Fields, Barbara. "Ideology and Race in American History," in J. Morgan Kousser and James M. McPherson, eds., *Region, Race and Reconstruction: Essays in Honor of C. Vann Woodward*. New York: Oxford, 1982: 143–177.

Fredrickson, George. *The Black Image in the White Mind: The Debate on Afro-American Character and Destiny, 1817–1914*. New York: Harper & Row, 1971.

Gerstle, Gary. *American Crucible: Race and Nation in the Twentieth Century*. Princeton: Princeton University Press, 2002.

Glenn, Evelyn Nakano. *Unequal Freedom: How Race and Gender Shaped American Citizenship and Labor*. Cambridge, MA: Harvard University Press, 2002.

Gross, Ariela. *What Blood Won't Tell: A History of Race on Trial in America*. Cambridge: Harvard University Press, 2008.

Guterl, Matthew. *The Color of Race, 1900–1940*. Cambridge: Harvard University Press, 2002.

Harris, Cheryl. "Whiteness as Property." *Harvard Law Review* 106 (1993): 1709–1795.

———. "Finding Sojourner's Truth: Race, Gender and the Institution of Property," *Cardozo Law Review* 18 (November 1996): 309–409.

James, Stanlie and Abena Busia, eds., *Theorizing Black Feminisms: The Visionary Pragmatism of Black Women*. New York: Routledge, 1993.

Marable, Manning. *How Capitalism Underdeveloped Black America: Problems in Race, Political Economy and Society*. Boston: South End Press, 1999.

Mills. Charles. *The Racial Contract*. Ithaca: Cornell University Press, 1997.

Moraga, Cherrie. *This Bridge Called My Back: Writings by*

Radical Women of Color. New York: Kitchen Table Press, 1984.

Rubio, Philip. *A History of Affirmative Action, 1619–2000.* Jackson: University of Mississippi Press, 2001.

Saxton, Alexander. *The Rise and Fall of the White Republic: Class Politics and Mass Culture in Nineteenth-Century America.* New York: Verso, 1990.

Stefancic, Jean and Richard Delgado, eds., *Critical White Studies: Looking Behind the Mirror.* Philadelphia: Temple University Press, 1997.

Takaki, Ronald. *A Different Mirror: A History of Multicultural America.* Boston: Little, Brown, 1983.

Williams, William Appleman. *Contours of American History.* Chicago: Quandrangle Books, 1996.

CHAPTERS 1 AND 2

Allen, Theodore. *The Invention of the White Race*, 2 vols. New York: Verso, 1994.

Batou, Jean. "From Plantation to Plant: Slavery, the Slave Trade, and the Industrial Revolution. At http://mercury.soas.ac.uk/hm/pdf/2006confpapers/papers/Batou.pdf

Blackburn, Robin. *The Making of New World Slavery: From the Baroque to the Modern.* New York: Verso, 1997.

Blackburn, Robin. *The Overthrow of Colonial Slavery, 1770–1823.* New York: Verso, 1988.

Block, Sharon. *Rape and Sexual Power in Early America.* Chapel Hill: University of North Carolina Press, 2006.

Brown, Kathleen. *Good Wives, Nasty Wenches, and Anxious Patriarchs: Gender, Race, and Power in Colonial Virginia.* Chapel Hill: University of North Carolina Press, 1996.

Calloway, Colin. *The American Revolution in Indian Country: Crisis and Diversity in Native American Communities.* Cambridge, GB: Cambridge University Press, 1995.

Carney, Judith. *Black Rice: The African Origins of Rice Culture in the Americas.* Cambridge, MA: Harvard University Press, 2001.

Davis, David Brion. *The Problem of Slavery in the Age of Revolution, 17701823.* Ithaca: Cornell University Press, 1975.

Du Bois, W. E. B. *Dusk of Dawn: An Essay Towards the Autobiography of a Race-Concept.* New York: Harcourt, Brace and Company, 1940.

———. *The Suppression of the African Slave Trade to the United States of America, 1638–1870* (originally 1896) at http://www.gutenberg.org/etext/17700

Edmund Morgan. *American Slavery, American Freedom: The Ordeal of Colonial Virginia.* New York: Norton, 2003.

Frey, Sylvia. *Water from the Rock: Black Resistance in a Revolutionary Age.* Princeton: Princeton University Press, 1991.

Gomez, Michael. *Exchanging Our Country Marks: The Transformation of African Identities in the Colonial and Antebellum South.* Chapel Hill: University of North Carolina Press, 1998.

Holton, Woody. *Forced Founders: Indians, Debtors, Slaves, and the Making of the American Revolution in Virginia.* Chapel Hill: University of North Carolina Press, 1999.

Jennings, Francis. *The Invasion of America: Indians, Colonialism and the Cant of Conquest.* Chapel Hill: University of North Carolina Press, 1975.

Kaplan, Sidney. "The 'Domestic Insurrections' of the Declaration of Independence." *Journal of Negro History*, Vol. 61, No. 3. (Jul., 1976): 243–255.

Lepore, Jill. *The Name of War: King Philip's War and the Origins of American Identity.* New York: Knopf, 1998.

———. *New York Burning: Liberty, Slavery, and Conspiracy in Eighteenth-Century Manhattan.* New York: Knopf, 2005

Linebaugh, Peter and Marcus Rediker. *Many-Headed Hydra: Sailors, Slaves, Commoners, and the Hidden History of the Revolutionary Atlantic.* Boston: Beacon, 2000.

McDonnell, Michael A. *The Politics of War: Race, Class, and Conflict in Revolutionary Virginia.* Chapel Hill: University of North Carolina Press, 2007.

Melish, Joanne Pope. *Disowning Slavery: Gradual Emancipation and Race in New England, 1780–1860.* Ithaca: Cornell University Press, 1998.

Morgan, Jennifer. *Laboring Women: Reproduction and Gender in New World Slavery.* Philadelphia: University of Pennsylvania Press, 2004.

Parent, Anthony. *Foul Means: The Formation of a Slave Society in Virginia, 1660–1740.* Chapel Hill: University of North Carolina Press, 2003.

Okoye, F. Nwabueze. "Chattel Slavery as the Nightmare of the American Revolutionaries." *The William and Mary Quarterly,* 3rd Ser., Vol. 37, No. 1. (Jan., 1980): 328.

Rawick, George. *From Sundown to Sunup: The Making of the Black Community.* Westport, CT: Greenwood, 1972.

Schama, Simon. *Rough Crossings: Britain, the Slave Trade, and the American Revolution.* London: BBC, 2005.

Schloesser, Pauline. *Fair Sex: White Women and Racial Patriarchy in the Early American Republic.* New York: University Press, 2002.

Sobel, Mechal. *The World They Made Together: Black and White Values in Eighteenth-Century Virginia.* Princeton: Princeton University Press, 1987.

Taylor, Gary. *Buying Whiteness: Race, Culture, and Identity from Columbus to Hip-Hop.* New York: Palgrave Macmillan, 2005.

Waldstreicher, David. *Runaway America: Benjamin Franklin, Slavery, and the American Revolution.* New York: Hill and Wang, 2004.

Walker, Juliet E. K. "Whither Liberty, Equality or Legality? Slavery, Race, Property and the 1787 American Constitution." *Journal of Human Rights* 6 (Spring 1989): 299–352

Wills, Garry. *Negro President: Jefferson and the Slave Power.* Boston: Houghton, Mifflin, 2003.

Wood, Peter. *Black Majority: Negroes in Colonial South Carolina from 1670 to the Stono Rebellion.* New York: Knopf, 1974.

Wray, Matt. *Not Quite White: White Trash and the Boundaries of Whiteness*. Durham: Duke University Press, 2006.

CHAPTER 3

Bailey, Ronald. "'Those Valuable People the Africans': The Economic Impact of the Slav(ery) Trade on Textile Industrialization in New England," in David Roediger and Martin Blatt, eds., *The North and Slavery*. New York: Garland, 1997: 331.

Cheyfitz, Eric. "Savage Law: The Plot Against American Indians in *Johnson and Graham's Lessee v. M'Intosh* and *The Pioneers*." *The Cultures of United States Imperialism*. Donald Pease and Amy Kaplan, eds. Durham: Duke University Press, 1993: 109–128.

Dublin, Thomas. *Women and Work: The Transformation of Work and Community in Lowell, Massachusetts, 1826–1860*. New York: Columbia University Press, 1979.

Esch, Elizabeth and David Roediger. *Race and the Management of Labor in US History*, forthcoming from Oxford University Press.

Foner, Eric. *Free Soil, Free Labor, Free Men: The Ideology of the Republican Party before the Civil War*. New York: Oxford University Press, 1995.

Guterl, Matthew. *American Mediterranean: Southern Slaveholders in the Age of Emancipation*. Cambridge: Harvard University Press, 2008.

Huginnie, Yvette. "A New Hero Comes to Town: The Anglo Mining Engineer and 'Mexican Labor' as Contested Terrain in Southeastern Arizona, 1880–1920." *New Mexico Historical Review* 69 (October 1994).

James, C. L. R. "The Atlantic Slave Trade and Slavery." In John Williams and Charles Harris, eds., *Amistad 1*. New York: Vintage Books, 1970.

Johnson, Walter. *Soul by Soul: Life Inside the Antebellum Slave Market*. Cambridge: Harvard University Press, 1999.

Jung, Moon-Ho. *Coolies and Cane: Race, Labor, and Sugar in the Age of Emancipation*. Baltimore: Johns Hopkins University Press, 2006.

Lawrence, Ken. "Marx on American Slavery." Originally 1976 at http://www.sojournertruth.net/marxslavery.pdf

Litwack, Leon. *North of Slavery: The Negro in the Free States, 1790–1860*. Chicago: University of Chicago Press, 1965.

Lott, Eric. *Love and Theft: Blackface Minstrelsy and the American Working Class*. New York: Oxford University Press, 1993.

Lowe, Lisa. *Immigrant Acts: On Asian American Cultural Politics*. Durham: Duke University Press, 1996.

Mandel, Bernard. *Labor: Free and Slave: Workingmen and the Antislavery Movement in the United States*. New York: Associated Authors, 1955.

Portnoy, Alisse. *Their Right to Speak: Women's Activism in the Indian and Slave Debates*. Cambridge: Harvard University Press, 2005.

Roediger, David. "Race, Labor and Gender in the Languages of Antebellum Social Protest." In Stanley Engerman, ed. *The Terms of Labor*. Stanford: Stanford University Press, 1999: 168–87.

Rogin, Michael. *Fathers and Children: Andrew Jackson and the Subjugation of the American Indian*. New York: Knopf, 1975.

Sanchez-Eppler, Karen. *Touching Liberty: Abolition, Feminism, and the Politics of the Body*. Berkeley: University of California Press, 1993.

Starobin, Robert. *Industrial Slavery in the Old South*. New York: Oxford University Press, 1970.

Streeby, Shelley. *American Sensations: Class, Empire, and the Production of Popular Culture*. Berkeley: University of California Press, 2002.

Takaki, Ronald. *Iron Cages: Race and Culture in Nineteenth-Century America*. New York: Oxford University Press, 2000.

CHAPTER 4

Bederman, Gail. *Manliness and Civilization: A Cultural History of Gender and Race in the United States, 1880–1917*. Chicago: University of Chicago Press, 1995.

Drinnon, Richard. *Facing West: The Metaphysics of Indian-Hating and Empire Building.* Minneapolis: University of Minnesota Press, 1980.

Du Bois, W. E. B. *Black Reconstruction in America: An Essay toward a History of the Part Which Black Folk Played in the Attempt to Reconstruct Democracy in America, 1860–1880.* New York: Harcourt, Brace, 1935.

DuBois, Ellen. *Feminism and Suffrage: The Emergence of an Independent Women's Movement in America, 1848–1869.* Ithaca: Cornell University Press, 1978.

Jacobson, Matthew. *Barbarian Virtues: The United States Encounters Foreign Peoples at Home and Abroad, 1876–1918.* New York: Hill and Wang, 2000.

Kramer, Paul. *The Blood of Government: Race, Empire, the United States, and the Philippines.* Chapel Hill: University of North Carolina Press, 2006.

Lemann, Nicholas. *Redemption: The Last Battle of the Civil War.* New York: Farrar, Straus and Giroux, 2006.

Leon Litwack. *Been in the Storm So Long: The Aftermath of Slavery.* New York: Knopf, 1979.

Litwack, Leon. *North of Slavery: The Negro in the Free States, 1790–1860.* Chicago: University of Chicago Press, 1961.

Loewen, James. *Sundown Towns: A Hidden Dimension of American Racism.* New York: New Press, 2005.

Montgomery, David. *Beyond Equality: Labor and the Radical Republicans, 1862–1872.* New York: Knopf, 1967.

Rable, George. *But There Was No Peace: The Role of Violence in the Politics of Reconstruction.* Athens: University of Georgia Press, 1984.

Roediger, David and Philip S. Foner. *Our Own Time: A History of American Labor and the Working Day.* New York: Verso, 1990.

Rydell, Robert. *All the World's a Fair: Visions of Empire at American International Expositions, 1876–1916.* Chicago: University of Chicago Press, 1984.

Saxton, Alexander. *Indispensable Enemy: Labor and the Anti-Chinese Movement in California*. Berkeley: University of California Press, 1971.

Shugg, Roger. *Origins of Class Struggle in Louisiana: A Social History of White Farmers and Laborers during Slavery and After, 1840–1875*. Baton Rouge: Louisiana State University Press, 1939.

Stanley, Amy Dru. *From Bondage to Contract: Wage Labor, Marriage and the Market in the Age of Slave Emancipation*. Cambridge: Cambridge University Press, 1998.

Trelease, Allen. *White Terror: The Ku Klux Klan Conspiracy and Southern Reconstruction*. Baton Rouge: Louisiana State University Press, 1995.

Vincent, Charles, ed. *The African American Experience in Louisiana from the Civil War to Jim Crow*. Lafayette, LA: Center for Louisiana Studies, 1999.

Whites, Leeann. *Gender Matters: Civil War, Reconstruction and the Making of the New South*. New York: Palgrave Macmillan, 2005.

Woodward, C. Vann. *Origins of the New South, 1877–1913*. Baton Rouge: Louisiana State University Press, 1951.

CHAPTER 5

Babb, Valerie. *Whiteness Visible: The Meaning of Whiteness in American Literature and Culture*. New York: New York University Press, 1998.

Barton, Josef. *Peasants and Strangers: Italians, Rumanians, and Slovaks in an American City, 1890–1950*. Cambridge: Harvard University Press, 1975.

Brodkin, Karen. *How Jews Became White Folks and What That Says about Race in America*. New Brunswick, NJ: Rutgers University Press, 1998.

Caban, Pedro. "Subjects and Immigrants during the Progressive Era." *Discourse* 23 (Fall 2001): 24–51.

Dyer, Thomas. *Theodore Roosevelt and the Idea of Race*. Baton Rouge: Louisiana State University Press, 1980.

Gómez, Laura. *Manifest Destinies: The Making of the Mexican American Race*. New York: New York University Press, 2007.

Guglielmo, Thomas. *White on Arrival: Italians, Race, Color, and Power in Chicago, 1870–1945*. New York: Oxford University Press, 2003.

Haney-Lopez, Ian. *White by Law: The Legal Construction of Race*. New York: New York University Press, 1996.

Hattam, Victoria. *In the Shadow of Race: Jews, Latinos and Immigrant Politics in the United States*. Chicago: University of Chicago Press, 2007.

Higham, John. *Strangers in the Land: Patterns of American Nativism, 1860–1925*. New Brunswick, NJ: Rutgers University Press, 1955.

Horsman, Reginald. *Race and Manifest Destiny: The Origins of American Anglo-Saxonism*. Cambridge: Harvard University Press, 1981.

Ignatiev, Noel. *How the Irish Became White*. New York: Routledge, 1995.

Jacobson, Matthew. *Whiteness of a Different Color: European Immigrants and the Alchemy of Race*. Cambridge, GB: Cambridge University Press, 1998.

King, Desmond. *Making Americans: Immigration, Race, and the Origins of the Diverse Democracy*. Cambridge, MA: Harvard University Press, 2000.

Knobel, Dale. *Paddy and the Republic: Ethnicity and Nationality in Antebellum America*. Middletown, CT: Wesleyan University Press, 1988.

Lee, Erika. *At America's Gates: Chinese Immigration during the Exclusion Era, 1882–1943*. Chapel Hill: University of North Carolina Press, 2003.

Lee, Robert. *Orientals: Asian Americans in Popular Culture*. Philadelphia: Temple University Press, 1999.

Meyer, Stephen. *The Five-Dollar Day: Labor Management and Social Control in the Ford Motor Company, 1908–1921*. Albany: State University of New York, 1981.

Mink, Gwendolyn. *Old Labor and New Immigrants in American Political Development: Union, Party, and State, 1875–1920*. Ithaca: Cornell University Press, 1986.

Montgomery, David. *Fall of the House of Labor: The Workplace, the State, and American Labor Activism, 1865–1925*. Cambridge, GB: Cambridge University Press, 1987.

CHAPTER 6 AND AFTERWORD

Abrams, Charles. *Forbidden Neighbors: A Study of Prejudice in Housing*. New York: Harper, 1955.

Bonilla-Silva, Eduardo. *Racism without Racists: Colorblind Racism and the Persistence of Racial Inequality in the United States*. Lanham, MD: Rowman & Littlefield, 2003.

Brown, Michael. *Race, Money, and the American Welfare State*. Ithaca: Cornell University Press, 1999.

Davis, Mike. *Prisoners of the American Dream: Political Economy in the History of the US Working Class*. New York: Verso, 1986.

De Genova, Nicholas. "Migrant Illegality and Deportability in Everyday Life." *Annual Review of Anthropology* 31 (2002): 419–47.

———. *Working the Boundaries; Race, Space and "Illegality" in Mexican Chicago*. Durham: Duke University Press, 2005.

Denton, Nancy and Douglas Massey. *American Apartheid: Segregation and the Making of the Underclass*. Cambridge, MA: Harvard University Press, 1993.

Dudziak, Mary. *Cold War Civil Rights: Race and the Image of American Democracy*. Princeton: Princeton University Press, 2000.

Edsall, Thomas and Mary Byrne Edsall. *Chain Reaction: The Impact of Race, Rights, and Taxes on American Politics*. New York: Norton, 1991.

Freund, David. *Colored Property: State Politics and White Racial Politics in Suburban America*. Chicago: University of Chicago Press, 2007.

Gilmore, Ruth Wilson. *Golden Gulag: Prisons, Surplus, Crisis, and Opposition in Globalizing California*. Berkeley: University of California Press, 2007.

Greenberg, Stanley. *Middle Class Dreams: The Power and Politics of the New American Majority*. New York: Times Books, 1996.

Guglielmo, Thomas. "Fighting for Caucasian Rights: Mexicans, Mexican Americans, and the Transnational Struggle for Civil Rights." *Journal of American History* 92 (March 2006).

Guitiérrez, David. *Walls and Mirrors: Mexican Americans, Mexican Immigrants, and the Politics of Ethnicity*. Berkeley: University of California Press, 1995.

Harrington, Michael. *The Other America*. New York: Macmillan, 1970.

Hill, Herbert. *Black Labor and the American Legal System: Race, Work and the Law*. Madison: University of Wisconsin Press, 1986.

Jackson, Kenneth. *Crabgrass Frontier: The Suburbanization of the United States*. New York: Oxford University Press, 1985.

Katznelson, Ira. *When Affirmative Action Was White: An Untold Story of Racial Inequality*. New York: Norton, 2005.

Lassiter, Matthew. *The Silent Majority: Suburban Politics in the Sunbelt South*. Princeton: Princeton University Press, 2006.

Lipsitz, George. *The Possessive Investment in Whiteness: How White People Profit from Identity Politics*. Philadelphia: Temple University Press, 2006.

Maclean, Nancy. *Freedom Is Not Enough: The Opening of the American Workplace*. Cambridge: Harvard University Press, 2006.

Morris, Roger. "The Undertaker's Tally." February 2007 at http://www.truthout.org/article/roger-morris-the-under-takers-tally.

Nelson, Bruce. *Divided We Stand: American Workers and the Struggle for Black Equality*. Princeton: Princeton University Press, 2000.

Ngai, Mae. *Impossible Subjects: Illegal Aliens and the Making of Modern America*. Princeton: Princeton University Press, 2004.

Oliver, Melvin and Thomas Shapiro. *Black Wealth, White Wealth: New Perspectives on Racial Inequality*. New York: Routledge, 2006.

Omi, Michael and Howard Winant. *Racial Formation in the United States: From the 1960s to the 1980s*. New York: Routledge & Kegan Paul, 1986.

Perlstein, Rick. *Before the Storm: Barry Goldwater and the Unmaking of the American Consensus*. New York: Hill and Wang, 2001.

Quadagno, Jill. *The Color of Welfare: How Racism Undermined the War on Poverty*. New York: Oxford University Press, 1994.

Roediger, David. "Gook: The Short History of an Americanism." *Monthly Review*, 44 (March, 1992): 50–54.

———. "*Guineas, Wiggers* and the Dramas of Racialized Culture." *American Literary History* 7 (Winter 1995): 654–668.

———. "The Racial Crisis of American Liberalism." *New Left Review* 196 (NovemberDecember 1992): 114–19.

Sitkoff, Harvard. *A New Deal for Blacks: The Emergence of Civil Rights as a National Issue: The Depression Decade*. New York: Oxford University Press, 2009.

Steele, Richard. "No Ethnics: Discrimination Against Ethnics the American Defense Industry, 1940–1942." *Labor History* 32 (Winter 1991): 66–90.

Sugrue, Thomas. *Origins of the Urban Crisis: Race and Inequality in Postwar Detroit*. Princeton: Princeton University Press, 1996.

Sullivan, Patricia. *Days of Hope: Race and Democracy in the New Deal Era*. Chapel Hill: University of North Carolina Press, 1996.

Takaki, Ronald. *Double Victory: A Multicultural History of America in World War II*. Boston: Little, Brown and Company, 2000.

Wilder, Craig Steven. *Covenant with Color: Race and Social Power in Brooklyn*. New York: Columbia University Press, 2001.

Williams, Linda Faye. *The Constraint of Race: Legacies of White Skin Privilege in America*. University Park, PA: Penn State University Press, 2003.

Wolfinger, James. *Philadelphia Divided: Race and Politics in the City of Brotherly Love*. Chapel Hill: University of North Carolina Press, 2007.

Index